SUNDAY &
HOLY DAY
LITURGIES

YEAR C

SUNDAY & HOLY DAY LITURGIES

YEAR C

Flor McCarthy, S.D.B.

DOMINICAN PUBLICATIONS

This edition published (1985) by
Dominican Publications
42 Parnell Square
Dublin 1

This reprint August 1994

ISBN 0-907271-62-6

Cover design by David Cooke

Printed in the Republic of Ireland by
Colour Books Ltd, Baldoyle, Co. Dublin.

Contents

Foreword

Effective preaching is a great challenge but it is hard work. Put in its simplest terms preaching is about using words. Of words Solzhenitsyn says: 'If they are not about real things, and do not cause things to happen, are they any better than the barking of village dogs at night?' Hence the challenge facing the preacher. Our task is to preach the Good News, but we have to do so in the present tense, that is, we have to preach it in the language of today and relate it to the problems of today. 'As it is handed down the Gospel must reach each one of us as brand-new, that is, as news and good news at that, or not at all.' (Thomas Merton).

There is an additional problem. The words we use to convey our thoughts must not only touch the minds but also the hearts of our hearers. A Hindu monk who was dying asked a Catholic priest to instruct him in the basics of the Christian faith. When the priest had done so the old monk remarked: 'You have filled my mind with beautiful thoughts but you have left my heart empty.'

For the sake of those for whom Cycle C will be their first acquaintance with this series let me briefly state the approach I have followed. In general a single theme is chosen for each Sunday or Holyday, which is naturally drawn from the readings of the day or the mystery being celebrated. This theme is introduced at the start of the Mass. It is developed in the homily. We are invited to pray about it in the prayer of the faithful. And it is reinforced in a short communion reflection.

I do not like to consider the homily in isolation. I like to see it as part of an entire liturgy. Hence the title of this series is not 'Sunday *homilies*' but 'Sunday *liturgies*'. Many, I fear, when they think about a Sunday liturgy think solely in terms of a homily. This leads to a great impoverishment.

Those who are familiar with Cycles A and B of this series will know that I make extensive use of stories. I want to repeat a point about the use of stories which I made before because it is of vital importance. Look for the moral of the story not so much at the end of the story as within it. Ideally the moral of a story comes unbidden, in the course of the narration. Hence the phrases and expressions used in the narration are all important. Each in its own small way helps to elucidate and drive home the lesson.

In this volume I have used a slightly different tactic. Instead of launching straight into the story at the start of the homily I have generally given an introductory paragraph. The aim is to set the listener off on a specific trail. In a Sunday homily time is very limited. If we give the listeners a clue as to the message, then, even before we come to the end of the story, hopefully they will have seen that message for themselves.

In listening to priests saying Mass one of the great faults I find is that many go too fast. They rush along from one thing to the next, giving nothing a chance to sink in. This applies not only to the homily but even more so to the prayers. The priest must realise that he is not just praying *for* the people but *with* them. It is up to him to set the pace. He must go slower than he normally speaks. This does not mean that he has to be ponderous. There is a happy mean. Priests saying Mass on the radio seem to get it about right. Why should this be? I believe it is because they realise that people have to hear what is being said if they are to participate. But the same applies to every Mass. Pauses are very effective and necessary for a good liturgy.

I know that, besides priests, catechists are using these books. I am particularly pleased to know this because I laboured for several years in that field and I know how demanding it is.

In Cycle C we are using Luke's Gospel. It might help to point out a few of the major themes of this Gospel. Luke is very concerned with the theme of universalism: the Good News is for everybody. He is at pains to highlight Jesus' concern for all those who are marginalised: the poor, sinners, outcasts, those who suffer, and so on. He is also very keen on the place of prayer in the Christian life, as well as on the role of women in the community. And finally he is very strong on the social implications of Christ's teaching.

With the writing of Cycle C I have come to the end of what for me has been a long and winding road. I'm not merely referring to the time spent in the writing of these three volumes. That was the shortest part of the journey. I'm referring particularly to the years of ministry that went into the making of them. What I have shared did not fall into my lap. I had to go and search for it. I am very conscious that these books contain many deficiencies. But then no single person has all the answers. I have tried as best I could to offer to others the fruits of my own search. In doing so I am only repaying a debt. Many others have enriched me with the fruits of their search.

In conclusion I would like to say a special word of thanks to Fr. Bernard Treacy, my editor at Dominican Publications. His wise advice and gentle guidance helped me at every step of the road.

Flor McCarthy.

Advent

FIRST SUNDAY OF ADVENT
Doing our winter work

INTRODUCTION AND CONFITEOR

As we begin Advent we naturally think of the coming of Christ. We live between two comings of Christ — his first coming in humility and weakness, and his second coming in majesty and power.

With each passing year, as St Paul says, 'our salvation is nearer than when we first believed.' Let us reflect for a moment on how much we need the Lord's salvation in our lives and in the world. (Pause).

The Lord lives on in his Church. Let us turn to him with confidence, asking him to make the salvation he won for us a reality.

You bring us wisdom, fresh understanding and new vision. Lord, have mercy.

You bring us the good news, and the power which will transform our lives. Christ, have mercy.

You bring us the truth, showing us the way to eternal life. Lord, have mercy.

HEADINGS FOR READINGS

First Reading (Jeremiah 33:14-16). The prophet says that a time will come when God will be true to his promise. The Son of David (that is, The Messiah) will stand among his people. His reign will be marked by wisdom, justice and integrity.

Second Reading (1 Thess 3:12-4:2). Paul prays that the Lord may deepen the love the Thessalonians have for each other, a love that will then reach out to all people. Thus they will be ready for the second coming of Christ.

Gospel (Luke 21:25-28, 34-36). In language borrowed from the Old Testament Luke describes the final coming of Christ. Christians should not fear this. Rather, they should look forward to it and prepare for it through prayer and right living.

HOMILY

The dominant idea in today's readings is the second coming of Christ and the end of the world. But does it not seem a little strange that at the start of the Church's year our eyes should be directed, not towards the beginning, but towards the end of time? Not really, when you think a little about it.

At the start of her liturgical year the Church invites us to embark on a great journey — to follow the footsteps of Christ in all his mysteries so that we may live as he lived. Now if you want people to embark on a journey you have to give them some idea of the goal of that journey. And a vague shadowy goal is not much use. It must be real, concrete and desirable. That is the reason why on this day the Church directs our eyes towards the end, towards the second coming of Christ.

We are shown the end, not just of our individual journeys, but of the entire human family. The end is the coming of God's Kingdom in all its glory. God has a goal for the world. That goal will be attained. Christ, who once came in a humble and weak manner, will return in power and glory. What should be our attitude as Christians to the second coming of Christ, and how should we prepare for it?

A certain man owned a large garden. He needed workers to cultivate it. He had little trouble in finding spring workers. The days were lengthening, the sun shining and the birds singing. The blossoms of the fruit trees filled the air with their perfume. The soil was dry and didn't cling to your boots or tools. And the work consisted mainly of sowing things. And sowing is a beautiful occupation.

He had even less trouble in finding summer workers. By now the days were long, hazy and beautiful. The air was full of pleasant sounds and intoxicating scents. All the things that had been planted in spring were bursting with life. Every inch of the garden was full of green stalks, which were laden with flowers and young fruits.

It goes without saying that he had no trouble whatsoever in finding autumn workers. People were literally breaking down the gate to get in. For this was harvest time. The work consisted mainly in picking the ripe fruit. Not only did you get well paid for it but you could eat as much as you like and no one said a word to you.

Ah, but when the winter came, he could hardly find one who wanted to work in the garden. And what a lot of work there was to be done. Winter was an ideal time for cleaning up the garden. All that was used and useless could be taken away and burned. Anything that was broken could be repaired. Tools and machines could be cleaned and greased. And of course the beds had to be dug up. But the weather was wretched, the days short and the garden bleak and bare. And the wet heavy soil clung to your boots making them like lead.

It was no joke. The work was hard and unspectacular. At the end of the day you often had no visible results to show for your efforts, no fruits of any kind. You had to live on hope. How much nicer then to stay indoors by a nice warm fire.

Yet, of all the work, the winter work was the most important. If it remained undone or was badly done, then when spring came the sowing would be late and rushed, with the result that the harvest would be impoverished. But if one had done one's winter work well, it was a delight to await the coming of spring.

Even though Christ has come into our world, and remains with us, nevertheless we still live in a kind of winter. Of course there are many lovely things in the world but still there are lots of bare and bleak spots. We are waiting for the glorious spring of Christ's second coming, when he will bring to fruition all our efforts.

When this spring will come we do not know. Only the heavenly Father knows. Therefore we should not believe those who claim to have inside information. We know that it will come. We have Christ's word for it. That should be enough. We live in hope. What is uncertain is not the coming of Christ but our readiness and capacity to 'go forth to meet him'.

Meanwhile we must get on with our winter work. St Paul gives us a programme. (See second reading). He tells us to 'live the life that God wants, as you have learned from me.' First and foremost he places the command to love and care for our fellow Christians in the community of the Church. Then we are to reach out to others. As St John of the Cross put it: 'In the evening of life we shall be examined on love.' To love can be so unspectacular and so seemingly unrewarding. To love means to share the burdens and sorrows of others. This can be a sticky and messy business.

But if we have done our winter work well then we can look forward with joy to the spring. Christ urged his disciples, not to fear his coming, but to look forward to it. He said: 'Stand erect, hold up your heads, for the time of your liberation is close at hand.' Why should we not look forward in joyful hope to the definitive and complete victory of Christ our King over the powers of evil?

The last day will be a day of triumph for Christ and his true followers, a spring time of liberation and salvation. How strange that all the false prophets when they speak of the end speak of gloom, doom and damnation. But they are wrong. The love and the mercy of God are at the very heart of the Good News preached by Christ.

But we cannot live in the future. The future is in God's hands. The present is in ours. We have to get on with our winter work. But the risen Christ is at our side to encourage us and to give us hope.

'In the midst of winter I find in myself an invincible spring.'
(Albert Camus).

'No witness reaches our contemporaries more persuasively than
the witness of Christians who do what Jesus did.' (Anthony
Padovano).

PRAYER OF THE FAITHFUL

Let us pray to our heavenly Father that the salvation won for us
by Christ may be ours. *R.* Come, Lord Jesus.

For the Church: that it may continue to act as a beacon of hope
for the world, directing it towards Christ and his kingdom. (Pause).
Let us pray.

For all the leaders of the world: that they may speak and act in
a way that promotes justice and peace. (Pause).　　Let us pray.

For all those who live without faith and who are going through
a winter of despair: that the light of Christ may shine for them.
(Pause).　　Let us pray.

That we who recognise Christ as our Saviour, and who await his
second coming in joyful hope, may follow him in our lives.
(Pause).　　Let us pray.

For local needs.

Let us pray:

Heavenly Father, deliver us from every evil, and grant us peace
in our day. In your mercy keep us free from sin and protect us from
anxiety as we wait in joyful hope for the coming of our Saviour,
Jesus Christ. We ask this through the same Christ our Lord.

SIGN OF PEACE

Lord Jesus Christ, the night before you died, as you sat at table
with your friends, you said to them: 'Peace I leave with you, my
peace I give you. A peace which the world cannot give, this is my
gift to you.' Help us to live free from anxiety and fear, and grant
us the peace and unity of your kingdom where you live and reign
for ever and ever.

COMMUNION REFLECTION

Today, on a bus, I saw a girl with golden hair;
I envied her and wished I were as fair.
When suddenly she rose to leave I saw her hobble down the aisle;
she had one leg and wore a crutch, but as she passed — a smile.
O God, forgive me when I whine,
I have two legs the world is mine.

I stopped to buy some candy; the lad who sold it had such charm;

I talked with him; if I were late 'twould do no harm.
And as I left he said: 'I thank you, you have been so kind;
it's nice to talk with folks like you — you see, I'm blind.'
O God forgive men when I whine,
I have two eyes the world is mine.

Later, on the street, I saw a child with eyes of blue;
he stood and watched the others play, now knowing what to do.
I stopped a moment, then I said: 'Why don't you join the others,
   dear?'
He looked ahead without a word, and then I knew he could not
   hear.
O God forgive me when I whine,
I have two ears the world is mine.

With feet to take me where I'd go,
with eyes to see the sunset's glow,
with ears to hear what I would know,
I'm blessed indeed, the world is mine.

Author unknown.

SECOND SUNDAY OF ADVENT
Preparing a way for the Lord

INTRODUCTION AND CONFITEOR

Even though the sun may be shining brightly and warmly outside, unless you pull back the blinds it will not be able to fill your
house. In today's liturgy we hear the lonely but insistent voice of
John the Baptist urging us to 'prepare a way for the Lord'.

Christ has come into our world, and he will come to us during
this Eucharist. Let us pause to prepare our hearts and minds to
receive him. (Pause).

Lord Jesus, you come to reconcile us to one another and to the
Father. Lord, have mercy.

Lord Jesus, you heal the wounds of sin and division. Christ,
have mercy.

Lord Jesus, you intercede for us with your Father. Lord, have
mercy.

HEADINGS FOR READINGS

First Reading (Baruch 5:1-9). Jerusalem is told that she can forget the sufferings of the past. She will know the joy of seeing her exiled children restored to her. God will level out a highway to facilitate their return.

Second Reading (Philippians 1:3-6, 8-11). The central message of this reading is a call for unity, perseverance and unwavering witness to Christ and the Gospel. At the same time Paul's love for his fellow Christians shines through.

Gospel (Luke 3:1-6). This tells about the appearance on the scene of John the Baptist. The heart of John's message is that God is coming to save his people. The people are urged to prepare a way for him through repentance.

HOMILY

What a wonderful vision the Old Testament prophets had to offer. In today's first reading we hear Baruch say: 'Take off your dress of sorrow and distress, put on the beauty of the glory of God for ever. . . . Arise, Jerusalem, and see your sons reassembled from west to east at the command of the Holy One . . .'

We believe that Christ was the long-awaited Saviour. But was the vision of the prophets fulfilled in him? Look at the present reality of the world and at our individual lives. We live in fear of the holocaust of nuclear war — the total annihilation of life as we know it. However, the work of salvation goes on, but it is not as eye-catching as the work of destruction. It doesn't happen as fast, and it calls for a great amount of care and dedication. Any lunatic with a gun can shoot a man's arm off, but it takes a very skillful surgeon to sow it back on again.

It was Whit Sunday, May 21, 1972. The scene — St Peter's Basilica in Rome. As always a large group of people stood gazing at Michelangelo's Pietà. For nearly five hundred years this white marble statue of Mary holding the body of the dead Christ has been admired and loved by people from all over the world. They have marvelled at the delicate shape of Christ's body and at the beauty of Mary's sorrowful and youthful face.

Suddenly there was an uproar. A man carrying a hammer jumped over the altar rails and attacked the famous statue. Before he was overpowered he had hit it fifteen times. About fifty large pieces of marble and one hundred and fifty smaller ones lay scattered around the floor. The damage was very serious. Mary's left arm was broken off at the elbow and the fingers destroyed. Part of her nose was smashed. Her veil and left cheek were scarred in several places and her left eye was also badly damaged.

Sympathy, advice and money poured into the Vatican from many parts of the world. But a leading daily newspaper commented: 'The statue is ruined. It is beyond repair'.

But the head of the Vatican Museum did not agree. He got together a team of seven scientists and restorers and they spent ten months repairing this unique work. Their first task was to gather up the fragments, even the tiniest, each of which had to be sorted and labelled. Missing parts had to be made from exactly the same kind of marble as the original. Federici and his dedicated helpers worked long hours in their laboratory. He said: 'We felt just as though we were at the bedside of a person who was very sick and whom we loved very much. But there was joy in our hearts at being allowed to play a part in the recreation of this beautiful piece of art.'

At last, almost a year later, the work of restoration was complete. Except for a scar at the back of the veil, which was purposely left there as evidence of the attack, the Pietà was again perfect. On March 25, 1973, feast of the Annunciation, it was put on public display once more. The only difference was that now visitors would have to look at Our Lady's serene face through a bullet-proof glass screen. For the age in which we live is one of violence. Yet it is also an age in which a group of peaceful men, working with great care and marvellous skill, can restore lost beauty to the world.

Advent issues a great call to repentance. Each year we hear again John the Baptist's lonely voice crying out: 'Repent, for the kingdom of heaven is close at hand.' To repent means to recognise our brokenness and our consequent need of redemption, and to turn to God. Mankind in general is broken and fragmented. The unity of the human family is continually under siege. Indeed it has never been fully recognised, much less realised. And each of us in particular is damaged and wounded by sin. We have eyes that do not see; ears that do not hear; tongues that do not speak; and above all, hearts that do not love. And how many people suffer from anguish — the anguish of loneliness, inability to get on with others, and feelings of worthlessness.

Unless we are able to recognise this state of brokenness there is not much hope for us. What makes it all the more painful is the feeling that we are powerless to save ourselves. Left to ourselves we are incapable of performing even one Christian act. We are paralysed and afraid, yet conscious of what we should be doing.

But God has not abandoned us or forgotten us. In his love he has sent us a Saviour — Christ. First of all in his own person the damaged image of God was fully restored to its original perfection and innocence. Christ is the first of the new creation — man restored to God's friendship.

Then through Christ God's scattered children are being gathered into a single body. Thanks to him we form a single body, of which he is the head. 'Once you were not a people at all, but now you are the People of God.' (1 Peter 2:10). Look at us here this morning. We are gathered in Christ's name. Nothing else could cause us to drop everything and come together here. Here we realise we are brothers and sisters and that we have a common goal. We know that our unity is not perfect, but Christ will help us to work on it. Here no one should feel left out or unimportant. And here our individual wounds are healed. 'Through his wounds you have been healed.' (Peter).

The risen Christ is with us. The work of healing and restoring goes on in us and through us. God has not forgotten us. This is something to feel happy about. It means that the message of the prophets is being fulfilled. To be redeemed is not merely to be absolved of guilt before God, but to live in Christ, to be a new creature.

'Those in misery still wait for their Saviour under the appearance of the flesh and blood of a caring Christian.' (Jean Vanier).

'Our task is to seek and find Christ in our world as it is, and not as it might be.' (Thomas Merton).

PRAYER OF THE FAITHFUL

Let us pray to God our Father that he will help us to remove those obstacles to the healing work of Christ which exist in our lives and in our world.   *R.* Lord, graciously hear us.

For the Church: that it may be a sign of unity and an instrument of peace for all the world. (Pause).   Lord, hear us.

For all doctors, nurses and all those whose task it is to care for the sick and the wounded: that God may give them sensitive hands and compassionate hearts. (Pause).   Lord, hear us.

For those who are broken by sorrow and suffering, and for all those who are victims of violence or exploitation. (Pause).   Lord, hear us.

That through our work and cooperation with others we may continue Christ's work of saving and restoring the world. (Pause). Lord, hear us.

For local needs.

Let us pray:

Lord God, you have prepared fitting remedies for our weakness; grant that we may reach out gladly for your healing grace, and thereby live in accordance with your will. We ask this through Christ our Lord.

COMMUNION REFLECTION

By now winter has stripped the trees of their leaves.
How poor and bare they look.
All their flaws are plain to be seen.

Yet it is only when a tree has thus been stripped
that we can see and appreciate its true shape.
Nothing can hide in it.
The sunlight pours through it.
And how lovely it is.
to be able to look through its skeletal branches
to the blue sky beyond.

It is the same with ourselves.
When we have been stripped of all inessentials,
of all the flimsy things we use to hide our nakedness,
then all our warts and wounds appear.
At the same time,
it is only when all that is unimportant has been taken away
that our true worth is revealed.

Christ comes to strip us of all that is useless,
to expose our wounds so that he can heal them,
and to reveal to us our true dignity
as sons and daughters of the Father.

Thus God's light can pour into the world,
and we are able to look through it to the world beyond —
the world of the eternal.

THIRD SUNDAY OF ADVENT
What must we do?

INTRODUCTION AND CONFITEOR

As we gather in the house of our heavenly Father, Christ our Saviour is in our midst as he promised. St Paul says to us in today's second reading: 'The Lord is very near. So there is no need to worry. If you need anything, pray for it.'

Let us draw near to Christ our brother. (Pause). And let us with confidence confess our sins, especially those in which we offend against our brothers and sisters.

I confess to almighty God . . . etc.

HEADINGS FOR READINGS

First Reading (Zephaniah 3:14-18). Jerusalem is urged to rejoice because her salvation is at hand. God himself stands in her midst, the king and the protector of his people. We too should take heart from this message of hope.

Second Reading (Philippians 4:4-7). This urges us to rejoice in the Lord, to be free of anxiety and to live in a spirit of prayer and thanksgiving.

Gospel (Luke 3:10-18). John the Baptist tells various groups of people the works of justice and charity they must do in order to prepare for the Lord's coming and to escape his searching judgement.

HOMILY

John the Baptist obviously was a very practical man. When the people asked him: 'What must we do to prepare for the coming of the Messiah?', he gave them very down-to-earth advice. He said to all: 'Share your surplus food and clothes with the starving and the naked.' To tax collectors he said: 'Do not rob the people — just collect what you are entitled to and no more.' To soldiers he said: 'Do not abuse your power. Do not intimidate people or use violence against them'.

Christianity is a very practical religion. The foundation of everything is of course our relationship with the Father in and through Christ his Son. To strengthen and deepen this relationship we need prayer. But for too many people it all ends there. It does not flow over into their ordinary lives and show itself in the way they treat other people. Without this second dimension religion is little better than smoke without a fire or blossoms without fruit.

In a certain town there lived a very honest cobbler called Martin. He lived in a tiny basement room. Its only window looked out onto the street. Of the passersby all he could see was their feet. But since there was hardly a pair of boots or shoes that had not passed through his hands at one time or another for repair, Martin was able to identify the passersby by looking at their shoes.

But life had been hard on Martin. His wife died, leaving him with a young son. However, no sooner had the son reached the age when he could be of help to his father than he fell ill and died. Martin buried him and gave way to despair, taking to the bottle at the same time. He gave up the practice of his religion. But one day an old friend of his dropped in. Martin poured out his soul to him. At the end of if his friend advised him to do a little reading from the Gospels each day, promising that if he did so light and hope would come back into his life.

Martin took his friend's advice. At the end of each day he would take down the Gospels from the shelf and read a little. At first he meant only to read on Sundays, but he found it so interesting that he soon read every day. Slowly his life changed. He gave up drink. The words of Christ created new hope for him, and the deeds of Christ were like lights that drove out his darkness.

One night as Martin sat reading he thought he heard someone calling him. He listened and heard clearly: 'Martin, Martin, look out into the street tomorrow for I will come to visit you.' He looked around the tiny room, and since there was no one to be seen, he reckoned it must be the Master himself who had spoken to him.

So it was with a great sense of excitement that he sat down to his work next day. As he worked he kept a close eye on the window. He scrutinised every pair of shoes or boots that passed above him. He was looking for something or someone special. But nothing exciting happened. Just the usual people passed by going about their everyday business.

The day wore on and nobody special passed by. In the early afternoon he saw a pair of old boots that were very familiar to him. They belonged to an old soldier called Stephen. Going to the window he looked up and saw the old man hitting his hands together for it was bitterly cold outside. Martin wished that he would move on, for he was afraid he might obstruct his view and that he would not see the Master when he passed. But old Stephen just stood there by the railing. Finally it occurred to Martin that maybe Stephen had nothing to eat all day. So he tapped on the window and beckoned him to come in. He sat him by the fire and gave him tea and bread. Stephen was most grateful. He said he hadn't eaten for two whole days. As he left Martin gave him his second overcoat as a shield against the biting cold.

But all the time Martin was entertaining Stephen he had not forgotten the window. Every time a shadow fell on it he looked up but nobody extraordinary passed. Night fell. Martin finished his work and very reluctantly closed the window shutters. After supper he took down the Gospels and, as was his custom, opened the book at random. There his eyes fell on these words: 'The people came to John and asked: "What must we do?" And he said: "If anyone has two coats he must share with the man who has none, and the one with something to eat must do the same".'

Martin put down the book and reflected. Then those other words of the Master came to him: 'I was hungry and you fed me. I was thirsty and you gave me a drink. I was naked and you clothed me . . .' He understood then that Christ had indeed come to him that day in the person of Stephen, and that he had made him welcome.

And his heart was filled with a peace he had never before experienced.

Will Christ come for me this Christmas? Do I wait for him? Do I want him? Do I need him? Of course Christ has already come and we can encounter him any time and any place. But still Christmas provides us with a unique opportunity in the whole year to draw close to him. The only thing is that as we approach the day itself our daily lives get more and more hectic. There are so many things to be done that there is very little time or room for the Master. We do not have time to look towards the window. And how we need him when we consider our spiritual poverty, our darkness, our wounds, our fears and despairs.

But how do we expect Christ to come? Of course he comes bearing gifts for us. But he also comes, and at the oddest times and places and wearing off-putting masks, as the one in need. So then we might do well to ask: Who is passing by my window unnoticed? Who am I excluding from my life? Who am I treating unjustly?

Martin had already received Christ into his life through a prayerful reading of the Gospels. So the second step followed naturally: to make room for him in the person of a needy neighbour.

'No one can claim to be a follower of Christ and remain entirely unlike the Master whom he professes to love.' (Anthony Padovano).

'If I am hungry, that is a material problem; if someone else is hungry, that is a spiritual problem.' (Berdyaev).

PRAYER OF THE FAITHFUL

The Lord, our God, is coming. Let us put aside our fears, and prepare for his coming with generosity and joy.   *R*. Lord, hear our prayer.

For all Christians: that they may put the Lord at the centre of their lives and seek to imitate him in his love for the Father and for others. (Pause).   Let us pray to the Lord.

For all members of the army and police force: that they may never abuse their power, but that they may be true keepers of the peace. (Pause).   Let us pray to the Lord.

For all those who, blinded by materialism and self-sufficiency, do not experience any need of God in their lives. (Pause).   Let us pray to the Lord.

That we may realise that the Lord is always passing by our window in the person of the one who needs our help, and in the person of the one we are rejecting or treating unfairly. (Pause).   Let us pray to the Lord.

For local needs.

Let us pray:
Lord, with sorrow we confess our sins, unworthy servants that
we are. Heal our wounds and bring us joy by the coming of your
only Son who lives and reigns with you and the Holy Spirit, one
God, for ever and ever.

COMMUNION REFLECTION
(Today being Gaudete Sunday, here is a thought on joy).

A lot of people confuse joy with pleasure,
but there is a world of difference between them,
and unless you know this difference,
you have not yet begun to live.
People who have tasted real joy are suspicious of pleasure,
because pleasure sometimes can be the death of joy.

Joy consists in having a love affair with life.
It is having a heart aglow with warmth
for all your companions on the road of life.

It is a blend of laughter and tears.
It is knowing how to share with other people.
It is looking for the happiness that comes in small packages,
knowing that big packages are few and far between.

It is making the most of the present,
enjoying what is at hand right now.
Joy is love bubbling over into life.
And, surprisingly, it can coexist with pain.

Joy is the flag you fly
when Christ, the Prince of Peace,
is in residence within your heart.

FOURTH SUNDAY OF ADVENT
The Lord is at the door.

INTRODUCTION AND CONFITEOR
In a few days we celebrate the birthday of Christ our Saviour.
We are asked to prepare our hearts to receive him like Mary did.
She will help us. Let us turn to her. (Pause).
Christ came most readily to those who had most need of him,

that is to the unfortunate, the sinful, the destitute — those who were 'empty'. Let us come to him in our sinfulness and emptiness.
Shepherd of Israel, you rouse your might and come to our help. Lord, have mercy.
Lord, you let your face shine on us and we are saved. Christ, have mercy.
You give life to all who call upon your name. Lord, have mercy.

HEADINGS FOR READINGS

First Reading (Micah 5:1-4). Jerusalem was under siege and David's dynasty was in jeopardy. But the prophet said that salvation would come from a comparatively insignificant place — Bethlehem. From there a new leader would come to gather together the scattered exiles and unite the nation once more.

Second Reading (Hebrews 10:5-10). The sacrifices of the Mosaic Law were unable to purify people from sin. Only Christ, through his obedience and sacrifice of self, was able to bring about the reconciliation between God and his people.

Gospel (Luke 1:39-45). This deals with Mary's visit to Elizabeth. Enlightened by the Holy Spirit, Elizabeth praises Mary and hints at the uniqueness of the child she has just conceived.

HOMILY

Christmas is very near. What does it mean for us? It means different things for different people. For some it is a time of heightened loneliness, feverish activity, and ephemeral and selective goodwill. Here are some examples of what I mean. (Ideally these parts should be spoken by different people. The priest (P) could put the questions).

Mr. O'Brien is an elderly bachelor who lives alone.
P: How did you spend last Christmas?
O'B: I spent it alone like I spent the last eight Christmases ever since my sister died.
P: How did you feel?
O'B: Very lonely. The loneliness gets worse at Christmas.
P: Have you got TV?
O'B: I have but it's no use. My sight isn't good.
P: Are you looking forward to Christmas?
O'B: To tell the truth I dread it. It's hard to be alone at Christmas. You see other families drawing closer together. This makes you feel like an outsider at a feast.
P: Thank you Mr O'Brien. I think he is typical of the many old people who spend Christmas on their own. (Brief pause).

Mrs Hughes is a housewife with a young family.

P: What does Christmas mean to you Mrs Hughes?

H: A mountain of extra work! Cards to be written, presents to be bought, wrapped and delivered. The house has to be cleaned and decorated. The Christmas shopping has to be done. With the increasing traffic this gets worse every year. Then, of course, there is the turkey to be prepared and cooked. If the turkey doesn't turn out right then for some the whole Christmas is ruined.

P: Spiritually what does it mean to you?

H: Very little. Don't get me wrong. I'm as good a Catholic as the next. It's just that I don't have the time. I'm lucky if I can get three minutes to pop into confession on Christmas Eve and a half hour to go to Mass on Christmas morning.

P: You don't relish Christmas, then?

H: There are some things that I enjoy about it and I don't deny its spiritual importance. But there is too much fuss, too much worry attached to it, at least for a mother. You have to try to keep everybody happy. But then you see so much of your work wasted or not appreciated — food left over, toys cast aside . . . Honestly I'm glad when it's all over. (Brief pause).

Anne Carey is a young student.

P: What do you think of Christmas?

C: It is supposed to be a family feast. But in our house people are so busy that we haven't time to talk to one another. Either that or we are all glued to the TV or everybody is half drunk. Christmas is also supposed to be a time of peace and goodwill. But this goodwill hardly survives the morning, and is rarely extended to enemies. For instance in our family there is an uncle who never gets a card because of a row that happened twenty years ago. That kind of thing. There is a lot of hypocrisy attached to all this hand-shaking and exchange of 'Happy Christmas'. If people really meant it they would carry it over into the new year.

P: Do you think your family is typical in that respect?

C: Yes. From listening to my friends I believe it goes on all over the place. (Brief pause).

P: But for other people Christmas is not so bleak. It is a time for caring, family joy, and spiritual renewal. Mr McCann works for the Vincent de Paul.
Mr McCann what is your view of Christmas?

McC: I think it brings out the best in a lot of people. We hold a special collection for the poor at this time and we get more then than we get during the rest of the year together. Christmas somehow touches people's hearts.

P: What do you do with this money?

McC: We provide coal, food and clothes for needy families. We distribute a number of hampers to the poor. We pay for the rental of TV sets for struggling families. That kind of thing.

P: This must take up a lot of your menbers' time?

McC: Yes, but I've never heard one of them complain.

P: What precise meaning then do you see in Christmas?

McC: Well, when Christ came he came poor. There was no room for him in the inn. We have to make sure that the poor are not forgotten at this time, otherwise there is still no room for Christ. (Brief pause).

Mrs Goff is also a young mother and housewife.

P: What is Christmas like for you?

G: I agree with Mrs Hughes that there is a lot of extra work to be done but we try to share it out. That way it brings us closer together as a family. The children do most of the cleaning and decorating. My husband and I do the shopping. I do the cooking, but then I am not allowed touch the washup! Then we all sit down and watch the TV shows.

P: You don't find them contrary to the spirit of Christmas?

G: Not at all. They are generally of a joyful and uplifting nature.

P: And what about the spiritual side of Christmas?

G: We do not neglect it for we consider it very important. We all go to confession and Communion. At the centre of the home is a little crib built by the children. Each evening we gather for a little family prayer in front of it. (Brief pause).

Mr Deans is a business man, married with a family.

P: I understand that last Christmas was a special one for you?

D: That's right. I was brought up a Catholic but I drifted away from the practice of my religion in my twenties. Last Christmas Eve I was passing a church when suddenly I felt the urge to go inside. Before I knew it I was queueing for confession. I made my peace with God and I had the happiest Christmas of my life.

P: What had Christmas to do with your conversion?

D: There's something about Christmas. Somehow God seems very near to you and very friendly. If you are estranged from him you feel the pain of it and I think you get a special grace at this time to put things right with him.

P: Do you think there are others like you?

D: I'm certain there are. There is an enormous spiritual attraction about Christmas. I believe that many prodigals return to God's friendship at this time.

PRAYER OF THE FAITHFUL

We celebrate Christmas not just as individuals but as a community. We benefit from each other's example and support. Let us pray to our heavenly Father, who so loved the world that he sent his only Son, not to condemn us but to save us. *R:* Come, Lord Jesus.

For all the followers of Jesus: that they may experience a renewal of their faith in him this Christmas. (Pause). Let us pray.

For all government leaders: that they may never despise any of their fellow human beings, since through Christ's coming we are all children of God. (Pause). Let us pray.

That all families which are scattered may be reunited: that those in distress may experience relief. (Pause). Let us pray.

That each of us this Christmas may extend the hand of understanding, forgiveness and friendship to all, but especially to those from whom we may be estranged. (Pause). Let us pray.

For local needs.

Let us pray:

Father, when your Son came among us he took upon himself a human nature like ours. Grant that having shared our human lives he may give us a share in his divine life. We ask this through the same Christ our Lord.

INTRODUCTION TO THE OUR FATHER

The coming of Jesus among us as a brother teaches us that we are all children of the one Father. Let us pray to our Father now as Jesus taught us.

COMMUNION REFLECTION

It has been claimed that,
except for some sincerely religious people,
Christmas has become an occasion of dusty sentimentality —
something pretty but not quite authentic.
There is more than a little truth in this.

There are people who all year long
scarcely give the teachings of Christ a thought,
much less live by them,
who on Christmas Eve
wallow in cheap and sentimental piety.

We have to be careful not to fall into the same trap.
Mary, who is at the centre of today's Gospel, will help us.
She is a great example.

No sooner has she said her 'Yes' to God than she arose
and went with haste to help her cousin Elizabeth.
Her religion was not a matter of mere sentimentality.
It was the expression of a genuine feeling,
a feeling that she converted into deeds.

By all means let us light the Christmas candles for our children
and sing the carols.
But let us not be content with mere sentimentality.
Let us demand more of ourselves.
If it is true that only love can redeem us.
then let our love be true,
and don't let us confine it to one day in the year.

Christmastide

INTRODUCTION AND CONFITEOR

'I bring you news of great joy, a joy to be shared by the whole people. Today . . . a Saviour has been born to you.'

These are the words of the angels to the shepherds. As we gather here this night (morning) our Saviour is present among us, not as a little helpless baby, but as our risen Lord. Let us draw close to him and be happy. (Pause).

On those who live in a world of deep shadow your light shines. Lord, have mercy.

To all who accept you, you give the power to become children of God. Christ, have mercy.

You are full of grace and truth; from your fulness we all receive. Lord, have mercy.

HEADINGS FOR READINGS

Midnight Mass

First Reading (Isaiah 9:1-7). This reading looks forward to the coming of a Saviour-child who will rescue his people from darkness and oppression, and enable them to live in security and peace.

Second Reading (Titus 2:11-14). St Paul reminds us of what is expected of us if we are to enjoy the salvation won for us by Christ.

Gospel (Luke 2:1-14). This tells about the birth of Christ in a manger and how the news of his birth was brought to simple shepherds by angels.

Dawn Mass

First Reading (Isaiah 62:11-12). With the birth of our Lord the Christian people can taste the joy of the exiles returning from Babylon.

Second Reading (Titus 3:4-7). We ourselves did nothing to merit the birth of Christ; rather, God sent his Son out of compassion for us.

Gospel (Luke 2:15-20). With Mary we are invited to ponder on the deep meaning of the birth of Christ so that, with the shepherds, we may be moved to glorify and praise God.

Day Mass

First Reading (Isaiah 52:7-10). This great hymn of exultation at the return of the exiles from Babylon is also a poem of joy for our redemption.

Second Reading (Hebrews 1:1-6). The whole history of God's dealings with his people in the past was a preparation for the coming of his Son at a particular moment in history.

Gospel (John 1:1-18). This is a great hymn to the Word of God, the source of all life, whose coming among us makes us children of God.

HOMILY

Some sixteen years have passed since three men set off on the longest journey ever undertaken by man. Their target was a quarter of a million miles away. They set off faster than man has ever dreamed possible. The eyes of the whole world were upon them. We waited and watched, hoped and prayed for them and for the success of their mission. Thanks to television we were able to follow every second of it.

Their craft was a rocket twenty-four storeys high and worth millions of pounds. It had some three million components put together by ten thousand skilled workers. I'm talking about Neil Armstrong and his two fellow astronauts who in July of 1969 took off for our nearest neighbour in space — the moon. Can you still remember it? It's not very long ago, yet now it seems so hazy that it might have been fifty years ago. Yet it made such news at the time.

They landed on the part of the moon known as the Sea of Tranquility. They found it exactly as they expected — lifeless and barren. What did they bring back? Not much — just a handful of rocks and dust. Yet they described their mission as 'one small step by us, but a giant leap by mankind.' I don't want to minimise their achievement, but only a decade and a half later we've almost forgotten that it ever happened. And the men whose names were then on the lips of everybody have disappeared into obscurity.

Today we Christians celebrate the mystery of the incarnation, that is, the coming into our world of Jesus, the Son of God. It is the central mystery of our faith, more important by far than the trip to the moon. If only we had been allowed to manage it, how differently we would have done things. What a splash we would have made. Christ would have come with a magnificent display of fireworks. We would of course have waited until the advent of TV so that all the world could see and know what was happening.

But this is not how God did it. God's Son came not so much

from 'above' as from 'below'. He sprang up among us, born of a humble maid from an obscure village. He was born at a time when communication was slow and in a small country, a country that was certainly no sea of tranquility but the scene of bitter wars and almost perpetual strife. There weren't many people on hand when he came — just a few and they were simple people — Mary and Joseph and the shepherds.

That is how Christ's birth happened, yet we still talk about it and celebrate it. Though Christ came among us weak and empty-handed, he brought us priceless and everlasting gifts. He came to teach us that we are not dust, but sons and daughters of the heavenly Father.

Neil Armstrong and the early astronauts got a view of the earth no one ever got before — a view from space. As they looked back at it they exclaimed: 'To see the earth as it truly is — small and blue and beautiful in the eternal silence where it floats — is to see ourselves as travellers on the earth together, brothers who now know that they are truly brothers'.

This is the vision the coming of Christ gives us. We truly belong to one another, not merely because we live on the same small planet, but because we have a common Father. Christ came to reconcile us to the Father and to one another.

The joy of this day fills our hearts and the whole world. Let us welcome Christ, the only Son of the Father, who has come as our Brother and Saviour. Welcoming him we also reach out to one another. Christ leads us on a far more daring and more important journey than that of the moonmen — the journey to the Father's kingdom and eternal life. It is a journey we do not have to make alone. We make it together, as members of God's people should, with Christ at our head.

'Children are grateful when Santa Claus puts toys in their stockings. Could we not be grateful to God who has put in our stockings the priceless gift of two miraculous legs.' (G. K. Chesterton).

PRAYER OF THE FAITHFUL

We have no other light but Christ. He came down from heaven to show us the way to the house of our heavenly Father. Let us pray to him with unlimited confidence on this joyful day. *R*. Save us through your birth.

For all who believe in Christ: that they may recognise their splendid dignity and strive to live up to it. (Pause). Let us pray to the Lord.

For all men and women of goodwill: that God may touch their

hearts and open their ears so that they may receive the message of salvation. (Pause). Let us pray to the Lord.

For all those who are poor or lonely or dispirited: that they may experience the loving presence of Christ in their lives. (Pause). Let us pray to the Lord.

For ourselves: that we may welcome Christ into our lives with the simplicity and love of Mary, Joseph and the shepherds. (Pause). Let us pray to the Lord.

For local needs.

Let us pray:

Father, when your Son came among us as man he scattered the darkness of this world and filled it with your glory. Grant that through his grace we may live as children of the light so that, when our earthly journey is over, we may come at last to the kingdom where he lives and reigns with you and the Holy Spirit, one God, for ever and ever.

SIGN OF PEACE

Lord, at your birth the angels sang: 'Glory to God in the highest, and peace to his people on earth.' Yet two thousand years later they still fight for possession of the land where you were born. Help us not to abandon the struggle for peace, and grant to us who have heard the message of the angels the peace and unity of your kingdom where you live for ever and ever.

COMMUNION REFLECTION

Spelling out the meaning of Christmas:

C stands for Christ. If we leave him out of Christmas
  it is like celebrating a wedding without the groom.

H stands for the hope he gives us —
  hope of a life without end.

R stands for the revolution he began:
  turning hate to love, war to peace,
  and everyone into everyone's neighbour.

I stands for Israel, the land where he was born.
  But it also stands for me,
  for Christ could be born a thousand times in Bethlehem,
  but it would all be in vain unless he is born in me.

S stands for the salvation he brought:
  those who lived in darkness saw a great light.

T stands for thanks — thanks to the Father for the gift of his Son.

The best way to say thanks
is to make room for him in our hearts.

M stands for Mary who brought him to birth.
She will help to bring him to birth in us also.

A stands for the angels who at his birth sang:
'Glory to God in the highest, and peace to his people on earth'.
It was the sweetest music ever heard on earth.

S stands for the star that led the wise men to Bethlehem.
Now Christ is the star we follow.
His light will guide us through the night
until the sun of eternal day dawns upon us.

FEAST OF THE HOLY FAMILY

INTRODUCTION AND CONFITEOR

As we assemble to celebrate the Eucharist on the feast of the
Holy Family of Nazareth, let us remember that we are not a bunch
of individuals without any close ties. Together we form the family
of the People of God. Let us pause to reflect on our unity and ask
God to remove the things that divide us. (Pause).

Lord Jesus, you came to unite us to one another and to the
Father.   Lord, have mercy.

Lord Jesus, you heal the wounds caused among us by sin and
division.   Christ, have mercy.

Lord Jesus, you continue to intercede for us at the right hand of
the Father.   Lord, have mercy.

HEADINGS FOR READINGS

First Reading (1 Samuel 1:20-22, 24-28). This deals with the birth
of Samuel and his consecration to God. Every child should be seen
as a gift from God.

Second Reading (1 John 3:1-2, 21-24). We are God's own
children and he has a wonderful destiny in store for us. We should,
therefore, respond by living a life that befits a child of God.

(Note: the readings from Year A may be used as alternatives).

Gospel (Luke 2:41-52). This relates the episode in which the
twelve-year-old Jesus got lost in Jerusalem. It shows how, even in
the best of families, hurtful misunderstandings can occur.

HOMILY

Children need sunshine. They need to play with other children.

They need someone to set them a good example. But above all they need love, even if it is only a tiny drop of love. Many children today are victims of broken homes, and are brutalised as a result of drunkenness, rejection and cruelty. Let us look at the incident in today's Gospel. It has many things to say about parenthood.

Jesus was twelve years old — time for him to take on the obligations of the Law. So Mary and Joseph took him with them to Jerusalem to celebrate the great feast of the Passover. It is the task of the family gradually to insert the child into the larger community and to teach him its traditions.

How exciting it must have been for a small boy from a remote village to join a large pilgrimage, to set foot in the holy city and to visit the Temple. We must never underestimate the importance of childhood memories and impressions in the formation of a person's character. The great Russian writer, Dostoyevsky, says that he never forgot a Mass he attended with his mother on the Monday before Easter. Though he was only eight at the time, he says he had a spiritual experience that planted seeds in his soul that flowered later on. Children need guidance. Above all they need to be shown a path to a spiritual well, otherwise they will always be thirsty.

But as Mary and Joseph set out on the return journey Jesus got left behind, and it wasn't until the end of the first day that he was missed. They began a frantic search for him. A young child, lost in a big city, sought by frantic parents. How often this happens today. No one was to blame. It was the result of a misunderstanding. Misunderstandings occur even in the best families.

Both of them were very worried. Having failed to find him among their fellow pilgrims, they returned to the city to look for him, their worry growing with each passing hour. They could not understand why he would cause them such anxiety. But a child doesn't stop being your child even when he or she causes you worry. Nor do you stop being a parent. In fact the test of a good parent is being a parent in bad times. We need to stay friends with our teenagers, even when their behaviour causes us worry. Friends are a very powerful influence.

Meanwhile Jesus was alone. But he wasn't utterly lost. A person is only lost when he has no home to go to or no one to care for him. But Jesus had a happy home. He had two people who cared deeply about him, and to whom he was important and precious. He was having an adventure. He knew where he was. He was in the Temple, God's house. Yes, the same Temple from which later he would drive out the merchants and the money-changers. But as yet he looked at the whole scene with the wonder and innocence of childhood.

When at last they found him, their first question was very understandable: 'Why did you do this to us?' And he replied: 'I did it because I must be about my Father's business.' It is interesting to note that they did not understand his explanation — at least not at once. Yet they didn't scold him. Had they done so they might have robbed him of the fruits of a marvellous experience, an experience in which he glimpsed his unique relationship with God. Sometimes parents don't know how to encourage their children even when they are interested in worthwhile things.

But Mary remembered his words and pondered them in her heart. Listening is a very important part of being a parent. We have to listen to what a child is saying with words and without them. Listening means searching for the real reasons behind the problem as opposed to seeking causes for condemnation. They say that for many young addicts drug-taking is a kind of silent cry for help. To get to know and understand our children we have to spend time with them. It is not enough to keep them busy with toys or to quieten them with TV. Nor is it enough merely to look in on them periodically to lay down the law. Everyone needs to feel that someone is watching over them, but there is a world of difference between that and the feeling of being watched.

Even though the whole incident was painful (at least for Mary and Joseph) it had the effect of bringing them closer together. Jesus appreciated how much Mary and Joseph cared about him, so he gladly obeyed them. It is not enough to command obedience, we have to try to be worthy of it. And for their part, Mary and Joseph began to realise what a special child Jesus was. And they began to give him scope to grow, even though it meant that he was growing away from them. Parents, having given life to their children, must not take it back. They must allow their children to live that life. Children are like kites. It takes a lot of time, patience and trouble to get them airborne. But when they are airborne only then will the parents know that they have done their job.

However, when all is said and done, the most important people in the family are not the children but the parents. The parents need to be able to find in the home the nourishment they need to grow as human beings. They have to take care of themselves and of each other. They need to support one another. Only then will they be able to take proper care of their children. Mothers especially often feel guilty about thinking of themselves. They think they are being selfish. There is a lot of difference, however, between being selfish and taking care of yourself.

Without the word 'we' there would be no community, sharing or togetherness. It is within the family that a child learns to use it for the first time.

'There is nothing a person cherishes more than the memories of early childhood in the home, provided there was at least a little love and harmony in the family.' (Dostoyevsky).

'I cry for parents so engrossed in giving their children all the material benefits of our affluent society that they neglect to give them the only thing that matters – God.' (Catherine de Hueck Doherty).

PRAYER OF THE FAITHFUL

Let us ask the Father, from whom every family in heaven and on earth takes its name, to send the Spirit of his Son into our hearts and our homes. *R.* Lord, in your mercy, hear our prayer.

For Christian parents: that the Lord may give them wisdom to guide their children, and integrity so as to be an example to them. (Pause). Let us pray.

For world leaders: that they may cooperate with one another for the good of the entire human family. (Pause). Let us pray.

For those families that have been orphaned or widowed or which are experiencing problems of any kind, that the Lord may comfort them. (Pause). Let us pray.

For ourselves: that like the child Jesus we may grow in wisdom and in favour with God and others. (Pause). Let us pray.

For local needs.

Let us pray:

O God, Father of every family, against whom no door can be shut, convert our hearts and our homes into fit dwelling places for Christ your Son, who lives and reigns with you and the Holy Spirit, one God, for ever and ever.

COMMUNION REFLECTION

A prayer for parents

Grant us children, O Lord,
who will be strong enough to know when they are weak;
who will be unbending in honest defeat,
yet humble and gentle in victory.

Grant us children,
whose wishes will not take the place of their deeds;
children who will know you and know themselves.

Lead them, we pray you,

not in the path of ease and comfort,
but rather in the path of difficulties and challenges.

Grant us children,
whose hearts will be clear,
whose goals will be high;
children who will master themselves
before seeking to master others.

And after all these things,
add, we pray, a sense of humour,
so that they can be serious,
yet never take themselves too seriously.
Give them the humility and simplicity of true greatness.
Then we, their parents, will dare whisper,
we have not lived in vain.

(Adapted from a prayer by General Mac Arthur).

SECOND SUNDAY AFTER CHRISTMAS
Presence

INTRODUCTION AND CONFITEOR

As we gather to celebrate the Eucharist we become present to one another. And Christ, who took upon himself our human condition, is present among us. Let us bring to him all our sins so that he may remove them. Let us bring to him all our burdens so that he may help us to carry them. (Pause).

Lord Jesus, by your presence you give light to all those living in darkness. Lord, have mercy.

Lord Jesus, by your presence you give us a share in the divine life of the Father. Christ, have mercy.

Lord Jesus, by your presence you fill us with grace and truth. Lord, have mercy.

HEADINGS FOR READINGS

First Reading (Ecclesiasticus 24:1-2, 8-12). This is a poem in praise of wisdom, a wisdom that has pitched her tent among God's chosen people.

Second Reading (Ephesians 1:3-6, 15-18). This reading introduces the theme of God's loving plan of salvation for us.

Gospel (John 1:1-18). As the Son of God, Jesus existed from the very beginning of time, sharing the divine life of the Father. But then he became man, sharing our human lives in order to give us a share in his divine life.

HOMILY

Once during a general audience Pope Paul VI told the following story. It concerned his time in Milan. One day during the course of parish visitation he found an old woman who was sick.

'How are you?' he asked.

'Not bad,' she answered. 'I have enough food and I'm not suffering from the cold.'

'You must be reasonably happy then?' he asked.

'No, I'm not', she said as she started to cry. 'You see, my son and daughter-in-law never come to see me and I am dying of loneliness.'

As he went away the phrase 'I'm dying of loneliness' came back to him again and again. And in his audience the Pope concluded: 'This shows that food and warmth are not enough in themselves. People need something more. They need our presence, our time, our love. They need to be touched, to be reassured that they are not forgotten.'

This is a simple truth, yet a profound one. There is nothing as important as *presence* to those we love. Gifts, letters and phone calls are good, but they cannot take the place of presence. Presence brings enormous comfort. The presence with me of a friend, one with whom I can share my most precious depths and secrets, one to whom I can open my heart with all its aches and pains. There are so few people in the world with whom we can do this, with whom we can feel totally at peace.

That woman in the story had no one to talk to. No one to satisfy the universal need we all have to be accepted and valued for the unique people that we are. She had no one to say to her: 'I love you', or if she had they did not back up their words with deeds. She had no one to reveal to her her beauty, her value; no one to rejoice that she was alive; no one to whom she was important and precious.

Real presence is precious but it is far from easy. In today's liturgy we celebrate the Good News of God's presence with his people. A great shout comes from it: *'He lived among us'*. In and through Christ, God is truly present among his people. But before starting his public ministry (which lasted a mere three years) what was Christ doing? He was not doing anything great or significant. He was working as a village carpenter. From a worldly point of view it would seem that he was wasting his precious time. Not so. During those years his contribution was his presence, that is, *himself*. Only later would he begin to speak and act. But then his words and deeds had enormous impact for he had first proved his love by simple presence.

He was being present among his people. He was doing the hardest thing of all — just being present, rather than running around trying to prove 'useful'. He didn't drop in, say 'hello', and disappear again. He came and lived among us. he joined us. He became an ordinary worker. His ministry lay more in powerlessness than in power. He shared fully our human lives in order that we might share his divine life.

To help the underdog, Gandhi believed you must first understand him. To understand him you must sometimes live as he lives and work as he works. This is what Christ did. And he didn't just dabble. So many dabble. A politician begins a clean-up of the city streets by sweeping a few feet of pavement, in full view of the TV cameras, then hands the brush over to someone else. The President plants a tree and then walks back to his residence and leaves someone else to care for it. Christ did not do this.

What a wonderful thing this is — Christ's presence among us. He joined us because he loved us. We must open our eyes to his continuing presence among us, like the two disciples did on the road to Emmaus. We must listen to him, and then like them, open our hearts to him and pour out our hopes and disappointments. Often we do the exact opposite. We hide from him and from others those things and parts of ourselves where we feel guilty, ashamed, confused, frightened and lost. We don't give him a chance to be with us where we feel most alone and cut off. Especially in moments of anxiety and loneliness we need a silent and loving presence — someone to be there, if not for us, then at least with us.

We must also try to be present to one another, especially to those we love. By all means if there is something that we can do let us do it; or if there is something that we can say, let us say it. But maybe all we can do, is just be there with the other person. We will feel clumsy, in the way, and useless. But still, we are there, there with our loved one. It's not easy to accept that often our main, and perhaps only, contribution is simple presence. What matters is the authenticity and intensity of our presence.

And, by being there, we make Christ's presence real for people. Through us his followers, and in us, he continues to live on in the world.

'I regard time as the best gift one can offer — time just to sit and share'. (Leonard Cheshire).

'If Christ is not really my brother with all my sorrows, with all my burdens on his shoulder and sadness in his heart, then there has been no redemption.' (Thomas Merton).

PRAYER OF THE FAITHFUL

Let us turn in prayer to Christ our Brother, who emptied himself to take upon himself our human condition. *R.* Lord, save us through your presence.

Through his coming Christ opened the new age which the prophets foretold. May we his followers grow in grace and in truth. (Pause). We pray to you, O Lord.

At his birth the angels proclaimed peace to the world. May he help all humankind to take the road of peace together.(Pause). We pray to you, O Lord.

Christ spent most of his life working as a village carpenter. May he help all workers to find dignity through their work; may he give courage and hope to those who are unemployed. (Pause). We pray to you, O Lord.

Christ was tempted in every way that we are, yet he remained sinless. May he help us to overcome all our temptations. (Pause). We pray to you, O Lord.

For local needs.

Let us pray:

God our Father, you are the light of every faithful soul. Fill the world with your glory, and reveal to all peoples the splendour of your presence. We ask this through Christ our Lord.

COMMUNION REFLECTION

When God became man
he didn't become a king or a great political leader,
as many thought the Messiah would be.
Instead he became a working man.

The Gospels show us Christ
as a healer, teacher and wonder-worker.
But these activities lasted only three short years.
For the rest of his life on earth
he worked as a village carpenter.

There was nothing spectacular about his work.
He didn't make benches and tables by means of miracles,
but by the hammer and the saw.
And, as far as we know, nothing he made
ever set any fashion trends or became collector's items.

Though many of us may see our daily tasks as dull and boring,
we must not underestimate their importance.
There is little we can say about them
that God's Son could not say
when he became man and lived among us.

Lord, by your continuing presence with us,
help us to see the value of our daily tasks,
and to do them faithfully,
so that we too may grow in wisdom,
and in favour both with God and with people.

EPIPHANY

INTRODUCTION AND CONFITEOR

The wise men came searching for Christ. They found him, worshipped him and offered him gifts. Since then millions of people
have followed in their footsteps and come to Christ. We are doing
just that this morning. We come to Christ to worship him and offer
him our gifts. (Pause).

But Christ is no longer a helpless baby. He is our Lord and
Saviour who enriches us.

Lord Jesus, you bring healing to the sick.   Lord, have mercy.

Lord Jesus, you bring forgiveness to sinners. Christ, have
mercy.

Lord Jesus, you give us yourself to heal us and bring us
strength.   Lord, have mercy.

HEADINGS FOR READINGS

First Reading (Isaiah 60:1-6). The exiles returned from Babylon
to find their beloved Jerusalem in ruins. The prophet cheers them
up with a vision of a restored city.

Second Reading (Ephesians 3:2-3, 5-6). Paul reveals the fact that
God invites all, Jews and Gentiles alike, to share on an equal
footing the salvation won by Christ.

Gospel (Matt 2:1-12). This relates how three strangers came from
a far country to pay homage to the Christ-child while the Jewish
leaders rejected him.

HOMILY

There are three separate ideas in what follows.

(1) The picture most people have of how the Magi came to

Bethlehem goes somewhat like this. They saw a bright star in the
eastern sky and began to follow it. The star guided them unfail-
ingly, first to Jerusalem, where it temporarily disappeared, and
then to Bethlehem where they found the Child Jesus. But if you
read the Gospel account carefully you will see that this was not the
case. They saw the star "as it rose". It says nothing at this point
about the star guiding them. Rather, it was no more than a sign that
something unusual had happened, that someone special had been
born. The next time the star is mentioned is when they were on the
road to Bethlehem, that is, as they neared the end of their journey.
The text says: "There in front of them was the star they had seen
rising." The impliction seems to be that in between they travelled
in darkness. They had to ask and seek and enquire. They had, so
to speak, to feel their way along. Their's was like a night-time
journey between two ports.

This has very important implications for us. We can identify with
them. When we start out on some road (whether it be following
Christ, or following a profession or a 'vocation') we too are
attracted by something bright — a bright ideal or vision or hope.
But this initial 'star' will not remain for ever in our sky. It will grow
dim. Clouds will get in the way and blot out its light, forcing us to
feel our way forward in the darkness. Perhaps we may get an occasional glimpse of it to keep us going. We must not be surprised
when this happens. We must not get discouraged or give up. We
must imitate the Magi. We must not be too proud to ask for
guidance. We must keep on going forward until the darkness passes
and once again we glimpse the initial star that beckoned to us and
which guided us for a while.

(2) When the Magi found Christ they 'opened their treasures,
offering him gold, frankincense and myrrh.' Then, having worshipped him, 'they returned to their own country by another route.'
When we find Christ and offer our love to him, he will help us to
open up the treasures of goodness that lie buried inside us, so that
we can offer 'gifts' to our brothers and sisters, especially those who
are poor like Christ was. And having met Christ and heard his
Gospel, we will travel through life by a different route. We will
have different attitudes, values and goals. It is impossible to
encounter Christ without it affecting the way we live. We who have
seen the light of Christ are obliged to make known his presence to
the ends of the earth. This we do not only by preaching the glad
tidings of his coming, but above all by revealing him in our lives.

(3) The feast of the Epiphany is a revolutionary feast. At the
Epiphany Christ was revealed as the Saviour, not of a few people
or a select group, but of all people. His star shines for all. His light

was 'the true light which enlightens all men.' The Epiphany broke down the age-old and seemingly impenetrable barrier between Jews and Gentiles. The Jews, because of the privilege of possessing the promise, became proud and egoistic. They erected a barrier in the temple so that Gentiles could not enter. They considered the Gentiles dogs and enemies; and the Gentiles for their part hated the Jews.

The Epiphany is a beautiful feast because it brings everybody together. 'All now share the same inheritance, they are part of the same body.' (Second Reading). This seems quite simple and straight-forward. In theory it is, but in practice no. It is surprising how, down the ages, Christians have appropriated to themselves the light of Christ, considering so many others as outsiders and strangers.

'If you run after two hares, you won't catch one.' (Proverb).

'True liberation is freeing people from the bonds that have prevented them from giving their gifts to others.' (Henri Nouwen).

PRAYER OF THE FAITHFUL

The Father made known the birth of the Saviour by the light of a star. We pray that he may continue to guide us with his light. *R.* Lord, hear us in your love.

For the Church: that she may continue to help people discover Christ as their Lord and Saviour. (Pause). We pray in faith.

For all of mankind: that Christ may be a beacon of faith and hope to all men and women of good will who are searching for truth and goodness. (Pause). We pray in faith.

For all those who are lost and who have no one to advise or guide them; for all those who have given up the search and who have settled for a life of material comfort and pleasure. (Pause). We pray in faith.

That we who have found Christ may try to live according to his teachings so that we may help others find him. (Pause). We pray in faith.

For local needs.

Let us pray:

Lord our God, on this day you revealed your Son to all the peoples of the world. Lead us from the faith by which we know you now to the radiant vision of your glory where we shall see you face to face. We ask this through the same Christ our Lord.

SIGN OF PEACE

Lord, of what use is it to extend our hand to our neighbour if at the same time we exclude him from our heart. It is like talking to a person at the doorstep on a cold day but not allowing him to enter into the warmth of the interior. Grant us a warm and accepting heart, so that we may enjoy the peace and unity of your kingdom where you live for ever and ever.

COMMUNION REFLECTION
Helen Keller, who went blind and deaf at nineteen months, wrote the following:
'I am often conscious
of beautiful flowers and birds and laughing children
where to my seeing friends there is nothing.
They sceptically declare that I see
"a light that never was on sea or land".
But I know that their mystic sense is dormant,
and that is why there are so many barren places in their
    lives;
they prefer "facts" to vision.'

Through her blindness
Helen Keller became a very wise woman,
and 'saw' more than many who have perfect eyesight.

The Magi were wise men,
not however in a worldly sense.
They were wise
because they recognised the Christ-child as their Saviour,
whereas some saw him as just another child,
and others, such as Herod, saw him as a threat.

Lord, help us to recognise you as our Saviour,
not merely here in church,
but out there in the world.
Thus we will never walk in darkness
but will always have a 'star' to guide us.

BAPTISM OF CHRIST

INTRODUCTION AND CONFITEOR
   Today we celebrate the day Christ, the sinless one, joined the ranks of us sinners by accepting Baptism from his cousin John. He did so in order to help us to live in the glorious freedom of the children of God.
   He joins us now as we meet to celebrate the Eucharist in his

name. Let us draw near to him who is a messenger of the Father's love and mercy. (Pause).
You open the eyes of the blind. Lord, have mercy.
You heal those who are broken-hearted. Christ, have mercy.
You set captives free and bring true justice to all peoples. Lord, have mercy.

HEADINGS FOR READINGS

First Reading (Isaiah 40:1-5, 9-11). The prophet is urged to deliver a message of hope and consolation to the exiles in Babylon. Like a shepherd caring for his sheep, God is coming to save his people.

Second Reading (Titus 2:11-14; 3:4-7). This talks about the kind of life the baptised should live and the kind of ambitions that should motivate them. Salvation, with its hope of eternal life, is a gift from God through Jesus Christ.

(Note: the first and second readings from Year A may be used as alternatives).

Gospel (Luke 3:15-16, 21-22). This reading gives us a snatch of John the Baptist's preaching and concludes with a brief account of the Baptism of Jesus.

HOMILY

Shortly before dawn on November 23, 1955, Russia exploded her first H bomb. It was so successful that a soldier and a small child were killed by the blast. But to the politicians and scientists that seemed a very small price to pay. That night a big banquet was held to celebrate the event. Present were government officials, military men, and of course scientists. Many speeches were made. Finally came the turn of the brilliant young scientist, Andrei Sakharov, whose work had made it all possible. His speech would put the cap on things. But to the surprise of everyone he introduced the only discordant note of the night when he made a plea 'that our handiwork may never be exploded over cities.'

His plea did not go down well. In fact he was gently but firmly reprimanded by his bosses. Still, he became a national hero overnight. Special privileges were showered on him — a luxury home, a chauffeur-driven car, the Stalin Prize, and a salary of £13,000 a year (colossal by Russian standards). Thus he became a member of the world of the so-called super-elite.

But he felt ill at ease. Up to this he had misgivings about the bomb. Now he was sure of its danger. What really worried him was the low moral values of the men who controlled it. He woke up one morning feeling (most likely he always felt) that the abundance which threatened to swallow him up was but dust and ashes. He saw no justification for the work he was doing. His soul longed for truth. He became a fierce enemy of the bomb and began to campaign to have it banned. Needless to say this did not help his image with his bosses.

At the same time he began to notice what was happening to others who dared speak out against the system — they were being locked away in mental institutions. He could no longer keep silent about them. He couldn't sit back and watch men he respected and admired being silenced. He took it upon himself to defend them, to become their voice. In effect he joined them. Thus he shut the door of what people call 'a future' in his own face, and chose to remain instead poor and insecure.

This finished him with the authorities. He was stripped of all his privileges. For the past thirty years he has been vilified by the Soviet press. His phone has been tapped, and his family hounded by the Secret Police. When his wife got an eye illness doctors refused to treat her so that she had to go to Italy. When he was awarded the Nobel Prize he was refused permission to go to Sweden to receive it. For many years he lived in a small flat in Moscow. It was constantly crowded with dissidents, people who, encouraged by his example, had begun to speak out for basic rights and freedoms. At persent he is living in internal exile in Gorky.

It was a miracle that a man of Sakharov's purity should appear in Stalin's Russia. They say that merely to see him, to hear his first words, is to be charmed by his look of absolute candour, bright glance, warm and gentle smile. Like a child he wandered unprotected away from his well-feathered nest, away from his own caste — the well-fed, corrupt, and unprincipled swarms of scientists who obeyed their bosses without a murmur — to join the ranks of the insulted and the injured. To his way of thinking, the only way to make a name for oneself was by serving, not by having privileges showered on you provided you sold your soul to the state.

As far as I know Sakharov is not a Christian. Nevertheless he is in many ways a most Christlike man. That decision of his taken back in the fifties (and he has never wavered from it) was a kind of 'baptism', and it helps us to understand the meaning for Christ of his own Baptism.

Up to this Christ had been doing the unspectacular work of a village carpenter. But all the while the seed of his Father's call was growing within his gentle and pure soul. His decision had been ripening within him. He could have had a quiet, peaceful and happy life at Nazareth. But now, at the urging of the Spirit, he left it all behind him. He could no longer go on with that kind of life.

The Father was calling him 'to serve the cause of right . . . to open the eyes of the blind, to free those in prison, and to bring out all those who languish in dark dungeons of despair and depression.' (First Reading).

He, the sinless one, didn't hesitate to be identified with sinners so that he might set them free. Thus it was that he was baptised by John. In doing so he too wandered away from the tribe and became, like all true prophets, a man without honour in his own country. But his only concern was to do the will of his Father — to be a messenger of his mercy to all his brothers and sisters, but especially the 'little ones'. His gentle voice was heard in the streets. He healed those who were broken and crushed. He sought out those who were lost. In the eyes of the authorities, however, he was a trouble-maker and a disrupter of the system. But the heavenly Father was pleased with him. That's all that mattered to him.

What does Baptism mean to us? We pay so little attention to it, as if it was all over and done with a long time ago. We celebrate birthdays lavishly, but never our baptismal day. Yet this is the day we were born as children of God. On this day he claimed us as his children. On this day his Spirit rested on us. On this day we became brothers and sisters of Christ.

Baptism is only a door. Once we go through this door, however, we can never see ourselves and our lives in the same way again. But since most of us were baptised when we were too small to know anything about it we must grow to understand it. It is like a seed planted in our souls. Let us hope that it will grow and one day burst into the bloom of Christlike living.

Baptism is not something that happens to me without any relation to other people. Every Baptism is a public event. By my Baptism I became a member of God's People. Hence forward I must never look upon myself as a loner. Nor must I see my obligations as ending with my own life. The lives of others become as dear to me as my own.

'Being baptised means choosing a life like that of Jesus.' (F. J. Heggen).

'For some Christians the command of Christ "Follow me" means nothing more than attending church.' (Dostoyevsky).

PRAYER OF THE FAITHFUL

Let us pray for a better understanding of the meaning of our Baptism and the grace to live up to it with joy and generosity. *R.* Lord, hear our prayer.

For all the baptised: that they may strive to live up to the dignity conferred on them in Baptism. (Pause). Let us pray to the Lord.

For all political leaders and scientists: that they may obey their conscience and seek at all times to promote truth and justice in society. (Pause).   Let us pray to the Lord.

For all those who are suffering persecution in the cause of right: that they may have the courage and strength to continue to bear witness to the truth. (Pause).   Let us pray to the Lord.

That each of us may treasure our Baptism and seek to grow in our understanding and living of it. (Pause).   Let us pray to the Lord.

For local needs.

Let us pray:

Lord, send us your Spirit to open our eyes blinded by selfishness, and to set us free from the prison of our fears and doubts, so that we can grow to maturity as caring sons and daughters of God our Father. For you live and reign for ever and ever.

COMMUNION REFLECTION

'You are my beloved Son, in you I am well pleased.'
Thus right from the start of his public mission
Jesus received affirmation from his Father.

One of the deepest needs of the human heart
is the need to be appreciated.
Every human being wants to be valued.
We all need someone who will help us unfold.
We need someone to believe in us,
who will help us to be ourselves.

We need someone who understands us,
someone who can see the hidden self in us
that is perhaps afraid to come out into the open.
Only such a person will help us to share all we are,
making us believe in our own goodness,
and awakening in us a desire to share it with others.

At our Baptism we too became children of the Father,
and we received the gift of the Holy Spirit.
The Spirit will help us to unfold and grow,
bringing his love to our brothers and sisters.
Thus we will become more and more pleasing
in the sight of our heavenly Father.

Lent

FIRST SUNDAY OF LENT

We can approach Christ with great confidence that he understands us because, as today's liturgy reminds us, he shared our human weaknesses and temptations. Yet he did not sin. He remained faithful and true to his Father. He will help us who know that we have sinned, to be faithful also. (Pause).

Lord Jesus, you experienced the same human weaknesses as we experienced. Lord, have mercy.

Lord Jesus, you experienced the same temptations as we experience. Christ, have mercy.

Lord Jesus, you experienced the same frustrations and difficulties as we experience. Lord, have mercy.

HEADINGS FOR READINGS

First Reading (Deuteronomy 26:4-10). This describes the ceremony of the offering to God of the first fruits. Through it the people recognise all that God has done for them especially in the Exodus. Our worship of God is also a recognition of his favours to us.

Second Reading (Romans 10:8-13). The core of the Christian *credo* is that Jesus is our risen Saviour. If anyone, Jew or Gentile, can say that and live by it, he or she will be saved.

Gospel (Luke 4:1-13). Jesus was tempted like we are but he did not sin. Through his grace we too can resist temptation and overcome sin.

PARALITURGY FOR THE START OF LENT

(*Note:* Lent is a very important time. Many people try to do something special during it. But it usually lacks an ecclesial dimension. This is a pity. We are not isolated individuals who hope to save ourselves alone. We are members of the new People of God. Besides, the support of the community is essential for the crossing of the desert. As well as undertaking something on an individual basis, would it be possible for a parish community to undertake something *as a parish?*

A brief word of introduction may be necessary. But if taken slowly this liturgy should speak for itself. It would be a great help if each person had a copy of the text).

I. Christ our model

At the start of the holy season of Lent the Church puts before us the tempting of Christ in the desert. This is where our Lenten exercise begins.

Having heard the voice of the Father calling him to bring the Good News of salvation to his brothers and sisters, Christ was led by the Spirit into the desert. He needed to reflect on the nature of this mission and to prepare himself to carry it out.

First of all he had to get his *goals* right. Secondly he had to purify his *motives*. Thirdly he had to decide what *means* to use. To this end he embarked on a programme of prayer, reflection and fasting. It was only to be expected that at this crucial moment he would be tempted by Satan. After all, he had come to overthrow the kingdom of Satan, and to free God's children from the slavery of sin and the worship of false gods. Christ overcame Satan but not without a prolonged struggle.

Let us reflect for a moment on the loneliness and pain of this struggle. Picture Christ in the solitude of the desert. Everybody wants to seek something for themselves . . . pleasure or glory or honour or power. Everybody recoils from the cross. Christ was not play-acting. His tempting was for real. (Brief pause).

With the word of God to enlighten him, and the Holy Spirit to strengthen him, Christ was victorious over Satan. We rejoice in his victory, a victory which he wants to share with us. *R.* Praise to you, Christ our Saviour.

You refused to turn stones into bread, saying: 'Man does not live on bread alone but on every word that comes from the mouth of God.' Thus you rejected a kingdom based soleiy on material things. *R.*

You opted to preach the Good News to all your brothers and sisters. *R.*

You refused to throw yourself off the temple, saying: 'You must not put the Lord your God to the test.' Thus you rejected the false gods of fame and popularity. *R.*

You refused to take the easy option and to seek your own glory. *R.*

You refused the kingdoms of the world and to worship Satan, saying: 'You must worship the Lord your God, and serve him alone.' Thus you rejected the false gods of power and glory. *R.*

Having refused to worship Satan, you declared yourself the obedient and loving servant of the Father, and committed yourself to do his will in all things. *R.*

And so, after forty days, you emerged from the desert purified and strengthened, ready to gather the new People of God together and to lead them to the promised land of the kingdom of God. We want to be part of this great pilgrimage. We do not want to belong to the kingdom of Satan, the kingdom of darkness. We want to belong to the kingdom of God, the kingdom of light.

II. Reflecting on our lives

The American writer, Thoreau, lived by himself for two years in the woods of New England. He tells us why he did so: 'I went into the woods to confront the essential facts of life, lest when I come to die I should discover that I had not lived.' Without some reflection we cannot hope to live worthwhile lives even on a human level, much less on a Christian level. But the age in which we live, full as it is of noise and haste, does not make it easy. However, Lent provides us with a great opportunity. And Christ offers us a wonderful incentive: deliverance from the slavery of sin so that we may enjoy the freedom of the children of God. He offers us a share, not only in his victory over sin, but also in his Easter victory over death. But we cannot hope to share in his victory unless we fight his battle.

To fight his battle we have to face the 'desert'. We have to fast and pray. We have to die to our old selves. This is a great season of grace. It calls us to conversion, to turn our minds and our hearts to God.

Let us have the courage to look at our actual condition, no matter how impoverished it may be. How many of us are happy with our present condition? Here are a few pointers which may give us some perspective on our lives and on our present condition.

We live too fast and too coarsely. No wonder we fall victims of anxiety and stress.

Are there values which we fear, from which we are trying to escape? Values like inner silence, concern for others, prayer . . .?

What receives our best time and our best energy?

What goals do we pour ourselves and our time into?

What are we committed to, what values do we live by?

In each of us there are really two people. One is the self which seeks easy gratification; the other is the true self, made in God's image. Which gets more attention?

Is our neighbour someone we genuinely care about or merely someone we avoid until we need him?

With whom or what group do we share ourselves and identify with?

What is our worst and constant temptation?

What place has God in our lives?

Let us ask God's grace to emend for the better in those things in which we have sinned, whether through ignorance, weakness or malice, lest suddenly overtaken by the day of death we seek space for repentance and are not able to find it. (Short pause).

III. Praying and deciding

Let us have the courage to face our real situation. If we have been living a shallow and indifferent life let us turn to God to taste his mercy. Without his help we are powerless to change our lives. If he asks us to give up something it is only because he has something better to offer us. If he asks us to die it is only because he wants us to live more fully. Whatever we undertake this Lent let it be something which will help us to die to self and live to God and to others. *R.* Put a steadfast spirit within us, O Lord.

That we may be delivered from the worship of material things which swallow up all thought of God and spiritual things. (Pause). Let us pray.

That we may not covet a life of pleasure and comfort. (Pause). Let us pray.

That we may not hunger after popularity and our own glory. (Pause). Let us pray.

That we may have a spirit of self-denial, to be faithful in what we have decided to give up this Lent. (Pause). Let us pray.

That we break with what must be broken with once and for all. (Pause). Let us pray.

That we may be able to show mercy to others, especially to . . . and so obtain mercy ourselves. (Pause). Let us pray.

That we may seek reconciliation with anyone from whom we are presently estranged. (Pause). Let us pray.

That we may be faithful to what we have undertaken as a community. (Pause). Let us pray.

(Pray silently for the grace to be faithful to what we have undertaken. The priest might bless the people with holy water, saying: 'May the Lord bless you in what you have undertaken and keep you faithful.').

Let us pray:

Support us, O Lord, in all that we have undertaken, and help us to support one another. Let your word guide us, and your Holy Spirit strengthen and inspire us, so that having died with Christ to sin, we may rise with him to a new and glorious life at Easter. We ask this through the same Christ our Lord.

COMMUNION REFLECTION
It has been raining since early morning.

I have been forced to stay indoors,
meditating on the shortcomings of life.
Our competitive world has made people selfish and uncaring.
I have made up my mind to do something about it.
I cannot hope to convert all those people.
I'd be happy if I could convert even one person.
I will begin with the person I know best — myself.

But where shall I begin?
Let me see.
I know that I am lazy and selfish,
vain, proud and unforgiving.
I could be kinder, gentler and more considerate.
But what's this?
I don't believe it.
It's just stopped raining.
So I can go outdoors again.
I need some fresh air.
I'll go for a long walk.
I can reform myself tomorrow,
that is, provided it's raining,
and I'm forced to stay indoors,
meditating on the shortcomings of life.

SECOND SUNDAY OF LENT
Faces

INTRODUCTION AND CONFITEOR
The apostles had a wonderful experience on Mount Tabor when they were given a glimpse of the inner glory of Christ. Each Sunday we should get a great boost from our celebration of the Eucharist. Here our faith in Christ is renewed. Here he enlightens us with his word. Here he nourishes us with the bread of eternal life. Let us reflect for a moment on what it means to us. (Pause).

Our sins disfigure us and tarnish the image of God within us. Let us ask pardon for them.

I confess to almighty God . . .

HEADINGS FOR READINGS
First Reading (Genesis 15:5-12, 17-18). In this reading we learn of the solemn covenant God made with Abraham which was the

fóundation of God's relationship with the people of Israel.
Through Christ we are the heirs to this covenant.

Second Reading (Phillipians 3:17-4:1). From this reading it is
obvious that even in the early Church not all lived up to the
demands of the Christian life. Paul, however, urges us to remain
faithful.

Gospel (Luke 9:28-36). On Mount Tabor, Peter, James and John
got a glimpse of the glory that was hidden in Jesus, and they were
delighted by it. Through faith we too glimpse the glory of the risen
Jesus who lives on in the Church and in each of us.

HOMILY

Luke tells us that on Mount Tabor as Jesus prayed 'the aspect
of his face was changed.' Matthew puts it more forcefully. He says:
'His face shone like the sun.' We sum it up by saying that Christ
was transfigured before the eyes of his three disciples, and this
showed up on his face. His inner glory shone through, and on seeing it, the three were overcome with joy. But as they came down
from Tabor they were conscious of leaving behind them something
beautiful and precious, which could never be repeated. And they
were sad.

Faces are a very interesting study. It's a pity we don't look at
them more often — our own face first of all, then the faces of
others, especially of our friends. While faces can't tell us everything
about other people, they can tell us quite a bit. The truth of this
is borne out by the many times we use the word 'face' in talking
about others.

We say: 'You should have seen his/her face when I said this!' In
other words, on the face we can read how they feel inside, how they
really are, what moves them, etc. We sometimes say that a person
is 'two-faced'. This is a very serious charge to level against anyone.
It implies that we think they are dishonest, they are not genuine but
false. We say that at last a person 'showed his/her true face.' Here
we imply that up to this they may have been dilly-dallying, or even
two-faced, but now at last they are forced to put their cards on the
table. And one of the worst things we can say about a person is to
accuse them of being 'faceless'. This implies that they are hiding
behind others or behind the system, and are too cowardly to come
out from the shadows and take responsibility for their actions.

The truth is that we do not have one face, but many faces. And
this is natural. It is part of being human, part of life. At different
times we wear the face of: happiness or sadness, courage or fear,
peace or unrest, hope or despair, weariness or relaxation, joy or
pain, friendship or hostility . . . There is nothing then to be

ashamed of in all this. The only thing we should be ashamed of is a false face. These other faces are all mine. I am behind each of them. They are real. But a false face tells a lie and may deceive. Why then are people so reluctant to let their real face (that is their real self) be seen? Why do they insist on putting on a mask, on pretending? Is it that they are afraid to be seen in their weakness? Hence the need always to wear a smile, even when they are crying inside.

It is easy to make the mistake of thinking that what the apostles saw on Tabor was 'the *real* Christ'. What they saw was real. It did reveal to them something of the inner person that at other times was hidden from them. But to say that it was the real Christ implies that all the other faces he wore were not real, and if they were not real then they were false.

Christ had all the faces that we have, except the false ones. His face often betrayed weariness: think of the time he fell asleep in the boat. His face showed disappointment: when the Nazarenes rejected him. It showed anger: when he cleansed the temple. It showed gentleness: with the children. It showed compassion: when he saw that the people were like sheep without a shepherd. It showed sadness: when he cried on the way to the grave of his friend Lazarus. It showed fear and anguish: in the garden. It showed pain: on the cross. And it was pale and frozen: when he was dead.

These are some of the many faces Christ wore, and they were all real. There wasn't a single one of them that was false. The face he showed on Tabor was indeed a very special one, but it was not the only face of Christ. But behind all these faces lay the person of Christ, human like us (sin excepted) but carrying within him also the splendour of his divinity. 'This is my beloved Son, listen to him.'

A lot shows up on the face. In a way everything shows up there, though some of what is inside may put in only fleeting appearances, so that only glimpses of it are revealed and even these may go unnoticed except by keen observers. Though we are all rather good at covering up what is going on inside us and how we really feel and are, we can't hide everything all the time.

Thus rottenness of soul, corruption of heart, eventually shows up on a person's face. When a tree is diseased inside, it eventually shows up on the leaves and the bark. The opposite is also true. A clean conscience, a pure heart, shines in the face, especially in the eyes. The inner health of a tree shows in the quality of the fruit.

But having said all this it is still true that the face, indeed the whole body, is only a case, a shell. Everything that is truly beautiful and worthwhile about another person remains invisible. We should then beware of judging others. We ought indeed to look into their faces, but not so that we may sum them up, categorise and judge them, but in order that we may be sympathetic towards them. We must not judge from what we see in the face. You can only begin to know and to understand other people if you can get behind the face. This means getting to know at least some of their biography. But they are not likely to open up and reveal their story to us if they see an unsympathetic face.

All faces keep a certain mystery. What lies behind a human face? What lies before it? We cannot tell unless the person lets us into the secret. At the deepest level every human being remains invisible to the rest of us.

Our true greatness is a matter of faith. It is hidden from us. Christ gave his disciples a glimpse of his inner glory on Tabor. He was the new Moses — God's new law-giver. He was the new and final prophet — the one who is the very Word of God made flesh. He is the presence of God among us — Emmanuel, God with us. He is God's Son, nothing more and nothing less. All we have to do is listen to him and follow him. And one day, as St Paul says, 'he will transfigure our lowly bodies into copies of his glorious body.' Meanwhile, like Abraham, we have to live by faith. The faith that assures us that behind the most ordinary human face lies a son or a daughter of God, a brother or a sister of Christ.

'There can be no happiness for us as long as the things we do are different from the things we believe in.' (Anon).

'God hasn't stopped talking. He talks through the lives of loving people.' (Michel Quoist).

PRAYER OF THE FAITHFUL

God our Father showed that he was well pleased with his Son Jesus. Let us then with confidence make our prayers to him through the same Christ our Lord and Saviour.   *R.* Lord, hear our prayer.

For the pope and the bishops: that they may sustain the People of God in faith, hope and love. (Pause).   Let us pray to the Lord.

For all those who exercise authority: that the Lord may watch over them and help them to fulfil their responsibilities worthily and well. (Pause).   Let us pray to the Lord.

For all the sick and the handicapped: that they may get the courage and strength they need so as to bear their cross with dignity. (Pause).   Let us pray to the Lord.

For each of us, the followers of Jesus: that we may listen to his words and put them into practice in our daily lives. (Pause).   Let us pray to the Lord.

For local needs.

Let us pray:
Merciful Father, fill our hearts with your love, and keep us
faithful to the Gospel of Christ. Give us the grace to rise above our
human weaknesses. Grant this through the same Christ our Lord.

SIGN OF PEACE
Lord Jesus Christ, you said to your apostles: 'I leave you peace,
my peace I give you.' We find it hard to give peace to others
because often we don't have it ourselves. Take pity on our
weakness, and grant us the peace and unity of your kingdom where
you live for ever and ever.

COMMUNION REFLECTION
On Mount Tabor the sky was clear.
Jesus was praying. As he prayed
his face shone and his clothes dazzled.
On one side of him was Moses — the great law-giver.
On the other side was Elijah — the greatest of all the prophets.
And as if that wasn't enough
there was the voice of the Father.
No wonder Peter exclaimed:
'It is wonderful for us to be here!'

But there came another day and another hill.
This time the sky was dark.
The face of Jesus was covered with sweat and blood.
His clothes did not dazzle —
they had been taken from him.
For companions he had two thieves.
There was no voice from heaven,
only the scoffers were heard.
The disciples were shattered
and wanted no part of it.

The only thing in common
was that once again Jesus was praying.
What sustained him in bright and dark moments alike
was his special relationship with the Father.

This special relationship is now open to us.
It will sustain us through all our dark moments
until the glory of Easter shines fully on us.

THIRD SUNDAY OF LENT
Unless you repent

Today in the Gospel we will hear the words of Christ: 'Unless you repent, you will all likewise perish.' To repent means to be converted, and conversion is the starting point of every spiritual journey, and is a prerequisite for entry into the kingdom of God.

It implies that we recognise the presence of sin in our lives and our world. Some of us may say we have no sins, at least no serious ones, in our lives. But what about our sins of omission? What about the good we could do but which we don't do? (Pause).

Let us confess or sins, especially those of omission, and ask Christ's forgiveness.

I confess . . .

HEADINGS FOR READINGS

First Reading (Exodus 3:1-8, 13-15). God has seen the miserable state of his people in Egypt. He takes pity on them and decides to free them through the leadership of Moses. It shows God's concern for those who are oppressed.

Second Reading (1 Cor. 10:1-6, 10-12). Though all the people of Israel were led out of Egypt and enjoyed God's protection in the desert, yet because of their infidelity most of them perished there. There is a great lesson and a warning in this for us Christians.

Gospel (Luke 13:1-9). Jesus says that the misfortunes which befall people are no indication that they are sinners. Yet, to his Jewish hearers, he stresses the necessity of repentance and tells them that time is running out.

HOMILY

Christ started his mission with a summons to repentance. 'Repent,' he said, 'for the Kingdom of Heaven is at hand.' Today, through the voice of the Church, he issues the same call to us. The call to repentance is at the heart of the Gospel. Christ addressed it, not merely to people like the rich tax collector, Zacchaeus, the public sinner, Mary Magdalen, and the thief on the cross. He addressed it to ordinary people who were not thieves or adulterers, but what you might call decent, respectable people. More surprising still, he directed the call at those who prided themselves on their holiness and goodness — people like the Pharisees. In other words, the call to repentance was addressed to all without exception.

'Unless you repent, you shall *all* perish.' But you may ask: how can this be — that good people should need to repent? Thomas was a collector of walking sticks. He tells a story about one stick that came to him in a very strange manner. Once in winter, on a stormy night, there came a knock at his door. He went out, not a little annoyed att being disturbed at such a late hour. The wind blew the latch out of his hand. A drift of snow came into the hall. It really was a terrible night out there. On the doorstep stood a man. He knew him as old Joe. He often came by, knocked and held out his hand. He never uttered a word either of thanks or of greeting. He just stood there with his hand held out.

That night old Joe looked at him out of drunken, watery eyes and Thomas gave him what was nearest to hand — a few slices of bread along with a few coppers. Over his shoulder Joe carried a stick. At the end of the stick was a bundle which contained all his worldly belongings. But what was most upsetting was to see that he was bare-headed on a night like this. So Thomas took a woolen cap from the hook and Joe swayed a little as he pulled it down over his ears. Then he turned away without saying a word.

'That,' he said later, 'was the moment I should have thought about sending him away. I should have thought of my back room. Oh yes, I did think of it. In there was an empty bed all prepared, a table and a chair for a guest, and the room was warm and comfortable. There was soup in the kitchen, also bread and butter and a few bottles of beer. But immediately I thought of my clean house, and how this tramp would nose about inside it, wet and dirty and smelling of cheap wine. He would let his rags fall on the polished floor. No, that was asking too much. So I closed the door and left him out there in the storm and cold and dark. I refused to think where or how he was to pass the night. It just did not bear thinking about.

'Two days later the gravedigger came by and showed me a stick. It was an extraordinary piece of work, carved by hand from hazel wood. He asked me if I wanted it. I said yes, and we agreed on a price. It was then he told me he had just buried old Joe, and hadn't got a penny for his trouble — only the stick. "Actually he didn't die," he said, "I mean not from a disease or anything like that. He froze to death."

'When he went away I felt ashamed. And what I say now is meant only for myself. I do not want it to be a burden on anyone else. What I wish to say is this: the evil that we do, God will perhaps forgive. But the good that we fail to do, remains unforgiven.'

What disturbed Thomas most of all was not the evil he had done (for he hadn't done any), but the good which he had failed to do.

I believe this is the main thrust of Christ's parable about the barren fig tree. What is a fig tree for if not to produce figs? The owner is disappointed with the tree, not because of any poisonous fruit it has produced, but because it has produced no good fruit. It is judged and found wanting because of what it has failed to do.

Christians rarely ask themselves the question: what have I failed to do? I know we ask it in the Confiteor at the start of Mass, but generally we just skim over it. The call to repentance is not merely a call to turn away from evil, but a call to 'produce the fruits' of good living. That is why it is relevant for everybody. So often we are content with the former. We go to Confession, tell our sins, get rid of our guilt feelings, and then go out and live much the same as we did before.

This attitude reminds me of a man walking along a road who is being pestered by a pebble in his shoe. Finally, unable to bear it any longer, he stops, takes off his shoe, and removes the offending pebble. Then he puts on the shoe and continues walking in the same direction and at the same pace. He might have used the pause to see whether or not he is going in the right direction or whether what he is about is worthwhile.

Christ's call to repentance disturbs us. Inwardly we make the same cry as those possessed by devils made when Christ approached them: 'Leave us alone! Don't meddle with us!' In other words, we want to be left alone, left as we are. We don't want anyone, not even Christ, to disturb our quiet life, a life which may contain a lot of selfishness. We may not be guilty of great evil but yet we can be so selfish, instinctively demanding, totally inconsiderate, but we don't want to know, much less do anything, about this side of our nature. We are being called from being self-centred, to become other-centered and God-centered.

Perhaps we need an awakening. Perfectly good people can sink into a life of selfishness and pettiness slowly and imperceptibly. It is said that man has never been able to hold onto a single plateau he has attained. There are currents in life which will take us away from the values of the Gospel. In times of prosperity and ease we can make a lot of concessions to ourselves and a lot of compromises. But then, by the grace of God, we can be growing, however slowly, in awareness. We may not have any big moment of conversion such as Moses had. One day he was minding sheep. Next day he was leading an oppressed people to freedom.

But conversion is a joyful thing. It is good news, It is a call from the slavery of selfishness and every form of sin, to a life of grace and freedom. It is a call from a life of barrenness to a life of fruitfulness. It is a call to enter into the joy of the Kingdom. However, it is not something that is done once and for all. It calls for growth and development.

'The sin of omission is one of the worst things in the world.' (Adolfo Pérez Esquivel, Nobel Peace Prize Winner, 1980.

'If we fail to accomplish acts of love, all our good intentions will remain mere daydreams, and our whole life will slip by like a shadow.' (Dostoyevsky).

PRAYER OF THE FAITHFUL

Let us pray to our Lord that we may learn the lesson of his parable and be converted to the Gospel. *R*. Lord, hear us in your love.

It is by producing good fruit that a tree shows that it is healthy. Let us pray that all Christians may be prepared to give rather than to receive. (Pause). We pray in faith.

Christ was the gardener who asked that the tree be given another chance. That all those in authority may be kind and merciful towards those they serve. (Pause). We pray in faith.

For all those whose lives are barren and empty of the deeds of love: that they may get the grace to do something about it. (Pause). We pray in faith.

That in our lives we may not be content merely to produce the fruits of outward observance, but that we may strive to produce the fruits of humility, patience, forgiveness, generosity and peace. (Pause). We pray in faith.

That we may persevere with our efforts to renew our lives this Lent. (Pause). We pray in faith.

For local needs.

Let us pray:

Lord Jesus, you are that careful and patient gardener who can produce fruit from the most unpromising of trees. Help us to produce in our lives the fruits of true repentance. For you live and reign for ever and ever.

COMMUNION REFLECTION

What I fail to do.

It isn't the things you do,
it's the things you leave undone,
which give you a little heartache
at the setting of the sun.

The gentle word forgotten,
the letter you didn't write;

the flowers you might have sent,
are your haunting ghosts tonight.

The stone you might have lifted
out of your brother's way;
the little heart-felt counsel
you were hurried too much to say.

The tender touch of the hand,
the gentle and kindly tone;
which we have no time or thought for,
with troubles enough of our own.

FOURTH SUNDAY OF LENT
The prodigal son

INTRODUCTION AND CONFITEOR

In today's Gospel, we will hear once more Christ's famous story of the prodigal son. Prodigal means wasteful. We are all wasteful where God's grace is concerned. We misuse his gifts to us. We squander life's opportunities.

Let us pause to call to mind our failings. (Pause). Fortunately God is prodigal with his forgiveness. So we turn to him with confidence that he will forgive us once more.

Lord Jesus, you came to reconcile us to one another and to the Father. Lord, have mercy.

Lord Jesus, you heal the wounds of sin and division. Christ, have mercy.

Lord Jesus, you interecede for us with your Father. Lord, have mercy.

HEADINGS FOR READINGS

First Reading (Joshua 5:9-12). The Israelites, free at last from the humiliation they suffered in Egypt, enter the land of promise. Possession of the land becomes a reality when they eat of the produce of Canaan.

Second Reading (2 Cor. 5:17-21). The whole aim of Christ's mission was to bring about a reconciliation between God and humanity. It is the task of the Church to bring the benefits won by Christ to all people.

Gospel (Luke 15:1-3, 11-32). This contains Christ's immortal parable — the prodigal son.

HOMILY

Of all Christ's parables this is the most revolutionary. So much so that some have come to the conclusion that Christ got it wrong. That he went overboard. That we have to correct him. I mean what would happen if we opened our doors to every runaway, waster and squanderer? Isn't that what's wrong with the world today? We have too many prodigals, too many people who are all too willing to claim their rights but too few who are willing to consider their responsibilities?

Many people feel sorry for the older son in the story. They feel he got a raw deal from the father. They imagine him saying something like this:

'The way my father treated my younger brother was a slap in the face for me. Maybe he might have taken him back after a right good telling off. Taken him back, of course, as a servant, not as a son. I would have seen that he got the heaviest and dirtiest jobs, and I would have kept him there until I was satisfied that he had proved he was truly repentant. Then slowly, a little at a time, I'd have given him back some of his old status and privileges, but only on condition that he continued to walk the straight and narrow.

'But what happens? Out my father runs to meet him, and before the waster even had time to say he was sorry, he throws his arms around him and hugs him, and he still reeking of pig manure. And as if that wasn't bad enough, he orders that he be dressed out in finery. Then, to cap it all, he gives a big feast in is honour. I mean, it didn't make sense. He was acting like someone who had lost his senses.

'I mean, what impression would the servants get? They would surely conclude that in this house one could commit murder and get away with it. And who would blame them? And just how do you think he made me feel? I who had been faithful to him all those years, years in which I had to do not only my own work but that of my absent brother as well. When I came back from the fields that evening, and I all tired and sweaty from the heat and toil of the day, was he there to give me a little recognition? To say: "Well done, son!" That's not asking for much — just a little pat on the back. But he wasn't there. I took it that he had something important to do. But what was my surprise to discover that the reason why he wasn't there was that at that very moment he was falling all over the waster who had come back only because the money had run out and he was too lazy to work.

'I ask you to put yourself in my shoes. How would you feel if you were in my position? Would you not feel it was unfair? Would you not feel that you were hard done by? And how would you

react? You'd blow your top! If you didn't you wouldn't be human.
You'd shout: "This is not right! This is downright unfair! I won't
put up with it".'

I think a lot of people might agree with the above thinking. How
often I've heard it. I suppose it shouldn't surprise us to hear it from
teenagers who tend to have a black-and-white view of morality. But
one hears it from adults too. Does this not tell us something? Does
it not tell us how much of the Pharisee is in each of us? The older
brother in the story stands for the Pharisees — those austere men
who kept all God's commandments yet were without love and
mercy.

But now try to put yourself in the shoes of the younger son. If
you were in his place would you not be very happy at the way things
turned out? This is not to say that what he did was right. It wasn't.
It was wrong, selfish, and the height of ingratitude and irresponsibility. But that said, he paid a big price for his sins.

He was in a foreign country. When his money ran out he was
alone. And what a come-down he suffered! After his high life to
end up feeding pigs and being glad to eat the same food as they did.
For a Jew, feeding pigs was the lowest of all jobs. As an alien he
was being hopelessly exploited by his employer, but he had to work
if he wanted to stay alive.

It wasn't that he hadn't known any other kind of life. He had.
He thought back to the fine life he had back home. He thought of
the kind and loving father he had. Then shame, remorse and guilt
arose within him. He realised that he had done a terrible thing to
his father. So it was that he came to his decision to return home.

To come back home was no easy job. It called for a lot of
humility and courage. He knew well what people were thinking and
saying about him back there. And it wasn't just that he wanted to
come in from the cold. There was a marvellous quality about his
repentance. He realised that he had sinned, not only against his
father, but against God. He knew he did not deserve to be called
a son, and was quite willing to be accepted back as a servant.

That is how he felt as he got his first glimpse of home. But what
if his father should tell him to get lost? Then he would be really
humiliated, and he would have no one to blame but himself. And
what would life have to offer him then? Nothing — only the black
night of despair.

Repentance alone does not help. Grace cannot be bought with
repentance; it cannot be bought at all. But then he saw his father
coming towards him, and from the expression on his face he knew
that he was right to have come back, that everything was going to
be all right. As far as the father was concerned there was no need

of recriminations. The only thing that mattered to him was that his son had come home alive.

Who can describe the joy the prodigal son felt as the evening went on? We waste so much time in remorse. We become slaves to guilt. There's really only one thing to do when we've sinned, and that is to run to the Father, truly believing that he awaits us.

If we still find it easier to identify with the older son, then so be it. However, we should remember this: it is possible to keep all the commandments and still be far from God. But which of us can truthfully say that we have kept all the commandments, that we have served God 'all day long'? Have we not all been unfaithful at some time? Have we not all squandered at least some of our inheritance? Have we not made a totally inadequate response to God's love?

The prodigal shows us the way to the Father's house. He tells us what we have to do. 'I will arise and go to my Father's house, and I will say to him . . .' Millions have heard those words and, inspired by them, have come in from the cold, and found welcome and forgiveness from God. It is not simply that we are 'saved' and that God remits the debt contracted by our sins, but that we are *loved* by the Father.

'I pray incessantly for the conversion of the prodigal son's brother.' (Helder Camara).

'Through our own recovered innocence we discern the innocence of our neighbours'. (Thoreau).

PRAYER OF THE FAITHFUL

Let us pray that we may learn the lessons of this wonderful parable and put them into practice in the daily living of our faith. *R.* Lord, hear our prayer.

In his misery the prodigal son knew that his father's door was always open. That all Christians may be generous in forgiving those who have hurt or disappointed them. (Pause). Let us pray to the Lord.

For all the members of our society: that they may rid themselves of the utterly selfish attitude of the younger son who demanded his rights without the slightest thought for his responsibilities. (Pause). Let us pray to the Lord.

For all parents: that they may be able to create homes in which their children will know that they are loved unconditionally. (Pause). Let us pray to the Lord.

That we may all rise above the small and begrudging attitude of the older brother who had learned so little of his father's love and understanding. (Pause). Let us pray to the Lord.

For local needs.

Let us pray:

Heavenly Father, your door is always open to us; your light is always on for us; your hand is always stretched out towards us. Help us to remember this if we should go astray in life. Help us to return to you confident that you will welcome us, for Jesus your Son told us so. We make all our prayers through the same Christ our Lord.

COMMUNION REFLECTION

The prodigal girl.

Great poets have sung the beauties of home,
its comfort, its love and its joys;
how back to the place of its sheltering dome
I welcome the prodigal boy.

They picture his father with pardoning smile
and glittering robes to unfurl;
but none of the poets thought it worthwhile
to sing of the prodigal girl.

The prodigal son can resume his old place
as leader of fashion's mad whirl,
with never a hint of his former disgrace —
not so for the prodigal girl!

The girl may come back to the home she had left
but nothing is ever the same:
the shadow still lingers o'er the dear ones bereft,
society scoffs at her name.

Perhaps that is why when the prodigal girl
gets lost on life's devious track;
she thinks of the lips that will scornfully curl,
and hasn't the heart to come back.

Yes, welcome, the prodigal son to his place;
kill the calf, fill the free-flowing bowl;
but shut not the door on his frail sister's face,
remember, she too has a soul.

(Autor unknown).

FIFTH SUNDAY OF LENT
Stone-throwing

INTRODUCTION AND CONFITEOR

In today's Gospel we will hear the immortal words of Christ to the woman caught in adultery: 'Has no one condemned you? Neither will I condemn you. Go in peace and sin no more.'

Therefore we have no need to be afraid to let Christ see our sins. We have nothing to receive from him but forgiveness. Let us pause to call to mind our sins, especially the harsh and unfair judgements we sometimes pass on others. (Pause).

I confess to almighty God . . .

HEADINGS FOR READINGS

First Reading (Isaiah 43:16-21). This was addressed to the Jews exiled in Babylon. It assures them that there will be a new Exodus. Its message of hope should inspire us also.

Second Reading (Philippians 3:8-14). Frequently we see holiness as something that we can achieve by our own efforts. Instead we should try to see it as something that comes through faith in Christ and in the power of his resurrection.

Gospel (John 8:1-11). This relates the incident concerning the woman caught in adultery, and how Jesus told her accusers that they should look to their own sins before condemning her.

HOMILY

Isn't it strange that there is no more compassionate and understanding person towards those who fall than the genuinely holy person. This is exemplified in the lives of the saints, and of course especially in the life of Christ. The opposite is also true: there is no more judgemental and condemnatory person than the self-righteous phoney. The latter has such high standards where others are concerned, makes such exacting demands, brooks no excuses, exceptions or slip-ups, yet when it comes to himself he can be so blind and all-forgiving.

Anne and Mary were two cleaning ladies. They worked in a hospital. Their job was to clean the corridors and the operating theatres. And they not only knew their job but did it to the very best of their ability. When they had finished their cleaning there literally wasn't a speck of dust either on the floors or on the furniture. Everything was bright and clean. Everything was thoroughly disinfected. Even the walls shone. No one could possibly find fault with their work. They set very high standards.

But you should see the flat in which they lived. It's true that they were poor. They had only one large room which served as bedroom, livingroom and kitchen, and a small bathroom off it. But the state of the large room! Instead of having blinds on the windows they had old dust-covered blankets which they never removed. The walls were painted a dull, depressing and stale blue. Their beds were never made and the clothes on them were filthy. The sink was also clogged up with cigarette ends. There was a row of unwashed milk bottles on the window sill. And on the floor, close to the sink, was a plastic bag with all sorts of foul-smelling refuse spilling out of it.

I could go on but I won't. I think you have a picture of the squalor in which these two women were living — two women who were cleaning ladies by profession. (This is a true story and was told to me by a friend). Now I haven't the slightest intention of passing judgement on them. I merely want to use this incident as a kind of parable. Here you had two ladies who scrubbed the public corridors and theatres of a hospital while at the same time they lived in a room that was full of dirt. Here were two people who were experts at cleaning up the dirt of others but woefully inadequate when it came to cleaning up their own. It's not a nice story. It's dirty and messy.

The incident in today's Gospel is also dark and messy, reeking of moral squalor — sin. On the surface there appears to be only one sin involved — the sin of the woman who was caught in adultery. But there are other sins there, subtle and hidden and, to my mind, more serious. In fact the vindictiveness of the scene, its malice and moral squalor are overwhelming. It stinks to high heaven.

There was the horrible sin involved in the way the scribes and Pharisees treated the woman. What is so important is not the horrible meanness of it all, but the way it was done. They showed not the slightest regard for her feelings, not the tiniest shred of concern for her as a person. She was simply someone they could use in the hope of entrapping Christ. To them she was just like bait to fishermen. The bait is gladly sacrificed in the hope of catching a fish. To use another person in this way is a despicable thing. It bears out the truth of what Dostoyevsky said: 'No beast could ever be as cruel as man.' Yet this kind of thing happens all the time and is often not even recognised as being a sin at all.

Then there is the sin involved in their attitude towards Christ. Here are men who have consciously rejected the light and who are pursuing the path of darkness. They have only one aim — to get rid of Christ. In other words — murder. Of course they would object and protest in the strongest possible terms if you were to put it as bluntly as that. No doubt, like all those in high places who eliminate those who pose a threat to them, they would have a host of excuses and defences.

Christ exposed them, but on this occasion he didn't spell it out in public. He merely let them know that he was aware of their game, and that he read their minds and hearts. He invited them to look to their own sins. He didn't even judge them. He invited them to judge themselves.

But he was not content with that. He illuminated this dark scene with the radiance of his compassion. He will not judge the woman at the centre of the incident. His mission is about mercy and forgiveness, not judgement and condemnation. He did not come to expose the sores of people but to heal them. The kindness and compassion with which he treated the woman is a tremendous example for us to follow.

He did indeed correct her, but ever so gently. His approach was like that of a good surgeon: a combination of courtesy, gentleness and tenderness while using the scalpel. To correct the adulteress was much better than to stone her; to pardon and save her was much better than to condemn her.

We are innate stone-throwers. We cannot tolerate the sinner. Sin stinks when it is committed by others and we want to clean it up. But not so when it is committed by ourselves. We seldom measure the faults of others with the same rule or weigh them on the same scales as our own. But it is better to exercise mercy towards others. We're not saints ourselves.

Therefore we should try to look at our own house before we start throwing mud at others. It is impossible to throw mud without some of it sticking to your hand. This means that the very act of condemning others involves a sin on our part. We should be ready to extend to others the same compassion we would like to receive if we were involved in the same situation. And if there comes a time when we feel we have a duty to correct an erring brother or sister, let us remember that there is an art in doing so. This art consists in being totally kind and totally honest at the same time.

We might imitate St Paul. He does not spend his time judging others. Nor does he sit on his laurels. His only aim is to press on and finish the race he began when he set out on the road to imitate Christ, his Master.

'There is no more important thing in life than compassion for a fellow human being.' (Tolstoy).

'There is nothing harder in the whole world than frankness, and there is nothing easier than flattery.' (Dostoyevsky).

PRAYER OF THE FAITHFUL

Let us pray that we may learn from Christ's example to be kind, understanding and forgiving. *R*. Lord, hear our prayer.

That all who follow Christ may refrain from passing judgement on other people. (Pause). We pray to the Lord.

For all judges and lawyers: that in the exercise of their professions they may work to ensure that in all cases the truth is heard and justice done. (Pause). We pray to the Lord.

For all those who have been victims of unjust judgement and oppression. (Pause). We pray to the Lord.

That we may be saved from ever using the sins of others to justify our own. (Pause). We pray to the Lord.

For all those who are engaged in the warfare of Lent: that they may persevere in their efforts to reform their lives. (Pause). We pray to the Lord.

For local needs.

Heavenly Father, help us to keep our hearts pure, our minds clean, our words true, and our deeds kind. We ask this through Christ our Lord.

SIGN OF PEACE

Lord Jesus Christ, you looked with compassion on the woman caught in adultery and, even though you knew she was a sinner, you refused to condemn her; instead you sent her away in peace. Help us to be merciful and forgiving towards all those who sin against us, so that we may enjoy the peace and unity of your kingdom where you live for ever and ever.

COMMUNION REFLECTION

When her accusers had left
Jesus turned to the woman and asked:
'Is it true what these men said?'
She nodded her head.
'That means you were in sin then.'
Once again she nodded her head.
'To be in sin is to be in darkness.
And you were not made for darkness but for light.'
He paused, then added: 'Has no one condemned you?'
'No one, Sir,', she replied.
'Well then, neither will I condemn you.
Go in peace, walk in the light,
and do not enslave yourself again.'

A faint smile appeared on her tear-stained face,

and she began to move away.
She went slowly at first,
as if fearing that at any second he might stop her in her tracks
and recall her.
But then she picked up speed and bounded away
with all the enthusiasm of a reluctant school-goer
who had just been given an unexpected free day.

She was dismissed with infinite gentleness
and the most delicate of reproofs.
How differently it might have ended
but for the compassion of Jesus.

PASSION (PALM) SUNDAY
Redeeming suffering

INTRODUCTION AND CONFITEOR
Today we begin the week we call 'Holy Week' — the week in which
Christ died and rose. He died because of sin. 'Sin brought death
to the Son of God and it continues to bring death to the children
of God.' (Oscar Romero).

Let us pause to call to mind our sins, especially those by which
we hurt and betray others. (Pause).

The Lord died forgiving those who put him to death. He will
forgive us too.

Lord Jesus, you looked at Peter after he had denied you and he
wept for his sins. Lord, have mercy.

Lord Jesus, you forgave your enemies and your executioners.
Christ, have mercy.

Lord Jesus, you received the repentant thief into paradise.
Lord, have mercy.

HEADINGS FOR READINGS
Gospel for Procession (Luke 19:28-40). Christ enters Jerusalem
to receive a kingdom — not an earthly kingdom, but the kingdom
of God. His entry as messianic king is a sign that the peace and
salvation decreed by God is at hand. We are asked to declare our
loyalty publicly to him.

First Reading (Isaiah 50:4-7). The prophet suffers in carrying out
his mission, but he is convinced that God will eventually save him.

Second Reading (Philippians 2:6-11). Because Jesus took on himself our human condition and accepted death on a cross, the Father has made him Lord of heaven and earth.

Gospel (Luke 22:14-23:56). Luke's version of the Passion Story. As in the rest of his Gospel, so in his account of the Passion, Luke presents a Christ who is merciful and forgiving, even to his executioners. We are involved in the Passion Story too.

HOMILY

There is an awful lot of suffering in the world today and perhaps in the life of each of us. However, it should be a great consolation for all those who suffer to know that Christ suffered too. We've just read the Passion Story. But we tend to skim over it. We've heard it so many times that perhaps it fails any longer to make an impression on us. In any case we may be tempted to think that Christ's suffering was not for real. That somehow it was different for him. After all he was the Son of God. Besides, he was only carrying out the Father's plan. He did not choose it freely. It was all planned like that from long ago.

Straightaway, we must be clear about this. Christ's suffering was real. It was no play-acting. If anything, his suffering was more intense than others, given the fact that he was such a caring and sensitive person. It is the one who dares to love who leaves himself open to the possibility of very deep hurt if that love is rejected. Another thing: Christ's suffering was freely chosen. This said, let us now look briefly at some of the pain he endured during his passion.

He suffered the pain of being let down by his friends. 'This night all of you will abandon me.'

What is worse, he suffered the pain of being betrayed by one of them — Judas.

Consider the fear and anguish he suffered in the garden. It was so intense that he asked his Father to remove it from him. And he had no one with whom to share his agony. The three on whom he was relying were fast asleep.

He suffered the hurt of being arrested and tried for something he never did (break the law or cause trouble).

He was falsely accused and subjected to a barrage of lies.

He endured insults, blows, taunts, spits; then the lash of the whip and the piercing of the thorns.

Finally came the shame of being condemned to death like a common criminal. As he died he had to endure more taunts, insults and mockery. And where was God? Wherever he was, he kept his silence.

Who could plumb the depths of what Christ suffered? Yet all this suffering would have been wasted, and would not have redeemed even one small corner of the world, if he had not endured it with love. It was not Christ's suffering that saved the world. It was his love — the love with which he bore and offered his sufferings to the Father for us.

He showed us how to bear our sufferings. 'Some people,' says Helder Camara, 'are like sugar-cane, even when crushed in the mill, completely squashed, reduced to pulp, all they yield is sweetness.' Christ was like that. Even though surrounded by darkness the lamp of his love was still burning brightly, and thus he was able to enlighten others. He prayed for his executioners. He welcomed the good thief to paradise. He got John to take care of his mother. With one look of compassion he brought tears of repentance to the eyes of Peter. He even elicited an act of faith from the Roman centurion who had conducted his execution. He died because he did the will of his Father — freely and out of love. He was the Good Shepherd dying because he loved his sheep.

Suffering that is merely endured does nothing for our souls except perhaps harden them. It only succeeds in turning us in upon ourselves and making us sorry for ourselves. Renunciation and sacrifice are worthless unless related to love. A mother would never by choice sleep in a wet bed but she would gladly do so in order to spare the dry bed for her sick child. It is the spirit in which we bear our burden that matters. All the coal and firewood in the world are no use without a fire. Two people can go through the same painful experience. It can destroy one and enrich the other.

Suffering gives us the opportunity to learn compassion. But many waste this opportunity. Self-pity robs them of the benefit of it. Self-pity is the first and normal reaction to suffering. But it is a cancer which erodes our courage and destroys our capacity to love. Our pain can bear fruit. Our suffering, properly borne, can become even a privilege, a call to the highest things. As Thoreau says: 'it defends you from being a trifler.'

It is not suffering that redeems us and the world, but love. This cannot be said too often. Some people seem to have a morbid love of suffering, but they tend to be rather dour people. It is love that Christ wants from us. Love can cause the greatest pain of all — heartbreak. But it also can cause the greatest joy of all.

'Mankind would perish if there were no exhibition anytime and anywhere of the divine in man.' (Gandhi).

'The Christian must not only accept suffering: he must make it holy. Nothing so easily becomes unholy as suffering.' (Thomas Merton).

PRAYER OF THE FAITHFUL

On this day when Jesus said that if the people kept silent the very stones would cry out, let us make our voices heard in prayer. *R.* Lord, hear us in your love.

For all Christian leaders: that they may not be afraid to show their loyalty to Christ in front of unbelievers and even cynics. (Pause). We pray in faith.

Jesus accepted a violent death to free us from sin: may all of God's children be able to live in freedom and dignity. (Pause). We pray in faith.

For all those in pain of any kind: that they may learn from the example of Jesus to bear their sufferings with courage and love. (Pause). We pray in faith.

That we may welcome Jesus into our hearts and into our lives with the same joy and enthusiasm as his disciples did on the first Palm Sunday. (Pause). We pray in faith.

For local needs.

Let us pray:

Today we see Jesus, our King, coming to us humbly riding on a donkey. Since he wanted so much to be like us, we should want to be like him. We ask this through the same Christ, our Lord.

COMMUNION REFLECTION

This week each year Christians are drawn to Jerusalem,
if not in body, at least in mind.
They stand at the foot of the cross,
beating their breasts,
and staring with pity at Jesus of Nazareth.
They listen with reverence to his voice.
as he prays for his killers:
'Father, forgive them, for they know not what they do.'
But when the week is over they return to their homes
to resume their deep-rooted spites
and the burden of things they can't forgive.

'Don't cry for me,' says Jesus.
'Cry for yourselves and for your children –
the children who will inherit
your fears, prejudices and hates.'

Let us not then weep for Jesus.
Rather let us follow the example of Peter,
who wept bitter tears for his own sins.
Then maybe we will be able
to forgive others who sin against us.

Eastertide

EASTER SUNDAY
Joy to all the earth

INTRODUCTION AND CONFITEOR
The joy of Easter fills all the earth. And this is the joy of Easter — that death has been conquered. Easter is the victory. Easter is the 'good news' which the apostles were sent to preach to the ends of the earth.

Christ overcame death, not only for himself, but for each of us and for all of God's people. Let us lift up our hearts as we draw near Christ our risen Brother who now dies no more but lives on among us. (Pause).

Lord Jesus, your victory over death brings joy to all the earth. Lord, have mercy.

Lord Jesus, your Easter victory brings hope to all who are downcast. Christ, have mercy.

Lord Jesus, your light, extinguished by death, shines brightly on us once more and will know no setting. Lord, have mercy.

HEADINGS FOR READINGS

First Reading (Acts 10:34, 37-43). This is part of an early sermon preached by St Peter. He tells us how he was a witness to the life, death and resurrection of Jesus. The risen Jesus is the Saviour of all those who believe in him, as well as the Judge of the living and the dead.

Second Reading (Colossians 3:1-4). Through our Baptism we already share in the risen life of Christ, though in a hidden and mysterious way.

Gospel (John 20:1-9). Early on Easter Sunday morning some of the disciples discover that the tomb in which Jesus was buried is empty. Then the truth of what the Scriptures had foretold begins to dawn on them, namely, that Jesus would rise from the dead.

HOMILY

(This is very short because the main emphasis is on the renewal of our baptismal promises. That ceremony, well done, should speak loud and clear).

Viktor Frankl spent three years in that grim place — Auschwitz. Statistically his chances of survival were only one in twenty-eight. But he did survive, though his wife and family perished. He tells how one day shortly after the liberation of the camp by the Allies he went for a walk through the country towards the market town a few miles from the camp.

The meadows were full of spring flowers. Larks rose into the sky and he could hear their joyous singing. There was no one to be seen for miles around. There was nothing but the wide earth and sky, the singing of the larks, and the freedom of space. He stopped, looked around him, and then up into the blue sky. Then he went down on his knees to give thanks to God for his liberation. As he prayed he was lost to himself and to the world. Only one sentence came to mind that could express what he was feeling. It was this: 'I called on God from my narrow prison and he answered me in the freedom of space.'

How long he knelt there repeating that sentence he could not tell. But he said later: 'On that day and in that hour my new life started. Step by step I progressed, until I again became a human being.'

Now that Lent is over we can emerge from the desert to enter into the promised land of Christ's resurrection, to taste even here on earth the joy and freedom of the new life he won for us through his death and resurrection, a life that will know its full flowering only beyond the grave. It is fitting that we should renew our promises to follow the risen Christ, and to try to be true to the new life he won for us at so great a price.

(It would help if each one could have a candle, lit from the paschal candle, and a copy of the text).

RENEWAL OF BAPTISMAL PROMISES

My dear brothers and sisters:

On a people who lived in darkness and in deep shadow a light has dawned. That light is the light of Christ, a light which even the darkness of death failed to overpower.

His light was opposed by those who lived in the darkness of evil and who did not want to change. But it was welcome by all those who longed for truth, goodness and freedom.

We ourselves were in darkness once, but God the Father, in his great love for us, called us out of darkness into the wonderful light of his Son. We must therefore try to live as children of the light. The effects of the light are seen in goodness, right living and truth.

Now that we have successfully completed our Lenten exercises, and the light of Easter has dawned upon us, let us renew our belief in the light of Christ, our risen Lord, and our determination to follow it faithfully. This, after all, is what we promised at Baptism when this light was first kindled in our hearts.

Response: We do.

Do you believe in God the Father, the one true God and source of all light, and in his love for you?

Do you reject the many false gods the modern world offers for your adoration?

Do you reject Satan, the prince of darkness?

Do you reject his works, namely, sin?

Do you reject the false lights by which he seeks to lure you from the path of the Gospel: greed for material things, lust for pleasure, craving for popularity?

Do you believe in Christ, the light of the world?

Do you believe that Christ has entrusted his light to us, and that he now depends on us to let the light of goodness shine in the world today?

Do you promise, then, that where the darkness of hatred reigns you will let the light of love shine?

That where the darkness of injury reigns you will let the light of pardon shine?

That where the darkness of doubt reigns you will let the light of faith shine?

That where the darkness of despair reigns you will let the light of hope shine?

That where the darkness of falsehood reigns you will let the light of truth shine?

Do you believe that through his resurrection Christ overcame the darkness of death, and that we can do the same if we have faith in him?

Do you believe in the Church, the community of believers in the light, brothers and sisters in the Lord?

Do you believe in the Holy Spirit who dwells within us, to console us in times of sorrow, to strengthen us in times of difficulty, and to bind us together in the love of Christ?

Do you believe that Mary, the Mother of Jesus, is also our Mother, and the Mother of the entire Christian community?

And now, my brothers and sisters, I say to you in the name of Christ, our risen Saviour: hold up your heads. Never be ashamed of this light. Carry it with pride and honour, with joy and love. If you do this, then Christ will not be ashamed of you before his Father in heaven.

May the Lord bless you and keep you faithful. But if in your human weakness you fail Christ, and fall back into the old ways of darkness, know that you can turn to him at any time. He will forgive you and help you to walk in the light once more.

(The priest now blesses the people with holy water. This water is a reminder of the waters of our Baptism. We should pray silently for the grace to be faithful to Christ).

Let us pray: (together).

Heavenly Father, we thank you for the light of grace and love which Jesus, your risen Son, brought into our world. We are still overwhelmed by its brightness. Help us to keep his light burning brightly in our hearts and in our lives. On seeing this light others will find their way, and so you will be glorified. We make our prayer through the same Christ our Lord.

SIGN OF PEACE

Lord Jesus Christ, on Easter Sunday evening, the doors being shut where the disciples were gathered, you came and stood among them and said: 'Peace be with you.' Then you showed them your wounded hands and side, and they were filled with joy. Grant us the peace and joy of your kingdom where you live for ever and ever.

COMMUNION REFLECTION

We all experience moments of dying in our lives.
We get a foretaste of death
when we live in bitterness,
when prejudice blinds us,
when loneliness enfolds us,
when fears oppress us,
when sadness overwhelms us,
and when we give in to despair.
In those moments the world is closing in on us,
and we have one foot in the grave already.

But we also experience moments of resurrection in our lives:
when we know true love,
when we are accepted,
when we are forgiven,
when we open our hearts to our neighbour,
and when hope returns.
In those moments our horizon is widening
and we are emerging from the tomb.

Lord Jesus,
may the power of your resurrection touch whatever is dead in us
and bring it back to life.
Let the splendour of your resurrection light up the world,
scattering the shadows of death,

and helping all of the Father's children
to walk in radiant hope towards the kingdom that is to come.

SECOND SUNDAY OF EASTER
Touching is believing

INTRODUCTION AND CONFITEOR

It is not always easy to believe that Christ is present in our world. Like Doubting Thomas, we all experience moments of doubt and uncertainty. But as we assemble here each Sunday to celebrate the Eucharist we ought to experience a great strengthening of our faith.

Let us not try to hide our doubts. Let us bring them to Christ, and he will do for us what he did for Thomas. (Pause).

Lord Jesus, you raise the dead to life in the Spirit.   Lord, have mercy.

Lord Jesus, you bring pardon and peace to the sinner.   Christ, have mercy.

Lord Jesus, you bring light to those living in the darkness of doubt and unbelief.   Lord have mercy.

HEADINGS FOR READINGS

First Reading (Acts 5:12-16). This tells of the high regard in which the apostles were held by the ordinary people, and of the cures they worked on behalf of those sick in body or in spirit.

Second Reading (Rev. 1:9-13, 17-19). John is the spokesman of the risen Christ who lives on among the congregations of believers. John is bidden to write a message, a message that has meaning for the Church until the end of time.

Gospel (John 20:19-31). By seeing and touching the wounds of their risen Lord, the apostles, and especially Thomas the doubter, are cured of their unbelief.

HOMILY

Physical contact with others is very important. We desperately need to have someone next to us — a friendly, comforting presence. Otherwise we experience confusion, hurt and damage. When you visit an orphanage the children fight for the privilege of touching you. How little we know about the power of physical touch.

Walter hadn't committed any crime. He was a prisoner of conscience. When first imprisoned he was placed in a horrible prison known as 'the dungeons', thrown in with common criminals. Conditions were so dreadful that the tide came in to a depth of three feet twice every twenty-four hours. With the tide came the rats. The only thing was that he had human companionship, such as it was.

Then he was transferred to a special prison where 'politicals' were interrogated for weeks, months, and even years on end. Here the physical conditions were much better but he was in solitary confinement. Because of this he found it more painful. What made it more painful was the lack of companionship. He had no one to exchange a word with, no one on whom to unload his worries and anxieties, no one to whom he could look for sympathy and support. There was nothing but the terrible silence and the endless gruelling interrogation sessions. It was hell.

Solzhenitsyn summed it up when he wrote: 'No one addressed a human word to you. No one looked at you with a human gaze. All they did was to peck at your brain and heart with iron beaks, and when you cried out or groaned, they laughed.'

At the beginning and end of each corridor there was a plywood cupboard. Thus if he was being walked along the corridor by a warder, to or from an interrogation session, and it happened that another warder with a prisoner appeared at the other end of the corridor, he would be hurriedly thrust into one of these cupboards and the door shut on him. Inside there was just enough room to stand. One prisoner was thus prevented from encountering another, in case he might draw comfort or support from the look in his eyes. How Walter longed for the dungeon where he was able to talk to the other prisoners. Here he touched no one and no one touched him. This was a far worse hell.

All this should help us to understand how Thomas and the other apostles felt when death robbed them of their Leader. They had pinned all their hopes and dreams on Christ. They had given up their jobs, they had left everything to follow him. But then a storm broke over them and suddenly he was gone.

What could they do but hide and wait. A feeling of hopelessness and futility gripped them. The more the reality of his death came home to them, the more clearly they saw how much he had meant to them, how indispensable he had become. It is a well-known fact that anything we lose assumes an exaggerated value and seems more important than the sum-total of what is left to us. This is even truer when the loss concerns, not a thing, but a person.

While Christ was with them they had known strains, and had experienced minor disillusionments, but never serious doubts. No migratory bird could be more sure of its goal or its mission than they. But now they were plunged into a terrible sadness and confusion, and they experienced real doubt for the first time. Everything now seemed to have become unreliable and doubtful. The value and meaning of everything was threatened: their comradeship, their faith, their whole lives. They were in a prison of despair, cut off and isolated from their Master.

And then the incredible happened — he was once more in their midst. The first thing he did was to show them his wounds. Why this? Because these were the proof of his love for them. Love, after all, is proved not by words but by deeds. Then he invited them to 'see and to touch'. When people have been hurt and let down they will not believe in words. They have to see and to touch before they will be convinced. Christ understood this need in his apostles, especially Thomas, and so he said: 'See and touch!'.

All of us have doubts and fears. We should learn from the example of Thomas. What a refreshing honesty he showed. He made no attempt to hide his doubts. He didn't pretend that all was well when it wasn't. Christ invites us to draw close to him in faith and to look at those same wounds of his. While it's true that we cannot touch him physically, we can draw close to him spiritually. He will help us to make contact with him and with one another. In his first meeting with his disciples he gave them the Holy Spirit and the power to grant divine pardon. The Spirit is the Spirit of love and unity.

And having been 'touched' by him he sends us forth to touch others who do not believe in him. The world today is full, not just of doubters, but of unbelievers. The only way they will be converted to belief is if they can 'see' him and 'touch' him in his followers. But if his followers have no wounds of love to show, if they live in insulated and selfish comfort, then how can the unbelievers be expected to believe?

But touching by itself is not enough. It is the *quality* of my touch that matters. The quality of my touch is a good measure of the kind of person I am. Helen Keller, being blind, had to rely heavily on the sense of touch. She said: 'I have met some people so empty of joy that when I shook hands with them it seemed as if I was shaking hands with an iceberg. But there are others who have sunbeams in them, so that their grasp warms my heart.'

And Thoreau said something similar. 'How often our ordinary contacts with one another are hollow and ineffectual. Surface meets surface. It is not words that I wish to hear or to utter, but relations I wish to stand in. It often seems to me that I go away from meetings unmet, unrecognised, ungreeted in my offered relation.'

We have to ask Christ to give us the gift of being able to touch people in such a way that, like him, we can bring faith, hope and life to them.

'My "Hosanna" has passed through a great furnace of doubts.' (Dostoyevsky).

PRAYER OF THE FAITHFUL

Let us pray to Christ that he may renew the faith of all those who believe in him, and that he may awaken faith in those who do not believe. *R*. Lord, hear our prayer.

For the Church: may the Holy Spirit make of it a community of brothers and sisters where all will find understanding, acceptance and pardon. (Pause). Let us pray to the Lord.

For all those in high positions: that they may show special concern for the poorer and more disadvantaged members of our society. (Pause). Let us pray to the Lord.

For all those with weak faith or no faith: that the Lord may touch their minds and hearts through the lives of committed Christians. (Pause). Let us pray to the Lord.

That our faith in Christ and in his love for us may continue to grow in spite of doubts and difficulties. (Pause). Let us pray to the Lord.

For local needs.

Let us pray:

Lord Jesus Christ, you rose from the dead so that all might believe and find eternal life. Grant us the will to reach out even when we do not want to; the love to comfort even when we are without comfort ourselves; the grace to see in darkness; and the faith to go on believing in you even in the midst of doubt. For you live and reign for ever and ever.

COMMUNION REFLECTION

Jesus says to us what he said to Thomas:
'See my wounded hands and side.
See the proof of my love for you.
So cease doubting and believe.'

Those who care about others
pick up a lot of wounds as they go through life.
Perhaps there are no great wounds,
but only a multiplicity of little ones —
a host of scratches, wrinkles and welts.
Yet these are only the visible wounds.

What about the myriad of invisible wounds:
the furrows left on the mind and the soul
by hardships, worries and anxieties?
And those piercing ones which affect
that most sensitive part of us — the heart —
things like disappointments, loneliness and ingratitude.

These wounds are not things we should be ashamed of.
They are the proof of our love.
Will anyone see these wounds
and come to believe in our love because of them?
Even if no one else sees them,
the heavenly Father sees them,
and he is proud of us,
for he sees that we are becoming like his Son.

THIRD SUNDAY OF EASTER
Stranger on the shore

INTRODUCTION AND CONFITEOR

We know how badly Peter acted on the night of the Lord's passion; how he denied his Master, not once, but three times. Yet in today's Gospel we will see how Christ restored him to where he was before and confirmed him as chief shepherd of his flock.

Let us pause to remember the times we have written people off or taken revenge on them when they disappointed us. (Pause).

Christ does not write us off. He gives us a chance to cancel out our failures by love.

Lord Jesus, you restore life to all those who sink into the grave of remorse and despair.   Lord, have mercy.

Lord Jesus, your anger lasts but for a moment; your favour lasts all life long.   Christ, have mercy.

Lord Jesus, you have changed our mourning into dancing by your loving forgiveness.   Lord, have mercy.

HEADINGS FOR READINGS

First Reading (Acts 5:27-32, 40-41). The apostles have been imprisoned and put on trial because of their preaching of the Gospel. But they are undeterred. In fact they are glad to suffer for Christ.

Second Reading (Rev. 5:11-14). This gives us part of the heavenly liturgies that are a feature of the book of the Apocalypse. It is a hymn in praise of the crucified and risen Christ.

Gospel (John 21:1-19). This relates an appearance of the risen Jesus to seven of his apostles on the shore of the lake of Gennesareth. The incident is built around Peter.

HOMILY

Often we write off other people on the strength of one bad experience or one unfriendly encounter with them. We rarely give them a second chance, much less a third or a fourth one. However, this is not only silly but downright unfair. Which of us would like to be judged on a single moment of our lives?

A certain woman was passing through an unfamiliar town. She looked through her tourist brochure in search of a good hotel in which to spend the night. She didn't have to go beyond page one. There she spotted an advertisement for the 'New Hotel'. It seemed to be exactly what she was looking for. It was right on the seafront. According to the brochure it was a Grade A hotel and had everything a tourist could desire.

When she got to it the hour was already getting late, and she was informed that there was only one room left. She took it. But she wasn't very impressed with the treatment she got from the receptionist. And the place seemed to be in chaos, with people rushing about all over the place. The fact was that there was a convention being held in the hotel, and the staff were run off their feet.

She had a bad night. The room was comfortable but there was so much noise coming from a late-night party in a room overhead that she got very little sleep. She got up early next morning. The first thing she did was pull back the blinds as she wanted to get a breath of sea air. But when she looked out she was horrified at the sight that met her eyes. Instead of looking out at the sea she found herself gazing into the backyard of the hotel. Right down below here was a horrible collection of half-covered refuse bins. The stench coming up from them was not pleasant.

She packed her bags and lodged a strong complaint with the management. But she was far from satisfied with the response she got. She got herself so worked up that she was unable to eat breakfast and left immediately. She departed in a vile mood, swearing that never again would she set foot in the place. 'Grade A hotel how are you! It doesn't even deserve a C!' was her parting remark.

Though we can feel some sympathy for her, she was wrong about the hotel and about the staff. She was unlucky to strike it at the moment she did. She couldn't have come at a more unsuitable time. In reality the hotel was a splendid one, the staff was first class, and the prices were not exorbitant. She judged the hotel and its staff on one bad experience. For her they would never be given a chance to redeem themselves.

As we said earlier, we ourselves tend to do the same to people. But by acting like this we can do them a terrible injustice. People are complicated. If we saw a fruit tree in winter time, stripped not only of fruit but even of leaves, we would make allowances. That is because we understand fruit trees. We don't show similar understanding where people are concerned.

Christ did not act like this towards Peter and the other apostles. In spite of his dismal failure Christ did not discard Peter. He didn't say: 'Ah, you're a nice one! The very time I needed you most, you deserted me. Go away from me! I'm finished with you!' Had he done so I think a lot of people would have agreed with him. They would have said: 'What other option had he but to cut him off? After all, he was the leader of the apostolic team. He had set a terrible example for the others. If he let the leader get off scot-free with his triple denial the others would surely conclude that it didn't matter whether one was loyal or disloyal. No, he was perfectly justified in discarding him.'

Not only did Christ not discard Peter, he didn't even give out to him. There were no recriminations as he restored him to where he was before. How hard it is not to blame someone who has let us down. How hard it is to try to see things from his point of view, and to say that in the same circumstances we would in all probability have done the same. Christ was able to see into the heart of Peter. He knew exactly how he felt. After all, did he not burst into tears of regret only minutes after his denial? Christ now saw that Peter was still feeling bad about his denial. He was full of remorse and the sense of failure. He was feeling down. And kicking a person when he is down doesn't help him to get up again.

This was not Christ's way of doing things. As long as there was even the slightest hope of rekindling the flame of the smouldering wick he would not extinguish it. Peter was overburdened with guilt. Christ came to lighten people's burdens, to lift up those who were bowed down and crushed. Furthermore, he knew that Peter's denial was caused by weakness and cowardice rather than by evil.

He did not go back over what had happened since Peter was only too painfully aware of the reality of it. Yet neither did he tell him: 'Just forget it — it was nothing!' So what alternative was left? To go forward. Love, we are told, keeps no record of offences. So Christ called Peter forward. He asked him to declare his love in public, since his denial had also been in public. The amazing thing is that love can co-exist with weakness and cowardice. So now Peter was asked to declare his love, and having done so, he was entrusted with the care of all of Christ's flock: 'Feed my lambs, feed my sheep.'

We can imagine that Peter made an excellent leader. A leader has to have the wisdom to know that his greatest enemy is himself. He has to have humility. Peter learned humility the hard way — through the experience of his own weakness. Thus ultimately the experience that might have ended it all resulted in a great step forward, a great purification. It rid him of his pride and his blind reliance on his own resources.

Peter's story is one of calling, falling and recalling. It shows that Christ's call doesn't exclude falls. It was said of Stalin that if you made one mistake it was like mishandling a detonator — it was the last one you made. We are all like Peter. We are not the rocklike characters we would like to be or that we sometimes think we are. We are weak human beings. We need someone who can understand our weaknesses, who realises that it may take time for us to overcome them, and who doesn't write us off because we don't produce the goods at once. We should be ready to extend the same understanding love towards others.

Peter repented, but what helped him to repent was the conviction that in spite of his denials Christ still loved him. It was love that brought Peter back to life. The only fall then is the one from which we learn nothing. I imagine that Peter learned more about life and about himself during that terrible night (in which he denied Christ) than in all his previous years.

'The heart of one person holds inexhaustible sources of life for the heart of another.' (Dostoyevsky).

'Diseases of the soul come on horseback, but leave on foot.' (St Francis de Sales).

PRAYER OF THE FAITHFUL

Let us pray to God our Father that he may help us to understand something of the height and depth of the love and forgiveness he has shown us in Christ his Son. *R*. Lord, hear us in your love.

For Church leaders: that they may rule the Church with love in a spirit of courage and right judgement. (Pause). We pray in faith.

For our political leaders: that they may fulfil their responsibilities worthily and well, by striving to please the Lord in all they do. (Pause). We pray in faith.

For all those who have been rejected or written off because of their mistakes, failures or sins: that the love of true Christians may breathe new life and hope into them. (Pause). We pray in faith.

That, remembering how kind the Lord has been to us, we may

in our turn be kind, understanding and forgiving towards all those who disappoint or fail us. (Pause).   We pray in faith.

For local needs.

Let us pray:

Father, our source of life, you know our weakness. May we reach out with joy to grasp the hand you extend to us in Christ, so that we may walk more readily in your ways. We ask this through the same Christ our Lord.

COMMUNION REFLECTION

Nobody likes to fail.
The apostles had failed.
But the Stranger on the shore got them to say:
'We caught nothing — we failed.'
If we can say these words in the presence of someone we trust,
then suddenly failure loses its power over us.
It is sometimes easier to say them
to a sympathetic stranger than to a friend.

Then the Stranger told them to let down the net once more.
They did so and made a large catch of fish.
This shows that even when Christ is only
a shadowy figure on the margins of our lives,
we are still okay if we do what he says.

But once Peter recognised the Stranger
he wanted to encounter him,
he wanted to be near him.

There is a world of difference
between those who have encountered the risen Lord,
and those who obey a stranger.
The risen Lord nourishes those who encounter him,
and he gives them a task to do.
He says to them:
'Feed my lambs, feed my sheep'.

FOURTH SUNDAY OF EASTER
The Good Shepherd

INTRODUCTION AND CONFITEOR

In today's Mass we have one of the loveliest gospels of the year

— that in which Christ describes himself as the Good Shepherd. He says: 'I know my sheep. They listen to my voice and follow me.'

We say we belong to the Good Shepherd; yet we don't always listen to him or follow him. Let us reflect for a moment on our failure to respond to his love and care. (Pause).

Lord Jesus, we are your people, the sheep of your flock. Lord, have mercy.

Lord Jesus, you continue to show us your merciful love even when we do not listen to your voice or follow you. Christ, have mercy.

Lord Jesus, you bind up the wounds of those who are injured and go in search of those who are lost. Lord, have mercy.

HEADINGS FOR READINGS

First Reading (Acts 13:14, 43-52). Everywhere they go, Paul and Barnabas preach the Gospel first of all to the Jews, but when the Jews reject it they turn to the gentiles who receive it with gratitude and joy.

Second Reading (Rev. 7:9, 14-17). This contains a vision of those who will come triumphantly through times of great tribulation and persecution. They will owe their victory to the care of Christ, the Good Shepherd.

Gospel (John 10:27-30). Christ is the true Shepherd, and no one will snatch from his care the sheep that the Father has given him.

HOMILY

There were two shepherds called Amos and Abel. Amos was in charge of a hundred sheep, all of which were his own. Abel was in charge of several hundred sheep, none of which were his own.

It is evening time and they have gathered their respective flocks into the common fold for the night. They cast a glance over the assembled sheep. Abel's glance is a hurried and superficial one. All he sees is a sea of faces. They all look the same to him. He knows practically nothing about them as individuals. However, as he brought them in he couldn't help noticing that a few of them were lame and obviously in pain. That others were desperately thin. That others were given to wandering off on their own and were ostracised by the others. But he doesn't know them well enough to be able to account for these differences, and he is not interested enough to find out.

Amos, on the other hand, casts a lingering glance over his sheep. Nothing escapes his trained and caring eye. To him they are not just a sea of faces, all of which look alike. Every face is special. Behind each face is an individual sheep whose life story is familiar to him.

His eye rests longer on the ones that need special care. He notices that such-and-such a one is lame. Tomorrow he will examine her foot to find out why. He sees another who is thin. Tomorrow he will give him a dose to fight off the worms. And so on.

It is the turn of Amos to guard the flock for the night. Pulling a blanket over his shoulders he lies down at the mouth of the pen. Though he is very tired, and has to fight to keep sleep away, he misses nothing. The smallest unusual sound and he is on his feet, listening intently. He creeps silently around the fold to make sure that all is well, to ensure that no thieves or wolves are about. Only last week when Abel was on guard thieves broke into the fold and stole several sheep. Where was Abel? He was asleep, though of course he strenuously denied this.

The next day finally dawns. Abel eventually shows up — late as usual. But Amos is not upset for he has used the time to take care of those of his sheep that needed attention — the lame one and the thin one in particular. As soon as he sees Abel approaching he begins to call his sheep. They look up at once and straightaway begin to follow him — every single one of them. He doesn't drive them. He leads them. Every now and then he pauses to give the stragglers a chance to catch up. He takes them a long way off to where the grass is lush and green and the water plentiful and pure. He sits down close by, weary but contented. Those sheep are a lot of trouble and at times can be so contrary. But he loves them. This soothes all his pains.

Meanwhile Abel, too, has been busy. He tries calling his sheep but they don't recognise his voice and refuse to follow him. So he has to drive them. It's no easy job and he has to dish out a few hurtful blows of his staff to the contrary ones. He doesn't go very far. He can't be bothered. He settles for the first bit of pasture land he encounters, though the grass is painfully thin and water nowhere in sight. But there's nobody to check up on him. And he's only in the job because of the money. He hasn't the slightest interest in the sheep. He's only waiting for promotion to an administrative job. He can't wait for evening to come. And when it does come he gathers up his flock without even bothering to count them, and heads for home. Ah, home! That's where his real life is. That's all he lives for.

Christ spoke of two kinds of shepherds — those who knew their sheep and who cared for them, and those who didn't know them and who didn't care for them. The first he called 'good'; the second he called 'hirelings'. Of himself he said without boasting: 'I am the Good Shepherd. I know my sheep. And my sheep listen to my voice and follow me.' Why do the sheep follow him? Certainly fear or force have nothing to do with it. They follow him in response to the love and care he shows for them. In my story Amos, of course, stands for Christ, the Good Shepherd. Abel stands for all the hirelings.

It is a pity that this Sunday is often limited to 'vocations Sunday'. The word 'vocation' in this context means vocation to the priesthood or religious life. But this leads to an impoverished understanding of one of the loveliest gospels of the whole year. All Christians have a vocation — the vocation to be loving and caring people. 'All vocations,' says Catherine de Hueck Doherty, 'are vocations to love.' And every Christian is called to love.

This Sunday, then, should be the feast of all those who care for others. If we single out any set of people it should be those in what are now called the caring professions. But I think it is a pity to limit it at all. It should be the day when we encourage and support all those who in their lives and dealings with other people are trying to imitate the Good Shepherd, and when we try to prod the consciences of the hirelings.

The good shepherd has to be able to forget himself (or herself), so as to think of others. First of all he must know his 'sheep'. This goes far beyond merely knowing their names, though this is not a bad start. To really know another person is to know where he comes from, that is, to be thoroughly familiar with his life story. But unless we show disinterested love for other people we will never know their stories because they will never trust us enough to tell them to us. But if they honour us by telling us their stories, this should lead to understanding, to tolerance of their idiosyncracies, and to acceptance of their uniqueness. But all this demands time, patience and sacrifice. To care in this way is costly. But it is immensely rewarding. The gardener who has done his tilling and sowing well will reap the benefits at harvest time.

Everything today tends to be big and centralised — all for the sake of economy. It is called 'rationalising' things. But it doesn't make knowing and caring easy, for everything is so impersonal. It doesn't encourage people to care, much less reward them for doing so. In this kind of system people are hired and promoted for efficiency, not for the love and care they are capable of showing.

How the world needs people who can care. Even if in my job I am mainly concerned with things, I can still imitate the love of the Good Shepherd in the way I treat my fellow workers. If Christ is truly the Good Shepherd for me, if I daily experience his love in my life, then surely I will be happy to mediate some of his love to others. And wherever we are, if we have the heart of the Good Shepherd, we will find an outlet for our love.

'Do not hire a person who does your work for money; instead

hire someone who does it out of love.' (Thoreau).
'If you feel no love, leave people alone. Occupy yourself instead with things." (Tolstoy).

PRAYER OF THE FAITHFUL

Let us pray to Christ, our Good Shepherd, that he may touch our hearts of stone and change them into hearts of flesh and blood, capable of loving as he loves. *R*. Lord, graciously hear us.

For the pope and the bishops: that they may faithfully and lovingly watch over the flock of Christ. (Pause). Lord, hear us.

For all those in positions of authority, and especially for doctors and nurses: that the Lord may fill them with a strong and unselfish love to work for the good of all people, but especially the weak and the wounded. (Pause). Lord, hear us.

For all those who have no love in their lives, and who are not important or precious to anyone. (Pause). Lord, hear us.

That each of us, wherever we are and no matter what our state in life, may strive to be people who love and care for others. (Pause). Lord, hear us.

For vocations to the priesthood and religious life: that the Lord may inspire men and women to devote their lives to caring for his flock. (Pause). Lord, hear us.

For local needs.

Let us pray:

Heavenly Father, grant that what we have said with our lips, we may believe with our hearts, and practise with our lives. We make our prayer through Christ our Lord.

SIGN OF PEACE

Lord Jesus Christ, you said: 'I am the good shepherd. I know my sheep, and my sheep know me. I am ready to lay down my life for my sheep. There are other sheep that do not yet belong to me. But they too will hear my voice, and there will be only one flock and one shepherd.' Good Shepherd, bind us to you and to one another so that we may enjoy the peace and unity of your kingdom where you live for ever and ever.

COMMUNION REFLECTION

Philip is handicapped
and was institutionalised when he was very young.
He is a deeply wounded young man.
He feels he has disappointed his parents.
He is deaf and stammers,
but these are only his visible wounds.

The deepest wound is that of the heart:
the feeling that he has not been loved,
that he is not precious to anyone.

We believe that we have hands that can make things,
and minds that can understand things.
Yet we don't believe that we have hearts that can give life.
But we are not sterile people.
We can give life to people who are inwardly broken.
We can show them that they are important,
and so bring life to them.

'I can do nothing for you:
all I can do is be your friend.'
The person who says that and means it,
has the greatest contribution of all to make.

Today, Good Shepherd Sunday, is also vocations Sunday.
All vocations are vocations to love.

FIFTH SUNDAY OF EASTER
Love one another

INTRODUCTION AND CONFITEOR
'Love one another as I have loved you.' Of all the commandments Christ gave us this as the most important. It sums up all the
others. In a sense the only failure in the life of a Christian is the
failure to love.
Let us think about the people we don't love . . . don't speak to
. . . don't forgive . . . don't associate with . . . (Pause).
Let us confess our sins against the commandment to love.
I confess to almighty God . . .

HEADINGS FOR READINGS
First Reading (Acts 14:21-27). Paul and Barnabas retrace their
steps encouraging the little communities of Christians which they
had founded.
Second Reading (Rev. 21:1-5). This is taken from the final part
of Apocalypse, and opens with the vision of a new world, and the
manifestation of a new Jerusalem. This new order of things has
been inaugurated by Christ.

Gospel (John 13:31-35). During his last supper with his apostles Christ left them a new commandment — to love one another as he had loved them.

HOMILY

We all like to think that we love unselfishly. But often we deceive ourselves. We love some people. We have our friends. So we think we love. But unfortunately, as Camus said, what passes for friendship is often no more than 'an effusion of feeling among people who get along together.' But this is neither real friendship nor real love. This is a selfish love. A selfish love seldom respects the rights of the other person. A selfish love withers and dies unless it is sustained by the attention of the loved one. True love seeks nothing at all, except the good of the other person.

Steve and Mark were brothers. Steve was twelve years old and was lame from polio. Mark was ten. Though they fought a lot, as boys will, deep down they were good to each other. They never went to sleep at night without settling a quarrel that had occurred between them during the day. Naturally, there were times when Steve was envious of his brother, especially of the fact that he had two good legs.

In his nightly dreams Steve often found himself exploring a deep and mysterious forest. One night he ventured deeper into it than ever before. Of course he was afraid, but his high excitement carried him forward in spite of his limping walk. Finally he came to a large opening in a rock wall. He went through and found himself in a dark cave. Creeping forward he eventually came into a hall-like cavern. At the centre of it a bright fire burned. Then out of the shadows came a man wearing a long robe.

Steve was frightened when the old man told him that he was the warlock of the forest. He asked Steve how he had found the entrance to his secret cave, but Steve told him that it was an accident. Then the warlock told him that as a reward he could have one wish fulfilled — just one wish, anything he desired. Steve didn't need much time to make up his mind. 'I wish that I may have two good legs,' he said in a voice that trembled with excitement.

With that the warlock threw his cloak around him and before he knew it Steve found himself back in his bed. He looked at the familiar surroundings. His brother was sleeping soundly in the next bed. Then the warlock got down to work. He lifted the blankets so as to expose Mark's legs.

'What are you doing?' asked Steve.

'I'm beginning the operation?' said the warlock.

'What operation?'

'The transference, of course. What's going to happen is this. When the operation is over you will have Mark's legs and he will have yours. But don't worry. No one will ever know. They will think that it was always like that.'

'I never thought it was going to be like this,' said Steve.

'Why, you hardly expected me to pluck a pair of good legs out of the air, did you?'

But Steve was in a state of deep shock. A picture flashed through his mind. He saw himself running freely along, and behind him, dragging his leg came his brother Mark. Tears came into his eyes at the sight. How could he live for the rest of his life knowing that he had done this to his brother, that he had robbed him of his good legs and given him crippled ones instead? He couldn't do that, at least not to his little brother.

'I can't do it. I don't want it,' he cried out.

On hearing this the old warlock was very angry. But finally he gave him his wish. But he warned him in future to stay out of the forest, and that he would pay dearly for it if he ever again entered the secret cave. Steve was happy to see the back of him. Next morning he awoke and looked across at his brother. Remembering his dream, he smiled. From that day on he never again felt envious of his little brother and he loved him more than ever.

What a lovely story about true love. Steve wanted to be happy. For him at that moment happiness meant one thing — having a pair of normal legs. But he refused to buy that happiness at the expense of causing misery to his brother. He rightly refused a false and momentary happiness that comes from the satisfaction of one's own needs irrespective of the pain caused to others. Such a happiness always leads to sorrow because it deadens the spirit. True happiness on the other hand is found only in unselfish love.

How difficult it is to love unselfishly. 'Love one another as I have loved you.' Christ showed us how to love. To really love is to put the other person first. It's simple and frightening at the same time. How many of us could claim to love like that? A few kind gestures, a commitment or two, and we have a good conscience. We give a little of ourselves, a few crumbs, and in no time we are so proud of ourselves. We brim over with self-congratulation.

True love, like true friendship, is more difficult. It calls for effort, and it causes pain. The effort called for consists in deeds. It is not enough to say 'I love you,' or 'I care about you', and then do nothing about it. The deepest pain comes when our love is not returned. When we meet with no response. Then it becomes really hard to go on loving. Often we flatly refuse to love those whom we consider, for some reason (often a trivial one), unworthy of our love.

It's not that we hate them. It's just that we refuse to accept them into our hearts.

It's interesting to note that (according to John) Jesus only started to talk about the new commandment when Judas had left. And he knew what Judas was about. But now that he had left he was free to open his heart to the others.. Though his heart was full of love it was also deeply wounded. And Judas's act of treachery left perhaps the deepest wound of all. When we meet with a lack of response we might take some consolation from the fact that even Jesus failed to touch some.

Love makes me an instrument of God's providence in the lives of others. Without my love for them they may perhaps not achieve the things God has willed for them. My love becomes the channel through which they will experience the love of God. 'By this (your love) all people will know that you are my disciples.' This means that as long as Christians love others, then people will be able to encounter Christ himself.

'Learning to love is hard and we pay dearly for it.' (Dostoyevsky).

'Without love the world is a very dark place.' (Catherine de Hueck Doherty).

PRAYER OF THE FAITHFUL

Everyone should know that we are followers of Christ by the love we have for one another. Let us pray for the gift of love. *R.* Lord, teach us to love.

For all the followers of Christ: that their love for one another may be sincere, generous and unselfish. (Pause). Let us pray to the Lord.

For all those who are well-off or powerful: that they may refrain from exploiting others; rather, that they may share with them, especially with the needy. (Pause). Let us pray to the Lord.

For all those who do not know Christ: that they may see him and meet him in the love of Christians. (Pause). Let us pray to the Lord.

That we may not be content merely to love our friends, but that we may try to be kind even to those who make life difficult for us. (Pause). Let us pray to the Lord.

For local needs.

Let us pray:

Heavenly Father, in your Son, Jesus, you gave us a wonderful example of love. Grant that as we hear his words and receive him in this Eucharist, we may follow his way of love in our daily lives. We ask this through the same Christ our Lord.

SIGN OF PEACE

Lord Jesus Christ, you said to your disciples: 'A new commandment I give you: love one another as I have loved you. Everybody will know that you are disciples of mine if you love one another.' Lord, touch our hearts so that we may be people who are able to love, and thus we will enjoy the peace and unity of your kingdom where you live for ever and ever.

COMMUNION REFLECTION

It is easy to love people who are far away.
It is not always easy to love those who are close to us.
It is easier to give a few pounds to relieve famine in Africa
than to relieve the loneliness of someone living next door.
In other words, it is easy to love at a distance,
but not so easy to love at close quarters.

But does Christ really expect me to love
that woman next door who never stops gossipping,
that stupid fellow I have to work beside every day,
that unfriendly bus conductor who never smiles,
that shouting party member or social climber,
that bad-tempered foreman,
that neighbour's cheeky spoiled brats . . .?

Ah, if only they were in China or India,
and they needed my help,
I would be moved with pity and send them something.
But they are right on my doorstep.

Yes, these are the people Christ asks us to love.
We must begin by loving the people near us.
That is where our love for each other must start.
But of course it doesn't have to end there.

SIXTH SUNDAY OF EASTER
Peace I leave with you.

INTRODUCTION AND CONFITEOR

As we assemble here I'm sure we all have our share of troubles and anxieties which rob us of that priceless gift — inner peace. In the Gospel of today's Mass we will hear Christ say to us: 'Do not

let your hearts be troubled. Peace I leave with you; my own peace
I give you.'

Let us look for a moment at the things that rob us of inner peace
and which make us difficult to live with. (Pause).

Christ will heal us and give us his peace.

Lord Jesus, you calm our fears with your words of hope. Lord,
have mercy.

Lord Jesus, you heal our troubled minds and restless
hearts. Christ, have mercy.

Lord Jesus, you guide us in all our doubts and uncertainties.
Lord, have mercy.

HEADINGS FOR READINGS

First Reading (Acts 15:1-2, 22-29). Many gentiles had accepted
Christianity as a result of the preaching of Paul and Barnabas. But
then a big question arose: how much of the law and traditions of
Moses should be imposed on the converts? This reading tells us how
the problem was solved at the very highest level.

Second Reading (Rev. 21:10-14, 22-23). This comes from near
the end of Apocalypse. It gives a majestic picture of the new
Jerusalem, the heavenly Church of the future, when God's
Kingdom will come in all its glory.

Gospel John 14:23-29). This contains yet another portion of
Christ's farewell discourse at the last supper. It is dominated by the
thought of his imminent departure.

HOMILY

Some people have an awful lot of anger inside them, for whatever
reason. The result is that much of life becomes a misery for them.
They enjoy very little peace of mind or serenity of soul. They are
to be pitied for they are robbed of so much. Often they stumble
along, blindly unaware that the roots of their unhappiness lie inside
themselves. But then you meet other people who, in spite of hardships and difficulties, have this inner peace, and what a difference
it makes to their lives.

There is an old story about two neighbours, James and John,
ploughing in adjacent fields. The ground was hard and stony which
meant the work was difficult. A hot sun beat down on them with
the result that sweat ran down their faces. The air was full of flies.
With both hands on the plough it was difficult to keep them at bay.
It certainly was no picnic. Though it was exactly the same for both
men, they reacted very differently to it.

James was in a black mood. He was thinking of how hard the
work was and about the pain in his arms and legs. His horse would

not go as fast as he wanted him to go so he lashed out at him again and again with his whip. The beatings only had the effect of making him more stubborn and uncooperative. James was convinced that his neighbour's wheat would grow taller than his. And everytime he looked across at him he got the impression that he was laughing at him. This made him even angrier.

He was completely oblivious to the singing of the birds and the bleating of the lambs. Nor had he eyes for the beauty which Spring had bestowed on the surrounding countryside. The work was hard but his mood was not making it any easier. Inside himself a battle was raging. He was full of anger and resentment. And even though at the end of the day he had finished the work, he derived no satisfaction from it. As he headed for home he experienced a terrible weariness of body and spirit.

It was not the work that was to blame, but his own agitated state. Agitation is a symptom of the inner confusion of a soul without peace. It not only destroys the spiritual usefulness of work, but leaves us exhausted and depleted.

John, on the other hand, was in a calm and serene mood. He worked quietly and well, in spite of the pains and aches. Every now and then he stopped to give his horse a rest. While doing so he would look behind him at the work he had done. It was good work. The sight of it encouraged him to go on. And the horse responded to his gentle promptings with an even and steady pull.

As he worked John's heart was lightened by the beauty that spring had brought to his world. He drank in the music of the birds and the fragrance of the flowers. He looked across at his neighbour. He bore him no ill-will. But he could see that he was in a very agitated state. He would have liked to help him but he knew that when he was like this it was better to leave him alone. When John finally had the job done he felt good. He patted the horse on the side of the neck and gave him some grain to eat. As he headed for home he was weary in body but felt happy and at peace with the world.

How do you account for the difference between the two neighbours? It was not in the outer circumstances but in their inner attitudes. John enjoyed inner peace and serenity. James had no order inside himself. He was in a state of inner turmoil, which spoiled life for him and for others around him.

The best most of us could say is that we have snatches of this inner peace. But how much unrest there is in each of us. How much we need the healing presence of Christ's Spirit of love and peace. Christ himself had this inner peace. Hence he was able to offer it to his disciples. What was the basis of his peace? It lay in the loving relationship he had with his Father. This was the unshakeable anchor that held him secure even when the barque of his soul was buffetted by the severest storms.

He offers us his peace: 'Peace I leave with you.' The peace he offers us is not the peace of escape from reality. It is the peace of conquest, something so deep that no sorrow or danger can rob us of it. In other words, it is independent of outer circumstances.

We can't give this peace to others, or have it with others, if we do not have it ourselves. Nothing is a greater obstacle to being on good terms with others than being ill at ease with oneself. Our inner state determines how we see the outside world and other people.

An old man was sitting on a bench at the edge of town when a stranger approached. 'What are the people in this town like?' the stranger asked.

'What were they like in your last town?' replied the old man.

'They were kind, generous, and would do anything for you if you were in trouble.'

'You will find them very much like that in this town too.'

Then a second stranger approached and asked the same question: 'What are the people in this town like?'

And he replied: 'What were they like in the town you have come from?'

'It was a terrible place', came the answer. 'I was glad to get out of it. The people there were mean, unkind, and nobody would lift a finger to help you if you were in trouble.'

'I'm afraid,' said the old man, 'you'll find them much the same in this town.'

Why do we sometimes see people in such a bad light? Because we are ill at ease with ourselves. A man who is not at peace with himself spreads a contagion of conflict around him.

First of all then we have to have peace with ourselves and our own reality. We have to have a right relationship with ourselves. Then we can have a right relationship with other people and with God, and we will find peace there too. Christ is the healer, the one who comes to bring us life and to liberate us from ourselves. He will help us to calm our fears and heal our anguish and hatreds. Then we will be able to look at the world with a still heart and an open soul.

'If you yourself are at peace, then there is at least some peace in the world.' (Thomas Merton).

'Real peace is more fruitful than any amount of turmoil.' (Philip Toynbee).

PRAYER OF THE FAITHFUL

Let us pray to Christ for the gift of peace, a gift he assures us he can give us and which no one can take from us. *R*. Lord, hear our prayer.

For the Church: that all its members may have the gift of inner peace through their efforts to live the Gospel in their lives. (Pause). We pray to the Lord.

For all political leaders: that they may take the path of peace and good will in a world which is dominated by wars and rumours of wars. (Pause). We pray to the Lord.

For all the homes of the parish: that they may be blessed with joy and peace. (Pause). We pray to the Lord.

Let us pray that we may have peace with our neighbours, and for the courage to seek to be reconciled with anyone we have fallen out with. (Pause). We pray to the Lord.

For local needs.

Let us pray:

Heavenly Father, grant us the serenity to accept the things we cannot change; the courage to change the things we can; and the wisdom to know the difference. We ask this through Christ our Lord.

SIGN OF PEACE

Lord Jesus Christ, you said to your disciples: 'Peace I leave with you, my own peace I give you. A peace which the world cannot give, this is my gift to you. So do not let your hearts be troubled or afraid.' Lord, take pity on our restless hearts and troubled spirits, and grant us the peace and unity of your kingdom where you live for ever and ever.

COMMUNION REFLECTION

To be glad of life, because it gives you a chance
to love and to work and to play
and to look up at the stars;
to be satisfied with your possessions,
but not contented with yourself
until you have made the best use of them.

To despise nothing in the world
except what is false and mean.
To fear nothing except what is cowardly.

To be guided by what you admire and love.
rather than by what you hate.

To envy nothing that is your neighbour's
except his kindness of heart
and gentleness of manners.

To think seldom of your enemies,
often of your friends,
and everyday of Christ.

And to spend as much time as you can,
with body and with spirit,
in God's out-of-doors.

These are little signposts on the footpath of peace.
The person who seeks God has already found him.

(Henry van Dyke).

THE ASCENSION

INTRODUCTION AND CONFITEOR

When Christ entered our world, St Paul tells us, 'he emptied himself, taking on the role of a servant.' But because he faithfully accomplished the mission on our behalf which the Father entrusted to him, the Father raised him up in glory.

On this day we celebrate the glorification of Christ, our Brother. He wants us to share in his glory when our earthly journey is ended. Let us reflect for a moment on the glory to which Christ calls us. (Pause). Often we allow the attractions of this world to dim our vision of the glory to come.

Lord Jesus, you are the Son of God and Prince of Peace.   Lord, have mercy.

Lord Jesus, you are the Son of God and Son of Mary.   Christ, have mercy.

Lord Jesus, you are the Word made flesh and splendour of the Father.   Lord, have mercy.

HEADINGS FOR READINGS

First Reading (Acts 1:1-11). Before ascending to heaven Jesus promised to send the Holy Spirit to his apostles. Now that he would no longer be bodily present among them, it would be up to them, aided by the Spirit, to be his witnesses in the world.

Second Reading (Ephesians 1:17-23). Paul describes the meaning of the ascension, which is that God has raised Jesus above all earthly powers, and made him not only head of the Church but Lord of creation.

Gospel (Luke 24:46-53). Before leaving his disciples Jesus sums up for them the meaning of his death and resurrection. Then he commissions them to preach this to all peoples. However, they must not start until they have received the Holy Spirit.

Long ago there lived a man who had twelve sons. Though he loved each of them he had a soft spot in his heart for the second youngest, a boy called Joseph. The others were very jealous of Joseph and one day they decided to kill him. However, at the last minute, they changed their minds and instead sold him to some passing merchants. They told their father that he had been devoured by a wild animal. The father was heart-broken on hearing this.

Poor Joseph was taken off in chains to a foreign country, there to be sold as a slave. He had a wretched life. To make matters worse, someone framed him and he ended up in the dungeons. Though surrounded by hardened criminals, Joseph continued to trust in God and to live a good life. He even made lots of friends among the criminals. Eventually he succeeded in clearing his name, and was released.

When he came out of prison, however, he could see that a famine was coming. He advised the king to get the people to start saving corn. Needing a wise and honest man to take charge of the operation, the king picked Joseph. Thus he rose from being a mere slave to being the king's right-hand man. But he didn't allow success to go to his head. He did a splendid job for the king. He saw to it that in the years of plenty the people stored away all the surplus corn. Thus when the famine hit they had nothing to fear.

But things were going badly for the people in the neighbouring countries. They came to Joseph's king looking for corn. The king would simply say to them: 'Go and ask Joseph. He will see to your needs.' One day who should show up begging for corn but Joseph's brothers — the very men who years previously had sold him as a slave. When they recognised him they trembled with fear, thinking that their goose was cooked. But instead of taking revenge on them, Joseph received them with extra kindness, precisely because they were his brothers. He hugged them and gave them as much corn as they wanted. He told them to come back and bring their father with them. Imagine the joy of the aged father when he discovered that his beloved son was not dead but very much alive.

A great treachery had been committed against Joseph by his brothers, and the father had been fed a pack of lies. But, thanks to Joseph and the kind of person he was, good came out of it all. Out of the misfortune of being sold as a slave, Joseph was able by his uprightness and goodness of heart, not only to save his brothers from the famine, but to re-unite the entire family.

What a brother Joseph turned out to be, and what a son he was. There was such a man as Joseph. We read about him in the book of Genesis. He is, of course, a figure of Christ. However, good and all as he was, he was still only a pale copy of Christ.

Christ was the Father's beloved Son. What a Son he proved to be. We are his brothers and sisters. And what a Brother we have in him. It was we who betrayed him, disowning him and putting him to death. But because of his sufferings and death Jesus was raised up by the Father and placed at his right hand in glory. Now, as we read in the Acts, there is no other name in heaven or on earth through which we can be saved. From his exalted position he saves us from sin and from every evil, even death itself. And he seeks to being together into one great family all of God's scattered sons and daughters.

This is the day the Church invites us to celebrate the ascension of Jesus to the right hand of his Father. It is a day of joy. When the apostles realised what had happened to Jesus they were filled with joy. (See Gospel). But we must not think that Jesus has abandoned us, that he once lived on earth but has now gone 'back to where he really belongs.' If this were so then Christianity would be no more than a remembrance religion. Jesus is risen. He is at the Father's right hand, but he also lives on among us. He continues to be born, to live and to die in us his followers.

So we must not look upon him as being far away from us. Because of the many people who do not have our faith, he needs us to witness to his presence in the world. These people will not believe unless, like Thomas the doubter, they see him and touch him in us. 'You must be my witnesses,' Jesus says to us. We witness to Jesus if, like Joseph, instead of seeking revenge we can forgive those who do evil against us. We are his witnesses if, in spite of living in difficult circumstances, we continue to trust in God and to live according to his will.

'Today's great deception is an unattainable happiness.' (M. Quoist).

'If a man is to strive with all his heart, the significance of his striving must be unmistakable.' (Antoine de Saint Exupery).

PRAYER OF THE FAITHFUL

Let us pray to the Father who raised his Son Jesus from the dead and seated him at his right hand in glory, that he may help us to follow his path in this life and so come to share his glory in the life to come. *R*. Lord, graciously hear us.

That Christ, taken up in glory, may enkindle in all his followers an ardent desire for his kingdom. (Pause). Lord, hear us.

On this day Jesus promised to send his Holy Spirit to his disciples: may he strengthen by the power of that Spirit all those who are working for a more just, peaceful and human world. (Pause). Lord, hear us.

In Jesus we see one who is crowned now with glory because he suffered death: let us pray to him for all those who have no faith in an afterlife. (Pause). Lord, hear us.

Christ is seated in the glory of heaven: may he intercede for us who put our trust in him and help us to bear witness to him in the world. (Pause). Lord, hear us.

For local needs.

Let us pray:

Heavenly Father, your Son Jesus lived in our world without power or prestige, the servant of all. Now, though he is at your right hand in glory, we believe that he is closer to us than ever before. And so we make all our prayers to you, through the same Christ our Lord, who lives and reigns with you and the Holy Spirit, one God for ever and ever.

COMMUNION REFLECTION

On Ascension Day Jesus withdrew
his physical presence from his disciples.
But physical absence does not mean absence of presence.
People can be very close to one another
even though separated by thousands of miles.

In fact, physical presence
can sometimes actually get in the way of intimate communication.
Many of our disappointments in life
are caused by the fact that seeing and touching
do not always create the closeness we seek.

For people to grow together
there must be periods of absence as well as presence.
In absence we see each other in a new way.
We are less distracted by a person's idiosyncracies
and are better able to appreciate his or her true worth.

When we think of each other with love
a spiritual bond is created between us,
and we enter into a new intimacy.
For those who love one another
there is no such place as 'far away'.

Lord Jesus, raised in glory to the Father's right hand,
may your Spirit create a bond of love between us and you,
so that when we think of you we will never be alone.

SEVENTH SUNDAY OF EASTER
Waiting

INTRODUCTION AND CONFITEOR

After Jesus left them, the apostles went back to Jerusalem and
'joined in continuous prayer' as they waited for the coming of the
Holy Spirit.

At the invitation of the Church, that is exactly what we are doing
during these days between the feasts of the Ascension and
Pentecost. Without the Spirit of Jesus to guide and inspire us we
simply cannot live the life of a Christian.

Let us briefly reflect on this. (Pause).

Lord Jesus, you raise the dead to live in the Spirit. Lord, have
mercy.

Lord Jesus, your Spirit beings pardon and peace to
sinners. Christ, have mercy.

Lord Jesus, your Spirit beings courage and hope to the weak and
the fallen. Lord, have mercy.

HEADINGS FOR READINGS

First Reading (Acts 7:55-60). This recounts the death of the first
martyr, Stephen. Like Christ, Stephen died forgiving his killers.

Second Reading (Rev. 22:12-14, 16-17, 20). The time has come
for God to reward his servants. Christ comes to give eternal life to
all those who have followed him.

Gospel (John 17:20-26). This is part of the great prayer which
Jesus made on behalf of his present and future disciples during the
last supper. He prayed especially for unity among them.

HOMILY

Before leaving his apostles Jesus told them that they were not to
start preaching the Gospel immediately. He told them to *wait* . . .

to wait until, they 'received *power* from on high.' By this he meant
the Holy Spirit. Why the wait? It helped to bring home to them
their utter need of the Spirit, while at the same time disposing them
to receive his gifts.

Waiting gives us an experience of our *powerlessness.* Think of
the times you stood in a queue that wasn't moving, waiting for
some place to open. There was nothing you could do but stand
there. Waiting is hard. Some find it harder than others. They
quickly become impatient and restless. Unable to stand still they
stamp their feet or walk up and down. What they can't bear is this
feeling of powerlessness. The actor, Rod Steiger, says: 'six to eight
weeks waiting for work and I feel as if I'm forgotten or like I can't
act anymore.'

People do not like waiting because it brings home to them their
inner emptiness and poverty. They do not like being totally dependent on someone else. They like being in control of things.
Sometimes, unable to put up with the waiting, people go away and
an opportunity is lost.

When Jesus made the apostles wait he wasn't being cruel to
them. Nor was he testing them. He was merely disposing them to
receive the Holy Spirit. As yet they simply weren't ready to receive
him. Without the Spirit their work would be barren. Unless they
realised this there wasn't much hope for them. It is only when we
have experienced a little hunger that we appreciate a meal. It is only
when we have experienced loneliness that we welcome the clasp of
a friendly hand. When the Spirit finally came the apostles welcomed him like desert travellers welcome water.

There are two kinds of waiting — *active* and *passive.* To
illustrate these let us take as an example the crews of two sailboats.
Each crew is waiting for the wind without which they cannot go
anywhere. In the first case the sail is down, the boat firmly
anchored in the harbour, and the crew ashore, fast asleep. That
is passive waiting. In the second case the boat has put out to sea,
the sail is up, and the crew is wide awake, ready and eager to go.
At the first puff of wind they are underway. That is active waiting.

What were the apostles doing while waiting for the Spirit? St
Luke tells us that after Jesus left them they went back to Jerusalem.
There they gathered as a group in the upper room and, joined by
several others, they 'joined in continuous prayer.' In other words,
they waited *actively.* We often pray to God for something but we
do nothing. We just sit back and wait for God to do everything for
us. But we must do what we can, even when it means just holding
ourselves ready and alert. We have to prepare ourselves to avail of
God's help when it comes. A small child once asked a sailor how

the wind worked. The sailor replied: 'I've no idea. All I know is how to put up a sail.' There is not much point in waiting for the wind to come if we can't even be bothered to put up a sail.

Sometimes waiting is a joyful thing. Think of waiting for the arrival of a friend. But at other times it can be a very trying time, filled with fear and anxiety. Think of waiting in a doctor's surgery for a diagnosis which could seal your fate for ever.

For the apostles their period of waiting was a joyful one. They had placed all their hopes on the word of Jesus. He would not disappoint them. And what he had promised was his very own Spirit. That was surely a tremendous reason to be happy. But at the same time their joy was tinged with anxiety. Ahead of them lay an extremely uncertain future. Then they were forced to wait behind closed doors because they were afraid of the Jewish leaders.

What was a great help to them was the fact that there was a group of them. They were able to encourage and support one another. It is terrible to wait alone, especially if bad news is in the offing. To be alone at an airport waiting to board a plane to take you to the bedside of a dying relative. To be alone in a hospital ward facing a serious operation. As followers of Jesus we must try to ensure that no one waits alone in cases like these.

What did the apostles expect to happen? We say that they were waiting for the 'gifts' of the Holy Spirit. But does this mean that they were like kids waiting for Santa Claus? Certainly not. I think it is true to say that the Spirit did not bring them anything, or give them anything, that they did not already have.

Spring does not give anything to the trees. All it does is help to bring out what is already within them, though only in a germinal state. So it was with the apostles. What the Holy Spirit did was awaken them to the gifts that God had already placed within them, and to bid them live and help them grow. Thus, while the action of the Spirit was mysterious, it was not magic (that is, something out of nothing). What was called for on their part was cooperation by way of openness, willingness and effort.

We have had our 'Pentecost' and so has the Church. We were given the Spirit at Baptism and Confirmation. But still, as individuals and as a community, we still await him. We always need him. We can't take even one step without him. That is where this week of prayerful waiting comes in.

'It is by desiring to grow in love that we receive the Spirit.' (Thomas Merton).

'It is in the faithful waiting for the loved one that we know how much he has filled our lives already.' (Henri Nouwen).

PRAYER OF THE FAITHFUL

Christ has ascended into glory. But he will not leave us orphans or without a guide. He will send us the one he promised, the gift of the Father, the Spirit of truth. Let us pray for the Spirit. *R*. Lord, send us your Spirit.

For all the Church: that the Holy Spirit may renew its life and make it radiant with hope. (Pause). Let us pray.

For all rulers and governments: that the Holy Spirit may guide them and help them to be wise and courageous. (Pause). Let us pray.

For all who suffer persecution for the name of Christ: that the Holy Spirit may help them to be strong in times of trial and difficulty. (Pause). Let us pray.

That the Holy Spirit may help us awaken to the gifts and talents God has given us and help us to use and develop them. (Pause). Let us pray.

For local needs.

Let us pray:

God our Father, your Son, at his ascension, promised to send the Holy Spirit to his apostles. Through his coming they received power and wisdom from heaven. Grant us also, we pray, the gifts of your Spirit. We make all our prayers to you through Christ our Lord.

COMMUNION REFLECTION

There was a bad flood
and the cellar of Thomas' house filled up with water.
A man came by in a canoe and said:
'Do you want a lift to safety?'
'No,' said Thomas. 'I have faith in God. He will save me.'

The water rose and flooded the ground floor.
Thomas was forced to go upstairs.
A man in a motor boat came by
and offered to take him to safety, but Thomas said:
'I have faith in God. He will save me.'

The water rose higher still
and Thomas had to take to the roof.
A helicopter came by
and the pilot offered to take him to safety.
But once again Thomas declined, saying:
'I have faith in God. He will save me.'
And he sat there waiting for God.

But the water continued to rise and he drowned.
On arriving in heaven he said angrily to God:
'I had faith in you, and still you let me drown.'
To which God replied:
'Not once, but three times, I sent you help,
and each time you refused it.'

We don't always recognise God's help when it comes.

PENTECOST SUNDAY
Emerging from the shadows

INTRODUCTION AND CONFITEOR

Today we celebrate the coming of the Holy Spirit on the apostles, and how as a result of that coming they went out to preach the Gospel to all the world. It is a mistake to see this coming as something that happened once and that can never happen again.

Through the prayer of the Church, the Holy Spirit comes to this roomful of people this morning. And how much we need him. We are weak and cowardly, lazy and selfish. Let us dispose ourselves to receive the Spirit. (Pause).

Lord Jesus, your Spirit is the Spirit of truth; he leads us into the fulness of your truth.   Lord, have mercy.

Lord Jesus, your Spirit is the Spirit of love; he helps us to overcome our selfishness and to love as you loved.   Christ, have mercy.

Lord Jesus, your Spirit is the Spirit of peace; he unites us and helps us to be ambassadors of your peace in the world.   Lord, have mercy.

HEADINGS FOR READINGS

First Reading (Acts 2:1-11). Here we have an account of the coming of the Holy Spirit on the apostles on Pentecost Day and the effects of that coming on them.

Second Reading (1 Cor. 12:3-7, 12-13). People have different gifts, but it is the same Spirit who gives these various gifts for the building up of the Christian community, which is the Body of Christ.

Gospel (John 20:9-23). On Easter Sunday evening Jesus breathes the Holy Spirit upon his apostles, a Spirit of forgiveness and of peace.

HOMILY

We all want to cling to someone we admire, love, and depend on. We can't bear the thought of their leaving. At the last supper Jesus told the apostles that he was leaving them and they were plunged into gloom. But he said: 'It is for your own good that I go away, because unless I go, the Spirit will not come to you, but if I go I will sent him to you.' (John 16:7). It must have been very hard for the apostles to see how his going away could be for their good. The following illustration may throw some light on the subject.

One evening in late November I was driving from Limerick to Dublin. It was crisp and cold even though the sun shone brilliantly. It was going down behind me as I sped along. It was a glowing orb of fire — bright, burning and beautiful. It filled the landscape with its golden light. It was so bright that to look directly at it was out of the question.

Then I spotted a near full moon halfway up the clear sky to my right. It was so pale and weak as to be practically invisible. Indeed it was only by accident that I noticed it at all. It didn't appear to be contributing anything whatsoever to the earth. The reason for this was that the sun had so outshone it that it was made to appear useless and utterly redundant.

But then the sun began to withdraw, and a curious thing happened. The lower the sun dipped, the brighter the moon became. By the time the sun had finally departed the scene, the moon was glowing brilliantly. Of course it could not compare with the sun. This was obvious from the fact that you could gaze directly at it without fear of suffering eye-damage. Yet its silvery light cast an enchantment over everything. A few hours ago you could barely see it by looking intently. Now it glowed, the brightest thing by far in the sky, so much so that you could not possibly fail to see it. Yet it was only when the sun had withdrawn that I could see what the moon was contributing. I was aware of course that it only reflected the light of the sun, now hidden from me. It still needed the sun, but the sun also needed it to reflect its light on the earth. But the sun had vanished leaving the moon to claim all the credit. That's what true love does.

Loving at times means distancing oneself from the person loved. This means that the person is free to develop in his own way. He is given a chance to give of himself. He is made to feel that he has a contribution to make, and also that he is free to receive from another.

Often, however, we do the exact opposite. We hug the limelight ourselves, and what is worse we do so in the name of love. We want to be there all the time. We do not know when or how to withdraw.

Thus, in a thoughtless and selfish way, we dominate other people. We stifle their development. Instead of encouraging them to open up and develop, we drive them into their shells. We force them to retreat into the shadows. We make them more conscious of their short-comings and inadequacies. We make them play second fiddle, feel inhibited, and as a result they remain underdeveloped.

When we act like this we are not loving anyone but ourselves. We are only thinking of ourselves. It's nice to be in the limelight. It's good for the ego to have people dependent on you. It gives you a sense of your own value when you are needed. But at what price to the other person? A lot of damage and hurt is caused. People can be made to feel second-rate, and in the end they remain but pale shadows of what they could become if they got encouragement and an opportunity to shine in their own right. We are loathe to let others be themselves. We justified this kind of thing by saying: 'Ah, you'd never manage without me.'

It is necessary for us to withdraw. It is truly good for the person we love. The work or whatever may suffer initially, but in the long run it will benefit. And our loved one will grow. He will not be kept in a childlike state of dependence, but will be given the chance to grow into an adult. Naturally when we withdraw there will be a vacuum. But the other person is forced to do something, and thus something new is born within him.

A lot of people suffer from feelings of inferiority. They lack self-confidence. This does not mean that they have nothing inside them. They just need someone to believe in them, someone who will help them to develop. Someone who knows when to let them get on with it on their own. There is an art in withdrawing. We have to do so in such a way that we do not give them the impression that we are walking out on them or abandoning them. We have to assure them that we are still within reach if needed, that they can still call on us if things should ever get out of hand.

Is this, then, what Jesus had in mind when he said it was necessary for his apostles that he should go, otherwise the Spirit would not come? Had he always remained with them in his physical presence they would never have come of age themselves. And when the Spirit came, what he did was bring out what was already inside them. His love awakened in them extraordinary energies that they themselves didn't think they were capable of. It was they who had to get on with it, but he was there to inspire, encourage and guide them.

No one ever showed more confidence in, or more respect for, people than Jesus. He did not dominate them. He gave them a chance to shine. He said: 'Let *your* light shine before men, so that seeing *your* good works, they will give glory to the Father in heaven.' He handed his entire work over to them. He knew that they still needed help. That was why he sent them the Spirit. After Pentecost the apostles were aglow with the Spirit, and went forth and did the work of Jesus. Stephen (cf. second reading) is a fine example of what the Spirit of Jesus can do to people.

We need the Spirit of Jesus. We need him to help us to realise the power we have within us. We need him to release that power so that we too can become fearless witnesses of Christ. Thus, even though he is no longer physically among us, his truth and his love can still illuminate the world.

'We meet at very short intervals, without having had time to acquire any new value for each other.' (Thoreau).

'I have nothing to give to another; but I have a duty to open him to his own life, to allow him to be himself.' (M. Quoist).'

PRAYER OF THE FAITHFUL

Let us pray for the coming of the Holy Spirit into our lives, into the Church, and into the whole world.   *R*. Spirit of the living God, fall afresh on us.

For all Christians: that the Holy Spirit may gather all the followers of Jesus into the unity of the Body of Christ and help them to be his witnesses in the world. (Pause).   Let us pray.

For all rulers and leaders: that the Holy Spirit may guide and enlighten them so that the earth may see the coming of justice and peace. (Pause).   Let us pray.

That the Holy Spirit may dry the tears of all those who mourn and may turn their sorrow into joy. (Pause).   Let us pray.

That the Holy Spirit may teach us wisdom and simplicity of heart, and help us to care for one another. (Pause).   Let us pray.

For local needs.

Let us pray:

God our Father, grant that the Holy Spirit may come to us to enlighten our minds, to purify our hearts, and to strengthen us in our resolve to follow Christ more closely, so that with his help we may do what we cannot do on our own. We ask this through our Lord Jesus Christ your Son, who lives and reigns with you and the Holy Spirit, one God, for ever and ever.

SIGN OF PEACE

Lord Jesus Christ, on Pentecost Day, you sent your Holy Spirit on your disciples, and, with hearts on fire, they went forth to preach the Gospel to the whole world. And people of good will from many different places heard the good news and welcomed it.

Send your Spirit of love on our world, to gather people of every race, language and way of life, into the peace and unity of your kingdom where you live for ever and ever.

COMMUNION REFLECTION

A child picks up a small bird
that has fallen from its nest.
He makes his hand into a nest
to keep it from falling
and doing further damage to itself.

But he does not make his hand into a cage,
for he has no intention of possessing the bird
or turning it into a pet.
Having reassured the bird that it is in safe hands,
he slowly raises it up and up.
Then, when the moment is right, he releases it.
He rejoices when it succeeds in keeping itself aloft,
and he is happier still when it flies off.
That is what love does.

Holy Spirit, on Pentecost Day,
you released the apostles from the prison of the upper room,
and they went forth with courage to do the work of Jesus.
Kindle within us the fire of your love,
and in our own humble way,
we shall renew some small corner of the world.

TRINITY SUNDAY

INTRODUCTION AND CONFITEOR

Today is the feast of the Blessed Trinity. But for a Christian every day is a day to love and honour the Father, the Son and the Spirit. The mystery of the Trinity is incomprehensible, yet it so simple when you live it. But do we live it? 'Don't bother proclaiming that you believe in God unless you live accordingly.' (Catherine de Hueck Doherty). Let us reflect on that for a moment. (Pause). Let us confess our sins and ask the Father's forgiveness.

I confess to almighty God . . . etc.

HEADINGS FOR READINGS

First Reading (Proverbs 8:22-31). This is a reading in praise of wisdom. We are not dealing with mere worldly wisdom but with the wisdom of God. This speculation about wisdom was a groping towards the revelation of the mystery of the Trinity.

Second Reading (Romans 5:1-5). Christ made it possible for us to have a relationship of love with the Father. This gives us the hope of sharing in his glory, a hope which sustains us even in time of suffering. It is the Holy Spirit who helps us to recognise the Father's love for us.

Gospel (John 16:12-16). The Holy Spirit carries on in the Church the work of Jesus. He helps us to grasp the full meaning of all Jesus said and did. What Jesus did was to reveal the Father to us.

HOMILY

It is very important to have a correct concept or image of God. If we get this wrong everything else will be out of focus. How can we pray properly, or how can we have a proper relationship with God if we have a false or inadequate image of him?

There's a story told about six blind men who were introduced to an elephant. None of them had ever before come in contact with such an animal, so they didn't know what to expect. But they were very curious to find out. Naturally their chief ally was their sense of touch.

The first man approached the elephant from the side. He felt himself up against a broad and very solid object, and concluded that the elephant was like a wall. He tried to climb it but failed, so he went away.

The second man also approached it from the side, but well forward. He reached out and his hands came in contact with one of the elephant's tusks, which appeared round, smooth and pointed. And he concluded that the elephant was like a huge spear, and he pulled back in fear.

The third approached it from the front. The first thing he felt was the elephant's trunk. As he touched it, it moved and squirmed. So he concluded that it was like an enormous snake. With that he drew back in terror from it.

The fourth man was rather short. As he reached out he came in contact with one of the elephant's legs. The leg was so thick that he could barely get his hands around it. He concluded that the elephant was like a tree. He didn't like trees as he often bumped into them and hurt himself.

The fifth happened to touch one of the elephant's ears. As soon as he touched it, it began to move back and forth creating quite a draught. So he concluded that the elephant was like a fan. Not liking cold, he stood well back from it.

And the sixth man approached the elephant from the rear. The first think he touched was the elephant's swinging tail. He concluded that the elephant was like a rope. Having no use for ropes he abandoned it.

Then the six men came together and shared their findings with one another. A long and loud debate followed. But at the end of it each of them stuck rigidly to his own picture of the elephant. What a pity. Each of them had a piece of the truth. If only they had been open to receive from one another they could have put all the pieces together and come up with a true picture of what this strange and mysterious animal was really like. And the way they saw the elephant determined their reaction to him.

Before God we are like those blind men. We can grasp little bits of the mystery of God and what he is like. Down the centuries people have come up with all sorts of weird ideas and images of God. This accounts at least in part for some of the distorted religious practices you come across. But God has not left us in the dark. He has revealed himself. Christians believe that he revealed himself in a very special and unique way in Christ.

So how can we tell who God is and what he is like? The answer is quite simple: look at Christ. Christ is the image of the invisible God. Jesus spoke about himself as being like a good shepherd, and he backed up his words with mighty deeds. Is there a lovelier image than that of the good shepherd? That is what Christ is like.

But what about the Father? We can tell what the Father is like by looking at the Son. 'Show us the Father,' the apostle Thomas pleaded during the last supper. And Jesus replied: 'Thomas, to have seen me is to have seen what the Father is like.' Christ is the Father's self-portrait.

And what about the Holy Spirit? The Holy Spirit is a gift from both. He is the bond of love between the Father and the Son, and between the Son and us. Ah, but you might say, all this is very complicated. Not really. The most important thing ever said about God was said by St John. He said: 'God is love.' So stop asking yourself whether you do or do not believe in God. Ask yourself instead whether you do or do not love. When we love, we experience God. We know God, and doubt disappears like an early-morning mist disappears before the sun. However, if we do not act according to our belief, then we lose a clear image of God until finally he seems not to exist any more.

The mystery of the Trinity is not something to argue about or even study. It is more something to pray about and to live. The Christian lives in the world of the Father, the Son and the Spirit.

This world is not somewhere in outer space. It is the same world
of every day.

God is my Father. I am his child. He loves me, even though I am
unworthy of his love. Christ, the Son of God, is my Brother. He
died and rose for me. Through him all other people have become
my brothers and sisters. And the Holy Spirit is the bond of love between us all. That's not too hard to grasp. Even a child could feel
at home with it. For a child knows what a parent is. A child knows
what a brother or sister is. And all children instinctively recognise
true love when they see it. There is everything, then, to be said for
keeping it simple. Simple, direct and childlike faith was praised by
Christ.

'Heaven is under our feet as well as over our heads.' (Thoreau).

'To understand God's purpose is beyond me. But to do his will,
inscribed in my conscience, is in my power.' (Tolstoy).

PRAYER OF THE FAITHFUL

United by the Spirit of Jesus, let us make our needs known to
our heavenly Father. *R.* Lord, graciously hear us.

For all Christians: that they may be united in praising and
honouring the Father, the Son and the Holy Spirit. (Pause).
Lord, hear us.

For all the human family: that, recognising their common
Father, they may see one another as brothers and sisters, and treat
one another accordingly. (Pause). Lord, hear us.

For all those who are searching for an unknown God: that the
light of Christ may help them to discover the Father. (Pause).
Lord, hear us.

That we may see God as a God of love who is always near us,
inspiring us to love one another. (Pause). Lord, hear us.

For local needs.

Let us pray:

Father, in your gentle mercy, guide our wayward hearts, for we
know that left to ourselves we cannot do your will. We ask this
through our Lord Jesus Christ your Son who lives and reigns with
you and the Holy Spirit, one God, for ever and ever.

COMMUNION REFLECTION

(John Henry Newman wrote this hymn when he was still a young
man, lost in a torment of doubt and indecision).

Lead, kindly light, amid the encircling gloom;
lead thou me on: the night is dark and I am far from home;
lead thou me on.

Keep thou my feet: I do not ask to see
the distant scene; one step enough for me.

I was not ever thus, nor prayed that thou
shouldst lead me on;
I loved to choose and see my path; but now
lead thou me on.
I loved the garish day, and, spite of fears,
pride ruled my will: remember not past years.

So long thy power hath blest me, sure it still
will lead me on
o'er moor and fen, o'er crag and torrent, till
the night is gone,
and with the morn those angel faces smile
which I have loved long since, and lost awhile.

Sundays of the year

SECOND SUNDAY OF THE YEAR
Water into wine

INTRODUCTION AND CONFITEOR
At a wedding in Cana Jesus changed water into excellent wine. Wine is a symbol of God's love and forgiveness. This wine came into the world with Christ, and is available in abundance to those who realise their need of it and who seek it with all their hearts.

Let us reflect on our need of this wine. (Pause).

Lord, you change the water of doubt into the wine of faith. Lord, have mercy.

Lord, you change the water of despair into the wine of hope. Christ, have mercy.

Lord, you change the water of selfishness into the wine of love. Lord, have mercy.

HEADINGS FOR READINGS

First Reading (Isaiah 62:1-5). When this was written Jerusalem lay in ruins and the plight of God's people was like that of a widow deprived of her children. It announces a joyful feast for God and his people.

Second Reading (1 Cor. 12:4-11). St Paul tells us that, though there are many different gifts among us, they all come from God's Spirit, and should be used for the good of all.

Gospel (John 2:1-12). This relates the first of the signs given by Jesus, when at a wedding in Cana he changed water into wine at the request of his mother.

HOMILY

The miracle stories of the Gospel do not just tell us about things which the historical Jesus did, never to be repeated. They tell us about things the risen Jesus continues to do for those who believe in him. If this were not so then the miracle stories would have no relevance for us today. How then might this apply to the miracle at hand — the changing of water into wine? What happened at Cana happens in every marriage — sooner or later 'the wine runs out,' and the couple are left with nothing but 'water'. This happens in spite of the presence with them of Jesus. And for those who have had a taste of wine, water is a very poor substitute. What do I mean when I say that 'the wine runs out'?

I don't mean this in a literal sense of course. At our modern wedding receptions there is little likelihood of the wine running out — or the beer or the spirits either. In any case, I'm not talking about the wedding reception but about the marriage as a whole. Let us look at a typical marriage.

It starts off with a feast of joy and enthusiasm. The couple are surrounded by a legion of friends and well-wishers who load them with gifts. Full of hopes and dreams, they set off on their honeymoon with the sound of music and dancing ringing in their ears. The wine is flowing freely. All are happy, but most of all the couple themselves.

But then they come back from the honeymoon and the real business begins — setting up a home and learning to live with one another. At first they find great joy in each other's company. The excitement and novelty of it all are intoxicating. There isn't a cloud in their sky. They are convinced that their love was preordained in heaven and meant to last for eternity. The wine is still flowing.

But when human beings are very close to one another problems inevitably arise. They start to squabble over trivial things. Where important issues are concerned they can usually agree. Not so, however, where the less important ones of day-to-day living are concerned. That is what makes it so frustrating. Tensions arise. The warts, wounds and cracks in each other begin to show up. They discover that they did not marry a perfect human being after all, but one deeply wounded by sin and selfishness. So they discover that marriage is no joke.

One day reality bursts in upon them and they are horrified at the poverty they discover in one another, and the thought that they are committed to sharing this for the rest of their lives becomes frightening. 'How did I marry such an ordinary person? How could I have walked into this with my eyes open?' one moans. And the other says: 'It's not what I thought it would be or what I bargained for. If I had known this in advance I would never have chosen it. I don't think I'll be able for this.'

In other words, the honeymoon is well and truly over. The wine has run out. There is little joy in their lives or in their relationship.All is dull and flat, routine, boring and difficult. All that they are left with is the 'water' of their own meagre resources. Incidentally, much the same thing happens in all careers, professions, and even in vocations such as the priesthood and religious life. The wine runs out there too. The first joy, enthusiasm and idealism ebb. And all that remains is the 'water' of routine, dullness and possible disillusionment. But because of the Gospel that's in it let us stick with the example of marriage. Now that the first wine has run out what are they to do? A crisis is upon them, but what are their chances of turning the water into wine?

The first thing is not to panic — not to run out with the wine! Many do so, crying: 'There is nothing in it for me, therefore I have decided to get out.' It sounds so reasonable that they may nor realise the selfishness that it implies. 'I expect wine, and I'm damned if I'm going to settle for water!' So off they go to enter another honeymoon.

If the truth were told, such couples desire rather than love each other. For them marriage is but a passing alliance of two selfish human beings. When they have taken all they can from each other, they begin to look elsewhere for more fruit that can be picked and eaten without effort or pain.

The first thing then is to acknowledge that the wine has run out. It is gone for ever. For the moment we will have to make do with the water. But now here is a surprising thing: it is necessary that the first wine should run out if the new wine is to be brought in. It is every bit as necessary as that the seed should die in order that the new flower may be born. So there is no need to despair or panic. We must hold on. Above all we must beware of looking for false substitutes — a career, climbing the social ladder, etc. — thus abandoning the relationship in which we could have grown as persons. Yes, we are faced with a crisis, but we are also being given a great opportunity.

Here is where the Good News comes in for those who have Christ present in their marriages — not just there at the wedding for the sake of respectability. Something new can begin — a real relationship. Real love can be discovered at this stage.

The first love (the first wine) was all very well. It made the couple feel so good. But it was mainly a physical and emotional thing, and it was not something that demanded much from them. It had to wear out if a deeper love was to be born. The new love enables us to put the other person first. It helps us to set out to give love, not merely to receive it. We must try to forget ourselves and find joy in making the other person happy. It is by giving freely to the other, on all levels, that we ourselves are enriched.

Love is an exciting but difficult adventure. It requires a lot of effort to transform it from *desire to receive* into a *desire to give*. It is impossible to unaided human nature. This is where we need Christ with us. Elsewhere he said: 'You can't put the new wine into old wineskins.' This means that, if the new wine is to flow, we ourselves must become new people — people who are capable of unselfish love.

So when marriages run into barren times there is no need to give up. It can mean that the couples are being given an opportunity of seeking the new wine. For those who know how to turn to Christ in their barrenness and poverty Cana still happens — he turns the water of selfishness into the wine of love for them. Only he can do this. Without love, no amount of wine will make a happy marriage.

'When we begin to love we become vulernable. We can be wounded if the person we love does not respond.' (Jean Vanier).

'True love seeks one thing only — the good of the loved one.' (Thomas Merton).

PRAYER OF THE FAITHFUL

Let us pray to God our Father that the miracle of Cana may happen in our families, in our communities, and also in the hearts of us all. *R*. Lord, hear our prayer.

For the leaders of the Church: that they may build it into a sacrament of unity, love and peace. (Pause). Let us pray to the Lord.

For all those in public office: that God may give them a strong and unselfish love so that they may work for the progress of all people. (Pause). Let us pray to the Lord.

For couples who are experiencing difficulty in their marriages: that in their need they may find the help of Christ. (Pause). Let us pray to the Lord.

That Christ may touch us and transform our lives, especially in moments of sorrow and hurt. (Pause). Let us pray to the Lord.

For local needs.

Let us pray:

Heavenly Father, may we experience your Son's gentle and loving presence in our lives so that, when our own efforts are not enough, he may support us with his grace and strength. We ask this through the same Christ our Lord.

COMMUNION REFLECTION

With the coming of Jesus
the wine of God's love, forgiveness, acceptance and peace
has come into the world.
It is made freely available
to all those who answer the invitation
to partake of the banquet of the Kingdom of God.

With his coming a great transformation happened.
Everywhere he went the old was made new.
At Cana he changed water into wine.
At Naim for a poor widow he changed tears into joy.
At Jericho for Zacchaeus he changed selfishness into generosity.

On Calvary for the good thief he changed despair into hope.
On Easter morning he changed death into life.

What a pity if we settled for the old wine
when the new wine is offered in such abundance
to all those who seek it in their need.

Change us, Lord, so that we may be able to contain the new
    wine,
and then through us it will flow to others,
and the world will know that you live among us.

THIRD SUNDAY OF THE YEAR
Good news for the poor

INTRODUCTION AND CONFITEOR

Jesus began his ministry by making his own the words of Isaiah:
'He sent me to being good news to the poor.' The good news is that
God's mercy is available to all those who hunger for it.

Let us not then be afraid to admit our sinfulness and spiritual
poverty before God, for Jesus made himself the friend of sinners
and of the poor. (Pause).   Let us ask the Lord's forgiveness for
our sins.

I confess to almighty God . . . etc.

HEADINGS FOR READINGS

First Reading (Nehemiah 8:2-6, 8-10). After the Jews returned
from exile in Babylon the nation had to be rebuilt. To Ezra fell the
task of re-establishing the Jewish religion. Here he reads the book
of the law of Moses to the people.

Second Reading (1 Cor 12:12-30). The human body is one
though made up of many parts. So it is with the Church. Though
it is composed of different members, coming from different
backgrounds and endowed with different gifts, it forms a unity in
Christ.

Gospel (Luke 1:1-4: 4:14-21). In the synagogue in his native
village of Nazareth Jesus makes the astonishing announcement that
in him the great prophecy of Isaiah is being fulfilled. He is the long-
awaited Saviour of the poor and the oppressed.

HOMILY

When a president or prime minister is being inaugurated he

usually makes a solemn speech. In it he outlines his policies. This is what Jesus did the day he stood up in the synagogue at Nazareth and read that passage from the prophet Isaiah. He picked that one because it neatly summed up his mission. It is a revolutionary passage and sounds like something out of a Marxist manifesto. The kernel of it could be put like this: *Good news for the poor and the oppressed.* Why should this be considered revolutionary? Because it could be seen as a threat by the rich and the powerful.

In a certain country, in which bread was the staple diet of the people, the wheat crop failed seveal years in a row. As a result famine raged throughout the land. The king, who was renowned for his kindness, was very concerned. As soon as the famine broke out he went abroad to look for bread for his people.

Naturally the famine affected the poor most of all. Skeletal children roamed the streets in search of bread that wasn't to be had. They died like flies. The rich also suffered from the famine, though not to the same degree. They had the money with which to buy bread from abroad. However, far from sharing it with their poorer brothers, they kept it jealously to themselves. But the foreign bread was clearly not the genuine article. It lacked some vital ingredient. While it kept those who ate it alive it did not nourish them. Those who ate large quantities of it ended up very bloated.

A cloud of gloom hung over the entire land, and it was the poor who were in the deepest shadow. They had placed all their hopes in the king. But why was he taking so long in coming to their aid? Then one day the king's messenger entered the capital and cried out: 'Rejoice! I come with good news for all the people.' 'Good news? You mean bread is on the way?' the people asked.

'Yes, my friends. The king is on his way with an unlimited supply of the finest bread.'

Could it really be true that what everybody needed and longed for was on its way at last? Spirits soared. The poor danced for joy in the streets. 'Long live the king!' they chanted, as tears of happiness ran down their faces.

The rich were a little more restrained in their manifestations of happiness, only a little. But then they suffered a change of mood. Someone claimed to have heard the royal messenger say that the bread would be free. Why should that upset them? Because it didn't make sense to them. It wasn't right!

'This can't be true,' they said. 'The king will charge for the bread. And it's only right that he should. People don't appreciate what they get for nothing.'

Thus it happened that a rumour spread to the effect that people would have to pay for the bread. This had a devastating effect on the poor. They had taken it for granted that the promised bread would be free. If that were not so, then they would be in a worse state than ever. They protested to the rich.

'But the royal messenger said that the bread would be for everybody. Presumably "everybody" includes us poor?'

'It will be for everybody who has *earned* the money to buy it,' the rich replied, emphasising the word 'earned'. To their way of thinking the poor were poor through a combination of ignorance, inefficiency and laziness. Whereas they were rich, not through circumstances, but through a combination of intelligence, hard work and efficiency.

'But that means then that it is only good news for those with money, in other words, for the rich. But the messenger said he had good news for everybody. Therefore the bread has to be free.'

'Don't be silly! No man would be so crazy as to give good bread away for nothing.'

The royal messenger was still in the country. So they sought him out and put the question directly to him. He answered like this: 'The bread will be absolutely free. I thought I made that clear. And one further thing: the distribution will begin with the poor.'

'But why begin with the poor?' asked the rich. 'Why not begin with us? Surely we are the more deserving? After all, we are his majesty's loyal subjects. We keep his laws and pay his taxes, unlike these others.'

The messenger replied: 'Why begin with the poor? Because they are the most needy.'

On hearing this the rich got very angry. They felt that they had been betrayed. The bread arrived and, as the messenger said, the distribution began with the poor. Many of the rich refused it. They could not get themselves to line up behind 'the common poor', as they called them, to accept what amounted to 'charity'. They left themselves no alternative but to go on eating the old bread, with the result that they got even more bloated. As for the poor, they lapped up the new bread and couldn't thank their king enough.

It's very important to get the Gospel right. The first thing is this: Jesus came with *good news,* not bad news. The Gospel is good news for everybody, but it is doubly good news for the poor. Who are the poor? They are all those who, realising their sinfulness, are hungering and thirsting for God's love and mercy. They will get them in abundance. It is not a question of whether or not one deserves them. To receive them is not a sign of worthiness, but a sing of God's goodness. This, of course, was a terrible blow to people like the Pharisees, who were convinced that one can be one's own light and one's own justification, and that God is there only for one purpose: to issue the stamp of confirmation on one's own rightness.

However, the good news must not be limited to spiritual blessings only. The poor are all the wounded and little ones; the blind, the oppressed, captives, and all those who are waiting for the liberator. Jesus did not come to minister to the wealthy, the privileged and the powerful. There is no liberation for those who, bloated with pride and the conviction of their own virtue, do not see themselves as sinners and in need of redemption. Nor is there liberation for those who, relying on things that counted for nothing with Jesus (power and privilege), think that they deserve it before everybody else. 'Happy are you who are poor: yours is the kingdom of heaven.' (Luke 6.20).

'I would rather be torn to pieces than to disown the suppressed classes.' (Gandhi).

'The Good News is God's love for us, and his one great commandment is to love'. (Catherine de Hueck Doherty).

PRAYER OF THE FAITHFUL

Let us pray to Christ our Saviour. We believe that through the power of the Holy Spirit he is still present and active among us. *R.* Lord, graciously hear us.

For the Church: that through its fearless voice, the poor and the downcast may hear the good news of God's love and care for them. (Pause). Lord, hear us.

For all the powerful and privileged of the world who are blinded by pride and materialism: that the Lord may open their eyes. (Pause). Lord, hear us.

For those whose hearts are broken with disappointment and misfortune: that the Lord may comfort them. (Pause). Lord, hear us.

That the Lord may keep us from coveting or relying on those things which counted for nothing with him — money, fame and power. (Pause). Lord, hear us.

For local needs.

Let us pray:

Heavenly Father, through Christ your Son we experience in our lives your love and healing, your forgiveness and compassion. May we share generously with others the blessings we have received from you. We ask this through the same Christ our Lord.

COMMUNION REFLECTION

'He sent me to bring good news to the poor.'
But who are the poor?

The poor are the hungry and the thirsty.
The poor are those who go about in rags.
The poor are the homeless.
The poor are the sick.

The poor are the physically and mentally handicapped.
The poor are the old.
The poor are the imprisoned.
The poor are the sad and depressed.

The poor are those who suffer injustice.
The poor arc the unemployed and those on low wages.
The poor are the rejects and unwanted.
The poor are the lonely and the unloved.

The poor are the alcoholics and drug addicts.
The poor are those who live on bread alone
and who never hear the Word of God.
The poor are those with hearts of flesh
but who do not love.

The poor, in one way or another, are we ourselves.
Before God we all are poor.
May we never see poverty as a curse from God.
Rather may we know that when we are poor
the Kingdom of Heaven is ours.

FOURTH SUNDAY OF THE YEAR
Rejecting the prophet

INTRODUCTION AND CONFITEOR

In the Gospel of today's Mass we read of the extraordinary incident in which Jesus was chased out of his native village of Nazareth. Why? Because they couldn't take the truth he was telling them.

None of us has any great desire to hear the truth, especially when it exposes unpleasant things about ourselves. We too reject the messengers God sends to us. Let us think about that for a moment. (Pause). Let us turn to Christ, the messenger of God's truth, love and mercy.

Lord, you came to heal the broken-hearted. Lord, have mercy.

Lord, you came to call sinners to repentance. Christ, have mercy.

Lord, you continue to plead for us at the right hand of the Father, Lord, have mercy.

HEADINGS FOR READINGS

First Reading (Jeremiah 1:4-5, 17-19). Jeremiah was one of the greatest prophets God sent among his people. This reading tells of his call by God and of his commission as a prophet.

Second Reading (1 Cor 12:31-13:13). This contains Paul's great hymn in praise of love. He says that for a follower of Christ love is by far the most important virtue of all.

Gospel (Luke 4:21-30). This tells how Jesus shared the fate of every true prophet: he was rejected by his own people.

HOMILY

When we hear the word 'prophet' we probably think immediately of someone who can tell the future by reading tea leaves or the stars. But this is not the biblical meaning of the word. In the Bible a prophet means someone who speaks for God. He is no magician. He is someone who, by means of a fundamental good sense and deep insight, is able to see things as they are.

Almost invariably the prophet is unpopular, especially among his own. Why is this? It is because he not only sees things as they are but he tells them as they are. In other words, he has the courage to tell people the truth. He dares to put into words what many people, deep down, see but are afraid to acknowledge as true. They do not want to face the truth because they find it too threatening and too demanding. But the prophet insists on telling it as it is. He shatters our illusions and exposes our pretenses. Unable to take the message, we chase away the messenger. To listen to the prophet's message would mean a willingness to admit that we were wrong and a readiness to change.

Once upon a time a group of people retreated from the world and went to live in a cave. The cave though deep and very dark was narrow and uncomfortable. But it was very safe. Its greatest asset was its darkness which acted like a wall around the people who lived in it.

The only time they left the cave was at night in search of food and other necessities. In time they grew so accustomed to the cave that, after a fashion, they learned to see in the dark. They looked on the outside world as a hostile place. They even pitied the people who had to live there. They were so deluded that they thought themselves were the saved ones — God's elect, rescued by him from a corrupt world! They closed their eyes to the limitations of their existence. They became blind to the smallness of their world, the narrowness of their horizon, and the fact that they lived in continual fear.

This went on for many years until one day a young man from their ranks, who had grown tired of the dark and who longed for the light, upped and left them. They looked upon him as a deserter and a traitor. The young man soon discovered that the world outside the cave was very different from what he had been taught. It was not the hostile place he had been led to believe it was. True, some ugly things happened there from time to time. But in the main it was a world warmed by sunshine and perfumed by the scent of wild flowers. A world filled with birdsong and the laughter of little children at play.

The young man took to it like a young bird leaving its nest takes to the freedom of the sky. What did he do? He simple spread his wings. He revelled in the light. He roamed free in the wide open spaces. He made lots of friends. But then his mind went back to his people in the dark cave. He felt sorry for them. He saw them as trapped in their cave existence.

So one day he decided to return to them to bring them the good news.He was determined to open their eyes to what they were missing. He longed to set them free from their self-made prison. So with a lamp in his hand he returned to the cave. But a strange thing happened. Instead of welcoming him they rejected him.

As soon as he set foot in the cave the old men put their hands over their eyes to shield them from the light. They screamed at the young man: 'Put out that light at once! You'll give us all away.' He tried to reason with them. But it was quite useless. They didn't believe him when he spoke about the outside world. Or was it that they didn't want to believe him? As he stood there he felt their hostility rising. He had committed the unpardonable crime of leaving the tribe. So what happened in the end? They rushed at him, smashed his lamp, and chased him right out of the cave.

That young man was a true prophet, and he met with the fate all true prophets meet — he was rejected by his own. How many prophets we as individuals, as a society and as a Church have chased away. Thus we save ourselves from hearing any truth not already familiar to us in case we might have to change in any way. A prophet is not necessarily someone with ideas, shouting them all over the place. A prophet is above all one whose very life is a word, a cry and a shout. A prophet can't help speaking. You would have to kill him to muzzle him. And even in death, his voice would echo throughout the world.

Thank God the prophets are still with us. Who are they? Here are a few of the outstanding ones. Mother Teresa is a prophet of the abandoned. Helder Camara is a prophet of the oppressed. Jean Vanier is a prophet of the handicapped. Andrei Sakharov is a prophet of human rights. All of these are paying a price for their witness, and some of them are without honour in their own country.

Christ, of course, was the greatest prophet of all. He was the very Word of God made flesh. And like a true prophet he too was rejected by his own. What truth did he tell his fellow villagers of Nazareth that they found so threatening that they made an attempt on his life? He pointed out to them that they were God's chosen people. That one would, therefore, expect to find some faith among them. Yet he told them that he found more faith among the pagans (the Gentiles). Hence, as happened more than once in the past, God's favours would be taken away from them and given to others who would welcome them. Unable to take this, they chased him right out of their village, and would have killed him if they could.

Each of us, as well as the world as a whole, needs the voice of a true prophet for there are so many things that we are blind to, so many things about which we delude ourselves. Sometimes it can be very painful to hear the truth about ourselves, but unless we hear it we are condemning ourselves to remain, like the cavemen of the story, forever in the dark.

Then, by virtue of our Baptism, we are commissioned to be prophets ourselves. That is, we are sent into the world to be witnesses in word but especially in deed to God's truth in a world of pretense and lies. We must expect to pay a price for our witness. If you stir up a stagnant pond you must expect a lot of mud to rise to the surface.

'A drowning man cannot save others.' (Gandhi).

'I shall become a Christian when I see Christians living their Master's teachings.' (Gandhi, on being asked why he wasn't a Christian).

PRAYER OF THE FAITHFUL

Let us pray that we may always receive Jesus and his message of Good News with openness and generosity. *R*. Lord, hear us in your love.

For the Church: that it may continue to be a fearless voice for truth, justice and freedom on behalf of all of God's children, but especially those who have no voice of their own. (Pause). We pray in faith.

For government leaders: that they may listen to the voice of the prophet who demands justice for the poor, the weak and the exploited. (Pause). We pray in faith.

For all those who are smug, complacent, and satisfied with a life of selfishness and mediocrity. (Pause). We pray in faith.

That we may never take our faith for granted, lest it become something that is barren and dead. (Pause). We pray in faith.

For local needs.

Let us pray:

Father, help us to receive Jesus, the one whom you anointed to bring good news to the poor, healing to the wounded, sight to the blind, freedom to captives, and to proclaim to all your favour and grace. We ask this through the same Christ our Lord.

SIGN OF PEACE

Lord, here in church it is easy to give a sign of peace, but in the real world it is often very difficult. We pause to see if maybe there is one person who at this moment is waiting for a sign of peace from us. (Pause). Lord, help us to give this sign of peace, so that we may enjoy the peace and unity of your kingdom where you live for ever and ever.

COMMUNION REFLECTION

For a Christian, love is the greatest
and the most important virtue of all.
Without it, all my words,
no matter how wise and clever they may be,
are just so much noise.

Without it, even if I had faith
strong enough to work a miracle,
that faith would be worthless.

Without it, all my deeds,
even if they were the greatest ever done on this earth,
would not do me the slightest bit of good.

Love means being patient and kind.
It means never being jealous or boastful.
It means never being rude or selfish.
It means that I do not take offence easily.
It means that I am not resentful.
It means that I rejoice in the goodness of others
and take no delight in their sins.

Love is not hard though it is tough.
It means that I am always ready to excuse,
to trust, to hope, and to endure whatever comes.

There are three things that last:
faith, hope, and love.
Love is the greatest of these.

FIFTH SUNDAY OF THE YEAR
A miraculous catch of fish

INTRODUCTION AND CONFITEOR

After the miraculous catch of fish Peter realised as never before
his own sinfulness and the holiness of Christ. He asked Christ to
depart from him. But Christ showed him that his sins and
weaknesses would not prevent him from sharing in his work.

While our sinfulness humbles us we should not let it get us down
or make us feel that we do not belong in the company of Christ.
Christ came to help us to overcome our sins. Therefore we come
to him with confidence and confess them. (Pause).

Lord Jesus, you forgive our sins and reconcile us once more with
the Father.   Lord, have mercy.

Lord Jesus, your strength helps us to rise above our
weaknesses.   Christ, have mercy.

Lord Jesus, your Spirit helps us to overcome our laziness,
selfishness and cowardice.   Lord, have mercy.

HEADINGS FOR READINGS

First Reading (Isaiah 6:1-8). When Isaiah was called by God to
be a prophet his first reaction was to declare his unworthiness. But
then, cleansed of his sins, he responded at once to God's call.

Second Reading (1 Cor 15:1-11). Paul energetically defends the
doctrine of Christ's resurrection from the dead. At the same time
he insists that he is the least of all the apostles.

Gospel (Luke 5:1-11). This relates the miraculous catch of fish
and the call of Peter to share in the work of Christ.

HOMILY

Today's three readings have the same idea and they are very
encouraging. We are dealing with three men who did great things
for God: Isaiah, Paul and Peter. Yet, strange as it may seem, all

three of them suffered from inferiority complexes. None of them were volunteers in the sense of offering themselves spontaneously. They were all called by God. They accepted that call somewhat reluctantly, feeling that they were unworthy of it.

Isaiah when called by God cried out: 'I'm not fit for such a task for I am a man of unclean lips.' Paul can never forget that once, drunk with self-righteousness and pride, he did the work of the devil rather than the work of God, and he said: 'Of all the apostles I am the least. In fact I do not even deserve the name apostle.' And Peter, after the miraculous catch of fish, declared: 'Lord, depart from me for I am a sinful man.' Each then starts by acknowledging his unworthiness, inadequacy and sinfulness but ends up by accepting God's invitation. And, relying not on their own resources but on God's help, they each do a splendid job.

Such a start is ideal. It is the people who start out believing that they can do great things for God through their own gifts and strength who usually grow discouraged and quite often end up doing more harm than good. Such people are only out for themselves. They seek their own glory, rely on their own resources, and desperately need to succeed. But human pride, self-sufficiency and self-righteousness are but sand, and the spiritual house built on them will surely fall. There is a great paradox in all this but it is true. Again it was Paul who said: 'When I am weak, that is when I am strong.' (2 Cor 12:10). The meaning is that when he recognises his own weakness the power of Christ becomes available to him and he is able to tune in to it. He never forgot what Christ had said to him: 'My grace is enough for you.'

This is, as I say, a great paradox. When we have experienced our own weakness, God can strengthen us. When we have experienced our own emptiness, God can fill us. When we have experienced our own poverty, God can enrich us. Then we become available to him to do his work, and to become channels of his riches to others. Conscious at all times of our own need of salvation we rely totally on God's grace and become instruments of salvation to our brothers and sisters.

But when we experience our own weakness, especially if this happens suddenly and dramatically as it did for Peter and Paul, at that moment we desperately need someone to believe in us, someone who will affirm us, but someone who will also challenge us and call us forward. Then we will make an amazing discovery: that power is restored to us. As Thomas Merton put it: 'The poorer our estimate of ourselves and the lower our expectations, the greater chance we have of using what we have. If we do not know how poor we are we will never be able to appreciate what we actually have. But, above all, we must learn our own weakness in order to awaken to a new order of action and of being, and experience God himself accomplishing in us the things we find impossible.'

Humility is a great starting point and it is only the truth. It's not that we are rotten through and through. Far from it. It's just that we are weak, poor and cowardly. We have a fallen nature, and without the grace of Christ we are unable to work out our own salvation, much less that of anyone else.

Each of us needs a true friend. A friend is someone who accepts us as we are. He or she doesn't write us off, much less condemn us, because of our sins and weaknesses. Yet we know that a true friend always expects more of us and makes us believe that we are capable of better things. As Thoreau said: 'A friend is someone who constantly pays us the compliment of expecting from us all virtues, and who can appreciate them in us.' What we all need then is not someone who will leave us the mediocre people we generally are, but someone who will give us the force, the motivation and the thirst for life.

Sometimes we use our sins and weaknesses as a cop-out, as an excuse for not even trying. Indeed, both Isaiah and Peter did the same at first. Isaiah asked God to choose someone else, someone with a clean mouth. Peter asked Christ to leave him alone because he was a sinner. When we do this we are excusing ourselves from making the effort to cooperate with God's grace, We are simply giving in to our weakness, laziness and cowardice. This is to take the easy way out.

But the three men we have been talking about did eventually cooperate with God's grace. They gave themselves to God. Isaiah said: 'Here am I. Take me.' Paul was able to say towards the end of his life: 'I have worked harder than all the others. By the grace of God I am what I am.' As for Peter, after that day by the lakeside his life would never be the same again. Every fisherman knew that the best time for fishing was the night time. Peter had fished all night long and caught nothing.But then in broad daylight Christ asked him to let down the net once more. He did so and made a large catch. When he had brought the fish to shore Christ called him to a new work and a new world. From now on he would be a fisher of men. And once again Peter obeyed. And again, in spite of some bitter failures, here too Peter would succeed through the power and the love of Christ.

This is the paradox — strength arising out of failure and weakness. It entails the loss of one's old life as a condition for finding a new one. Christ helps us to accept ourselves (and others) as we are: with all our defects, poverty, weakness and wounds; but also with our capacities, strengths, hopes and ambitions. He is forever calling us forward, calling us to start on a new and unknown course. This course is simply to take him at his word and to follow him wherever he asks us to go. Then, like Peter, we will be able to do things we never thought possible.

'Laziness and cowardice are the two greatest enemies of the spiritual life.' (Thomas Merton).

'I pine for one to whom I can speak my first thoughts, I know no one to whom I can be transparent instinctively.' (Thoreau).

PRAYER OF THE FAITHFUL

Jesus accepted Peter as he was. But at the same time he challenged him to grow. He accepts us as we are and challenges us to grow. Let us pray that we may cooperate with his grace. *R.* Lord, hear our prayer.

For the leaders of the Church: that they may challenge all the people of God to grow in holiness of life. (Pause). Let us pray to the Lord.

For all those who hold public office: that they may bring all their talents and energies to serving those for whom they work. (Pause). Let us pray to the Lord.

For all those who suffer from an inferiority complex and who have a low opinion of themselves: that they may find the acceptance which will help them to believe in themselves. (Pause). Let us pray to the Lord.

That we may face up to and accept our sins and weaknesses, but not be satisfied until we have tried to overcome them. (Pause). Let us pray to the Lord.

For local needs.

Let us pray:

Lord, may we realise how the quality of our presence, our looks, and our words brings happiness or misery, life or death to others; and, realising this, may we try to treat everybody as we ourselves would like them to treat us. We ask this through Christ our Lord.

COMMUNION REFLECTION

It was at the very moment Peter recognised his sinfulness
that Christ challenged hm to become a fisher of men.
Peter knew that the only thing he could rely on
was the word and the power of Christ.

We must not be put off by our weaknesses,
or make an excuse out of them for doing nothing.

Rather we must learn to turn them to our advantage.
Listen to how Paul did this.

'Though I could boast I won't.
It's true that I've had revelations,
but to stop me from getting too proud
I was given a thorn in the flesh.
Three times I pleaded with the Lord to take it away,
but he said: 'My grace is enough for you;
my power is at its best in weakness.'

So I am not only content with my weaknesses,
but I have actually learned to boast of them,
for it is when I am weak that I am strong,
because then the power of Christ is available to me.'

SIXTH SUNDAY OF THE YEAR
The world of the beatitudes

INTRODUCTION AND CONFITEOR
The Gospel of today's Mass plunge; us into the world of the
Beatitudes. Here we discover the values Christ held up before his
disciples. They are so different from tho se which are accepted as
desirable by ordinary sensible people that they take us into a new
world.

Which world do we belong to? For instance, when making
important decisions, do we ever consult Christ and his Gospel?
(Pause).

Lord Jesus, you teach us that we become truly rich not by receiving but by giving.   Lord, have mercy.

Lord Jesus, you teach us that the greatest person is not the one
who is served but the one who serves.   Christ, have mercy.

Lord Jesus, you help us to find peace of soul not by doing what
is popular or profitable but what is right.   Lord, have mercy.

HEADINGS FOR READINGS
First Reading (Jeremiah 17:5-8). The life of those who trust in
man is as precarious as that of a shrub growing in the desert.
Whereas the life of those who trust in God is as sure as that of a
tree growing by the waterside.
Second Reading (1 Cor 15:12, 16-20). The resurrection of Christ

is the foundation on which our faith and hope rest.

Gospel (Luke 6:17, 20-26)*:* This contains Luke's version of the Beatitudes. (Whereas Matthew has nine beatitudes, Luke has only four, with however four corresponding 'woes').

HOMILY

Christ faced people with a radical choice: they could either take the way of this world and its values (the pursuit of money, pleasure, popularity, power, prestige . . .) or they could take his way and live by the values of the Kingdom (poverty of spirit, cleanness of heart, capacity to show mercy, suffering in the cause of right . . .). This choice is put very starkly in the Gospel we just read. Solzhenitsyn has a story about a diplomat called Innokenty who during Stalin's regime was faced with similar choice.

Innokenty and his wife Dottie started their married life in very favourable circumstances. They belonged to that circle of society where such things as walking and taking the bus were unknown. In each post he was sent to, a lavishly furnished house awaited them. And how they lapped it all up. After all, you only live once! That was their philosophy. They ate every exotic fruit; came to know the aroma of every rare brandy; wore all the latest clothes; swam off every fashionable beach; went sailing and played tennis . . . etc.

For six years they had all they wanted from each other and from life. And these were the years during which humanity was being torn apart. Men died fighting and women and children were buried under the ruins of cities. Grown-up people, driven out of their minds, stole rations of bread as small as communion wafers. But not as much as a breath of the sorrow of the world touched Innokenty and his wife. They knew nothing about it and cared even less.

But in the sixth year of their marriage (the war was now over) Innokenty suddenly began to experience a sense of revulsion towards all the material fruits of the earth — all the things you can smell, touch, eat and drink. The feeling alarmed him and he fought it like a disease. But it still clung to him. He couldn't make out what was wrong with him. He had everything, yet he lacked something. Even his lovely wife Dottie was becoming a stranger to him. Their smart way of life he found embarrassing, though she wouldn't her of giving it up. Instead she insisted on piling up more and more possessions.

One day, while at home in Moscow, Innokenty started to go through some books that his mother had left him when she died. Prior to this his mother meant very little to him, and the world to which she belonged with its old-fashiond values seemed utterly remote from him. But as he read through her letters a strange thing happened. She came alive before him and he discovered a set of values that were in complete contrast with those of the world to which he belonged. Suddenly the values of his mother began to make sense to him. In her letters he came across passages in praise of compassion. In school he had been taught that compassion was a shameful thing. Other words began to crop up like 'truth', 'goodness', 'beauty', and so on. Then he came across this extraordinary piece: 'The most precious thing in the whole world is the consciousness of not participating in injustice. Injustice there will always be, but don't let it soil your hands.'

Sitting there before the dusty old books he suddenly discovered what had been missing from his life. And for days and nights he continued to sit there breathing in the values of his mother's world like a man breathes in new air. He was being shown a new world he never knew existed, and he liked what he saw. Dottie kept interrupting him to beg him to come to some party or other, but he just gave her a blank stare. He could not imagine himself as part of that pompous crowd, where everybody was the same and where they would all jump up to drink a toast to Comrade Stalin. It was all so stupid. He wanted no part of it.

It was as if he was leaving one world and entering another. His mind was being opened and he was being given a new way of seeing and of judging. Once started, he could not stop. Up to this his philosophy of life had been that we only live once. To put oneself out for another person was sheer folly. Now he was grasping another truth: that we have only one conscience and that a crippled conscience is as irretrievable as a lost life.

His new vision and the new values he had acquired obviously required a new way of acting and living. His new convictions were soon put to the test. There was an old doctor who had treated his mother during her last illness. Now famous, he was often sent abroad on delegations. In a day's time he was headed for Paris where he intended to pass on some medical secrets to the west because he believed all mankind had a right to know them. But a trap had been set for him. Innokenty knew about the trap. Should he save him by warning him? This was the dilemma which confronted him. Eventually he decided to tip him off. He made a phone call to the doctor. But the call was traced and he was arrested. And so it came about that the man who was so accustomed to soft living ended up in a small cell. Everything had been taken away from him and his future hardly bore thinking about.

What had happened to Innokenty was that he had experienced a great spiritual awakening in his life. He had left the world of comfort, riches, amusement, popularity . . . behind. He was now in the world of the poor, those who lack or who depend on others for the basic necessities of life, who are sad and crushed by their circumstances, and who are despised by the powers that be. He had entered unknowingly into the world of Christ and the Beatitudes.

How many of us who call ourselves Christians could say that we live by the values of the Beatitudes? In things that affect us directly — jobs, cars, comforts, homes, the future of our children — do we not live as the bourgeois live? We cannot live by the new values without renouncing the old ones. As said at the start, Christ offered his disciples a whole new set of goals and values. These are the exact opposite of those coveted by the world.

To enter the world of the Beatitudes, a world scarce in those things which many see as the very essence of life but paradoxically rich in freedom and happiness, we need a spiritual awakening. This spiritual awakening can happen very suddenly (as it did for Innokenty) or it can happen gradually. It brings us into a world with which the suffocating and materialistic world of the rich and pampered cannot compare. Riches and comforts in the end leave us in a spiritual wilderness. But we need a spiritual vision and spiritual values to live by if we are to achieve the fulfilment God intends for us. Otherwise, even on a human level, our deepest hungers will not be satisfied.

'The Beatitudes are terrifying when you try to live them.' (Catherine de Hueck Doherty).

"There's an awful lot of religion in Ireland, but very little real Christianity.' (Oft-repeated criticism one hears).

PRAYER OF THE FAITHFUL

Let us pray for the values, the outlook and the spirit Jesus not only preached but lived, and which he wants to see in the lives of us his followers. *R*. Lord, hear us in your love.

That the followers of Jesus may not seek after the things of this world but after those things that make them rich in the eyes of God. (Pause). We pray in faith.

For all those in positions of authority: that they may not be afraid to suffer in the cause of right, and not sell their souls for passing fame and popularity. (Pause). We pray in faith.

For those faced with life's sorrows: that they may not be afraid to show their hurt, because the tears of the just are precious in the sight of God. (Pause). We pray in faith.

That we may hunger for a good life, putting that even before eating and drinking, because then we will begin to taste real happiness. (Pause). We pray in faith.

For local needs.
Let us pray:
God our Father, you are the same yesterday, today and for ever.
Help us to have confidence in your unchanging love and goodness,
so that when things go wrong we may have the hope and strength
to persevere in goodness. We ask this through Christ our Lord.

COMMUNION REFLECTION
When you are rich,
when you have a name,
or when you are a member of a respected group,
you are never really oppressed.
When in difficulty,
only a phone call and everything is fixed up.

But when you have no friends,
when you are an immigrant and you speak the language badly,
you are quickly oppressed,
for you cannot defend yourself.
This is true of the sick, the handicapped, prisoners,
and all those who have no voice.

They are the oppressed ones,
and they are numerous in our society.
There are many without work,
with no security,
living off meagre wages,
living day by day in unbearable situations.

Each of us has met them.
They are all around us.
But what is frightening is that the disciples of Jesus
are so frequently in comfort.

On which side of the road was Jesus?
On which side of the road are his disciples?

(Jean Vanier, *Followers of Jesus,* © Alive Press Ltd., 8 Eramosa
Road, Guelph, Ontario, Canada).

SEVENTH SUNDAY OF THE YEAR
The enemy

INTRODUCTION AND CONFITEOR

'Treat others (even your enemies) as you would like them to treat you.' These words are taken from today's Gospel. We know exactly how we like others to treat us: we like them to be forgiving, merciful, generous and loving towards us. But how many of us could say that we treat others in that way?

Let us think about people we do not love as we should. (Pause).

Lord, you urge us to forgive others as you forgive us. Lord, have mercy.

Lord, you urge us to be generous to others as you have been generous to us. Christ, have mercy.

Lord, you urge us to be compassionate to others as you have been compassionate to us. Lord, have mercy.

HEADINGS FOR READINGS

First Reading (1 Samuel 26:2, 7-9, 12-13, 22-23). Saul, jealous of the young David, pursues him seeking to kill him. David gets an opportunity to kill Saul but he will not do so because he believes it would not be right before God.

Second Reading (1 Cor 15:45-49). Here we are dealing with the parallel between Adam and Christ. To Adam we owe the life of earth. To Christ we owe the life of heaven.

Gospel (Luke 6:27-38). Instead of seeking revenge on one's enemy this Gospel urges us to show forgiveness and compassion towards all.

HOMILY

In this Gospel Christ is asking us to be totally open, not just to our friends, but to all, even our enemies. A tall order surely? This openness calls for a large measure of defencelessness. It's easy, by adopting a vindictive attitude, to become poisoned by selfishness, hatred and fear. Hate robs us of so much. Whereas love awakens in us extraordinary energies and helps us to do what we thought we were incapable of. But is it possible, is it even desirable, to love someone who intends us evil?

A man lived with his wife and son at the edge of a large forest. The father was away from home a lot as he worked in the town. His son, a precocious lad, showed a keen interest in animals, not just tame ones but wild ones too. His parents didn't want him wandering off into the forest on his own, so right from his earliest years they filled his head with tales of the dangerous animals that lived in the forest, and what they would do to a little boy if they caught him. However, far from deterring him, this merely aroused his curiosity.

Now at the back of the house the father had a vegetable garden. The garden took up most of his spare time but rewarded him with excellent produce. It was inevitable that the garden would become a target for the animals that lived in the forest. He didn't mind the rabbits so much. But he blew his top when one day he discovered bear tracks in the garden.

'We'll have to get rid of this bear or he'll destroy the entire garden,' said the father. 'But surely we don't have to kill him?' said the son. 'Can't we just build a fence around the garden? That way we can have the garden to ourselves, and the bear can have the forest to himself.'

'That sounds nice, son, but we can never have peace while we have a wild bear as our nextdoor neighbour.'

That same day the father invested in a gun. In the days and weeks that followed he made several trips into the forest but, much to the delight of the son, failed to get near enough to the bear for a shot. So in the end he had to take the son's advice and erect a fence. However, each night before retiring he went out into the garden and fired a shot in the air — just to let the bear know that he wasn't wanted.

But the son was not content to leave things like that. Each evening, unknown to his father, he stole out and deposited some very tempting scraps of food just outside the fence. And how happy he was each morning when he found that they had been taken during the night, even though he couldn't always be sure that it was the bear that had taken them. But then one evening his father discovered his secret and was very angry.

'So you've been feeding the bear, have you?' he said. 'I was wondering how it was, that in spite of all my efforts to drive him off, he still kept coming back. Now I know! You must stop this at once, do you hear?'

'But I'm only trying to tame him,' the son protested meekly.

'Tame him? You won't tame him. You ought to be helping me to destroy him instead of hindering me,' said the father again.

'But, father, will I not in a sense be destroying him by taming him?' the son insisted.

'Take it from me, son, you'll never succeed in taming him. He's nothing but a wild brute. He'll never be any different.'

'I know he can be vicious,' the son continued, 'but that's only because he's convinced that we humans don't like him and want to kill him. Naturally he has to defend himself.'

'But bears have been known to attack humans without any provocation.'

'I still think that they only attack us because they fear us. And they have good reason to fear us considering the way we treat them.'

'So how should we treat them? Molly-coddle them?'

'I'm not sure. All I know is that by acting the way we do, we just bring out the worst side of them. But I believe that if we act kindly towards the bear we will see that he has a nice side too.'

In the end the father resorted to his authority, and forbade his son to have anything more to do with the bear. However, by adopting more cunning methods, the son continued to feed the bear, who rewarded him by becoming increasingly friendly towards him. Finally he came to the point where he actually took the scraps of food from his hand, giving contented grunts by way of thanks, before making off into the forest again. When the father discovered this he was glad to admit that his son had been right all along. So he gave his full approval to what he was doing. Thus it came about that the bear respected the garden, and the man respected the forest. And they lived as the very best of neighbours.

Most of us think we have done our Christian duty if we refrain from seeking revenge on our enemy. But Christ said that we should *love* our enemy, not just avoid doing harm to him or seeking retaliation against him. We know that this is repugnant to human nature. But that it is not beyond us we can see from the case of the youthful David (in the first reading).

And what a lot of sense the teaching of Christ makes, even on a purely human level. Revenge and retaliation only add darkness to darkness. Besides, when we hate our enemy we give him (or her) enormous power over us. The power of the enemy! There are a hundred people in a room. Ninety-nine are friends of ours, but one is an enemy. That one person casts a shadow over the entire room and the entire proceedings. Furthermore, we use up an awful lot of energy in hating, energy that we should put into loving. The highest aim we can have is (as the story brought out) the conversion of an enemy into a friend. But how often do we attempt this? Instead we put up a fence and keep out, not only our enemies, but people we do not like.

'He who is different from me does not impoverish me — he enriches me.' (Antoine de Saint Exupery).

'To use violence without love is like trying to put out a fire with a blazing torch'. (Helder Camara).

PRAYER OF THE FAITHFUL

Let us pray to Christ that, through the gift of his Spirit of love, we may be able to treat others, even our enemies, as we would like them to treat us. *R*. Lord, graciously hear us.

For all Christians: that they may be an example to the world in their tolerance of, and forgiveness towards, their enemies. (Pause). Lord, hear us.

For countries where there is war: that their leaders may think thoughts of peace and seek the way of peace together. (Pause). Lord, hear us.

For families that are torn with dissension and unhappiness: that they may be able to find peace and reconciliation. (Pause). Lord, hear us.

For those we find hard to love: that, remembering the Lord's goodness to ourselves, we may try to treat them in a more Christlike way. (Pause). Lord, hear us.

For local needs.

Let us pray:

Merciful Father, fill our hearts with your love and keep us faithful to the Gospel of Christ. Give us the grace to raise above our human weakness. Grant this, we ask, through the same Christ our Lord.

SIGN OF PEACE

Lord Jesus Christ, you said to your disciples: 'Love your enemies; pray for those who persecute you. In this way you will show that you are true children of your Father in heaven.' Help us to be merciful and forgiving towards all those who make life difficult for us, so that we may enjoy the peace and unity of your kingdom where you live for ever and ever.

COMMUNION REFLECTION

Smith and Jones approached the news-stand.
Smith greeted the newsman very courteously,
but got a most discourteous service in return.
Accepting the newspaper,
which was shoved rudely in is direction,
Smith smiled and wished the newsman a nice day.

As the two friends walked away, Jones asked:
'Does he always treat you so rudely?'
'Yes, unfortunately, he does,' Smith answered.
'Are you always that friendly to him?'
'I try to be.'
'Tell me, why are you so kind to him

when he is so rude to you?'
'Because I don't want him to decide for me
how I'm going to act.'

No matter how unchristian another person may act towards us,
we still have it in our power to act in a Christian way
towards him or her.

This, after all, is only what Christ expects of us.

EIGHTH SUNDAY OF THE YEAR
The plank and the splinter

INTRODUCTION AND CONFITEOR

At the start of each Mass we are invited to examine our consciences. This means, of course, examining *our own* conscience, not
the conscience of anyone else. And we must blame no one but
ourselves for our sins. (Pause).   Let us confess our sins to God and
to one another.

I confess to almighty God . . . etc.

HEADINGS FOR READINGS

First Reading (Ecclesisticus 27:4-7). Through three picturesque
comparisons, the reading makes one point: that a person reveals in
his speech the kind of person he or she is.

Second Reading (1 Cor 15:54-58). If we persevere in doing the
Lord's work, we need not fear death. When we die we will share
in Christ's victory over sin and death.

Gospel (Luke 6:39-45). As Christians we should of course be
concerned about others. However, we cannot guide another person
unless we see the way clearly ourselves.

HOMILY

Many people want to reform the world, but they go the wrong
way about it. They begin by trying to reform others instead of
reforming themselves. It is a well-known fact that nothing so blinds
us to our own faults as a preoccupation with the faults of others.
It has been said that the faults which we find most repugnant in
others are precisely the ones that plague our own lives.

Roddy, the Rhino, had some good qualities. But he had one
quality that certainly did not endear him to his fellow animals. In

fact it made him positively odious to them. Roddy was the victim of a great delusion — the delusion that he was perfect. Not that he had any proof of this or that he spent a lot of time in self-improvement programmes. It was just a feeling he had about himself: 'I feel I'm perfect — therefore I am perfect.'

Since he firmly believed that he was perfect he logically believed that he had an indisputable right, even a duty, to correct others. If only he did this with some sensitivity it might have been tolerable. But he did it in such a ham-fisted and high-handed way. He sounded so superior!

In any case he was constantly correcting his fellow animals, constantly alerting them to their faults and urging them to improve themselves. Even insignificant warts and spots did not escape him. But according to him the most serious defect was the wearing of any kind of horn. Horns he considered to be totally repulsive and unworthy of any decent self-respecting animal. Thus it was that those poor animals that had been born with horns became the main targets of his zeal for the betterment of the animal kingdom. The poor sheep, and goats and deer never got a moment's peace from him.

Now the amazing thing was this — and here is where the true magnitude of his delusion becomes apparent — all this time he had a big horn right on top of his, let's face it, thoroughly ugly nose. When you looked at Roddy it was the first thing you noticed. Yet he himself was unaware of it, though how this could be I do not know. However, none of the other animals had the courage to point it out to him, though they were for ever talking about it behind his back.

This situation might have gone on for ever were it not for the fact that finally one day someone did pluck up the courage to tell him. It happened like this. Roddy was drinking from a fast-flowing stream. A robin was perched on an over-hanging branch, singing its morning song. Now old Roddy hadn't a note in his head. He didn't like music either. Anything at which he didn't excel was anathema to him. In the middle of his drinking he looked up and said: 'Be quiet, you little twit! Can't you see I'm drinking.'

'You're not so handsome yourself,' said the robin. 'Some day you ought to take a good look at yourself in a clear pool of water, and you'll see what I mean.'

'What are you talking about? Why, everybody knows I'm perfect.'

'Perfect! That's the best joke I've heard in a long time. If only you hadn't got that ugly horn right on top of your nose. I can see you don't believe me. Well then, why don't you go to that quiet pool up there and take a look?'

Roddy was firmly convinced he had nothing to hide. So up he went and took a look at himself in the clear water. He was horrified at what he saw. Unable to take it, or indeed believe it, he plunged his blunt snout into the water and churned it up so that the unwelcome image disappeared. Then he sought refuge on the bank.

All next day poor Roddy wandered through the fields in a daze. His self-image was in smithereens. 'What hurts most,' he muttered to himself, 'is that everybody else knew about the existence of the horn, everybody but me. And there I was going around telling the sheep and the goats that they should be ashamed of their horns, and all the time I have this big horn right on top of my nose. How will I ever be able to face them?'

During the days that followed the other animals noticed that Roddy was acting strangely. He was going around, his head held low, talking to himself. 'I'm ruined,' he moaned. 'I can't face them and I can't face myself.' All this time he took great care to avoid crossing stagnant water.

But slowly and painfully it came home to him that he had no choice but to accept the truth. So on another bright day he made his way back to the pool in which he had first glimpsed his true image. He gazed steadily into the clear water, and it honoured him by telling him the plain truth. It showed him the horn in all its starkness.

'I was waiting for you to come back,' a voice said. It was the robin. 'It's not so bad after all, is it? You know one fault doesn't ruin you. In fact if you have any sense you can even turn it to your advantage. It can teach you humility.'

As Roddy stepped out of the water a slight smile crossed his large and furrowed face. Having plucked up the courage to face himself, it was comparatively easy to face the others. And face them he did. And what a different Roddy they discovered! A more charming fellow you could not wish to find. He was as open and radiant as a flower. He became renowned for one thing — acceptance of others, not as he wished them to be, but just as they were, warts and horns and all. As far as himself was concerned, never again would he pretend to be something he wasn't. Nor would he worry unduly about how others saw him. He would just try to be himself, to be the best that he could be.

It's only a story but I don't think it is utterly far-fetched. Jesus didn't seem to think so. He said that it was possible to notice a tiny splinter of wood in another person's eye while being unaware of a plank in one's own. It is a fact that we can be unaware of certain facts about ourselves which are perfectly clear to anyone who has ever lived in the same house with us or worked in the same office.

How can we be a guide to others (and as Christians we have a responsibility to show concern for others) if we are blind ourselves. In so far as we have any area of blindness then we will guide no one in that particular area. But the best thing we can do is not to guide simply by correcting but by example. By walking the right road ourselves and being a true friend – that is the way to guide. Others will follow. Our words then will flow from what we are. They will have a genuine ring about them and people will take notice of them.

'Never criticise your neighbour until you have walked for a mile in his moccasins.' (Indian Proverb).

'The fault-finder will find faults even in paradise.' (Thoreau).

PRAYER OF THE FAITHFUL

Let us pray that we may be able to see our own faults, and for the courage and grace to correct them, so that we may guide and help our brothers and sisters. *R*.Lord, hear our prayer.

For the pope and the bishops: that they may inspire and guide the flock of Christ by word and example. (Pause).   Let us pray to the Lord.

For all our temporal leaders: that they may fulfil the duties of their office with courage and integrity. (Pause).   Let us pray to the Lord.

For those who are lost on the road of life and who can find no hope or meaning or direction in life. (Pause).   Let us pray to the Lord.

For the grace to be able to accept others as they are, and for the courage not to accept ourselves until we have tried to be as good as we can be. (Pause).   Let us pray to the Lord.

For local needs.

Let us pray.

Father, open our hearts to your grace. Restrain us from our human waywardness, and keep us faithful to your commandments. We ask this through Christ our Lord.

COMMUNION REFLECTION

In the time when monks lived in the Egyptian desert,
one day a certain monk committed
what was considered to be a serious fault,
and the elders assembled to pass judgement on him.
They sent for their abbot to join them.

They sent him a message saying:
'Come, the community is waiting for you.'
So the abbot arose and started off.

He took with him an old basket which was full of holes.
Filling it with fine sand he carried it behind him.
Naturally, as he went along,
he left a trail of sand in his wake.

The elders came out to meet him
and asked him what he meant by this.
And he replied:
'My sins are running out behind me.
Everywhere I go I leave a trail of faults behind me,
only most of the time I don't see them myself.
And today you want me to sit in judgement on my brother.'

On hearing this the elders were ashamed.
They abandoned the trial,
and pardoned their brother.

NINTH SUNDAY OF THE YEAR
Faith like this

INTRODUCTION AND CONFITEOR

Our faith is the most precious thing we have, though we may not
always appreciate this. Faith is to us what a lamp is to a person
travelling in darkness. However, most of us are aware that our
faith is not as strong or deep or alive as it might be. We should not
be afraid to admit this. It is not easy to live by faith.

Let us turn to God and ask him to deepen our faith in his love
for us and in the value of our lives. (Pause).

Lord, where the darkness of doubt reigns you let the light of
faith shine. Lord, have mercy.

Lord, where the darkness of despair reigns you let the light of
hope shine. Christ, have mercy.

Lord, where the darkness of hate reigns you let the light of love
shine. Lord, have mercy.

HEADINGS FOR READINGS

First Reading (1 Kings 8:41-43). Solomon urges the people to
welcome all those foreigners who come to worship at the Lord's
Temple. It is a reminder to them that salvation was not something
intended for them alone but for all nations.

Second Reading (Gal 1:1-2, 6-10). Paul warns the Galatians against trouble-makers, that is, people who preach a different version of the Gospel to that which he originally brought to them.

Gospel (Luke 7:1-10). This relates the extraordinary faith shown in Jesus by a Roman army officer.

HOMILY

I think what is being emphasised in this Gospel is not so much the cure of the servant as the faith of the centurion. What made his faith so extraordinary was the fact that he was not a member of the Chosen People but a Gentile (a Roman officer). One would not have expected to find any faith at all coming from that quarter, much less faith of such a high quality.

Several times in the Gospel we find Jesus disappointed at the lack of faith he finds among his own people. In his native Nazareth he was unable to work any miracle because of their lack of faith. And he met pretty well the same fate in Capernaum: 'People came from the ends of the earth to hear the wisdom of Solomon, and there is something greater than Solomon here.' This is borne out again in today's Gospel where he says: 'I haven't found faith like this in all of Israel.' A strange thing about faith: it can blossom in unlikely places and wither in favourable ones.

Christ praised the faith of the centurion. What was so great about it? How are we to judge the quality of faith anyway? What should we look for? When we say: 'So-and-so has great faith,' what do we mean? There are a lot of misconceptions in this whole area. And it is so important to get it right. If we get a wrong idea of faith, we will get everything else wrong as well. So are there any definite signposts that could keep us going in the right direction? Any basics, any definite anchors or pillars? Let's have a look.

First of all we must not mistake religious practice for faith. Catherine De Hueck Doherty says: 'In our times a lot of people profess to believe but they believe *only with their lips*. When the chips are down they really don't. They attend Easter services and things like that. But their deeds are opposed to their beliefs. and nothing repels people from religion more than the hypocrisy of those who only give it lip service.' What you have here then is mere religious practice, not real faith. Indeed many non-believers surpass Christians in their purity of outlook and in their concern for their neighbour.

The quality, depth and strength of our faith must be reflected in the way we live, in the goals we pursue, in the values we live by, in all our dealings with other people. Our faith must show up in our life. One's life has to be transformed, however slowly, by what one believes. *The* quality then that our faith should have is *love*. A faith

that doesn't express itself in love is like a barren fruit tree or a lamp
that doesn't give light. Whatever it is it is not Christian faith. It is
some kind of fanaticism or superstition.

We often speak of faith as if it were a *thing*. Thus we talk about
'losing' one's faith, or 'finding' one's faith, or 'preserving' one's
faith, and so on. It's as if faith were some kind of charm to be worn
around the neck which will ensure us a safe and happy passage
through this life if worn faithfully. Faith is not a thing. It is a relationship with a person — with God (as Father, Son and Spirit). For
a Christian this relationship is one of love and trust. If I wish to
measure the quality and depth of my faith all I have to do is look
at the place God has in my life. What does he mean to me? Is God
real in my everyday life? Is he the one who makes sense of all my
strivings, the one to whom my life is flowing like a river to the sea,
the one around whom my life revolves?

This relationship with God is what faith is all about. Would then
that we could say with Carlo Carretto: 'I believe in God because
I know him.' How can I tell if God is real to me? By seeing if there
is love in my life. Again it is Carretto who says: 'Stop asking
yourself whether you do or do not believe in God. Ask yourself
whether you do or do not love. When we love, we experience God.'

This then is the heart of Christian faith — a relationship of
intimacy with God in all my daily undertakings, great and small.
God is interested in me and my life is important to him. This is
the star that guides me. This is the path that I follow. It is not a
complicated thing. One does not need to have studied theology to
live by faith. It is a simple childlike trust in God and a desire to do
his will.

Now let us look back briefly at the centurion's faith. For him
Jesus was not just some faith-healer or wonder-worker. He was an
agent of God. That's the first thing. Then it is obvious that his faith
was reflected in his life. See how he cared about his servant. In those
days servants were little better than slaves. See how he cared about
the people among whom he lived. He was a member of the forces
of occupation, yet he cared about the people and respected their
religious beliefs. And when we look at his humility we are simply
astounded. He was the most powerful man in the locality. He had
a lot of people under him. His word was law. Yet he did not think
himself worthy of a personal visit from Jesus. He was truly a rare
man, with an extraordinary purity of outlook and attitude.

Faith does not ensure us a comfortable passage in life. What it
does is give us bearings in a topsy-turvy world. It gives us hope that
all our sufferings and struggles have a meaning. That our lives have
a worthwhile goal. That a loving Father watches over us, whose

sons and daughters we are. To live by faith means to say our prayers and commit ourselves to life's uncertainties.

But, let's face it, our faith is often in danger of becoming just a smoke-screen with which we hide a fundamentally profane existence and attitude to life. We should not be afraid to admit this. If faith is a gift from God, we have no need to be ashamed to confess and to pray: 'Lord, I believe; help my belief.'

'Without faith in God we are like someone trying to read at night without a lamp.' (Carlo Carretto).

'To this faith I cling as to a lantern that will lead me safely home.' (Carlo Carretto).

PRAYER OF THE FAITHFUL

Let us pray to Christ that he may strengthen and deepen our faith in him so that it may transform our lives.   R.Lord, I believe; help my unbelief.

For all Christians: that they may bear witness to their faith in Christ and his Gospel, not just with their words but with their lives. R.. Let us pray to the Lord.

For all those who believe in and work for a world of justice and peace: that the Lord may support them in their vision and strengthen them in their struggles. (Pause).   Let us pray to the Lord.

For those with weak faith or no faith: that the light of Christ may illumine their minds and hearts. (Pause).   Let us pray to the Lord.

That the Lord may send us his Spirit to make us strong in faith and active in good works. (Pause).   Let us pray to the Lord.

For local needs.

Let us pray:

Heavenly Father, grant that what we have said with our lips, we may believe in our hearts, and practise in our lives. We ask this through our Lord Jesus Christ, your Son, who lives and reigns with you and the Holy Spirit, one God, for ever and ever.

SIGN OF PEACE

Lord Jesus Christ, the night before you died, as you sat at table with your friends, you said to them: 'Do not let your hearts be troubled or afraid. Trust in God still, and trust in me.' In the midst of all our anxieties and uncertainties, help us to go on trusting in the Father and in you, so that we may enjoy the peace and unity of our kingdom where you live for ever and ever.

COMMUNION REFLECTION

(This prayer was found on the body of a soldier, killed in action during World War I).

Look, God, I've never spoken to you before,
but now I just want to say 'hello'.
They told me you didn't exist,
and like a fool I believed them.

Last night I looked up at the sky from a shell hole.
When I saw the beauty of the stars,
and thought how big the universe is,
I knew that they were telling me a lie.

I wonder if you will shake hands with me when we meet?
Somehow I feel you will understand all my failures.
Strange how I had to come to this horrible place
to get to know you.
What was I doing before this?

There isn't much more to say,
but I'm sure glad I got to know you today.
I feel the zero hour will soon be here.
This is going to be a horrible fight.
Who knows but I may come to your house tonight.

I'm crying! Fancy me crying!
I never thought this could happen to me.
I have to go now.
Strange, since I met you, I'm no longer afraid to die.

TENTH SUNDAY OF THE YEAR
Death: encounter with Christ

INTRODUCTION AND CONFITEOR

There are many things that cause tears to fall, but without a
doubt the greatest offender is death. Death brought tears to the
eyes of Christ himself. But, as the Son of God, he is the one who
gives hope and consolation to all those who mourn the loss of a
loved one.

Let us draw close to Christ who at Naim dried the tears of a
widow crying for her dead son. (Pause).

Lord Jesus, you give comfort to all those who are sad. Lord,
have mercy.

Lord Jesus, you give hope to all who live in the shadow of
death. Christ, have mercy.

Lord Jesus, you brighten the horizon of all our tomorrows with your promise of eternal life. Lord, have mercy.

HEADINGS FOR READINGS

First Reading (1 Kings 17:17-24). Elijah restores the son of a widow to life. As a result the widow recognises Elijah as a true man of God and a prophet.

Second Reading (Gal 1:11-18). Here Paul is trying to prove to the Galatians that the Gospel which he has preached to them is not a human message but is the result of a revelation from Jesus Christ.

Gospel (Luke 7:11-17). This relates how Jesus raised to life the only son of a widow at Naim. The people recognise Jesus as a great prophet and, that through him and in him, God has visited his people.

HOMILY

We have many fears, but perhaps our fear of death is the real fear. To fear death is natural and understandable. Yet, if Christians have an excessive fear of death it is surely telling them something. It is telling them that their faith is superficial and that Christ is little better than a stranger on the margins of their lives.

A certain kingdom was ruled by a king who lived in a great castle in a remote part of the kingdom. Though reputedly the wisest and kindest of all kings, he was a strange king. Never once had he been seen by his subjects. It will come as no surprise, therefore, to hear that some of these subjects refused to believe in his existence. They dismissed it as nothing more than a pretty legend, and lived as they pleased. Some set themselves up as kings in their own right, laying claim to large tracts of land, and acting in a cruel and despotic way towards their fellowmen. They behaved as if they were accountable to nobody but themselves.

But there were others who had a rocklike belief in the existence of the king. Of course they were puzzled by his silence and inaccessibility. But what really bothered them was his apparent indifference to their lot. Why did he not defend those who were loyal to him? Why did he allow the strong to be so cruel and grasping and to lord it over the weak?

Though the king had never appeared in person among his people, it was widely believed that from time to time he had sent messengers or envoys to them. But most astounding of all was the belief held by some that he had once actually sent his own son among them. The purpose of his coming was not only to give them an example of how the king's subjects were expected to live, but to assure them of his love and concern for them. But he also brought the incredible news that after death all loyal subjects of the king would go to the Castle to live there for ever. Those who believed this henceforth saw death as a summons to the Royal Castle.

But even this was not always seen as good news by those who accepted it. What bothered them was the fact that often the summons was issued in a seemingly arbitrary and unfair manner. Some were called when their life's work was done, and were given plenty of advance warning. But to others the summons came suddenly and out of the blue, right in the middle of their life's work. And in still other cases it came before that work had even begun. Then others had difficulty in believing that the call to the Castle was anything other than a call to give an account of one's stewardship. In other words, instead of an encounter with a loving king, they saw it as a meeting with a stern judge.

Matthew was a typical believer. he understood that his whole life was a journey to the Royal Castle. At times he saw the castle as the goal of all his yearnings and strivings. But then at other times it was very unreal to him, not more substantial than a shadow.

Let me tell you about a man who entered Matthew's life. One day when he was a mere toddler he wandered into a wood and got lost. But then a man of about thirty, with a kind face and sympathetic manner, found him and brought him back into the bosom of his family, where he was the centre of attention and the cause of great rejoicing. That was the first time the man, who became known to him subsequently as 'The Stranger', entered his life. Naturally he remembered nothing of it since he was only a child at the time. The Stranger showed up again when as a young boy he was brought to their place of worship and given a mysterious food to eat.

The next time he met him was at his wedding, though who had invited him he did not know. But somehow he was glad he was there, for he definitely brought something to it that would otherwise not have been there. As the years went on he met him at the funeral of friends. And from time to time he got a fleeting glimpse, or thought he did, as their paths crossed briefly. But he never got close to him, though once when he was on a very lonely stretch of road, beset by fears and close to despair, the Stranger joined him and walked with him for a while. But then their paths parted and he lost sight of him once more.

Years passed. Then one day the thought of death burst into his life. He began to count up the number of years he had left. He was tormented by the thought that he might not have time to finish his life's work, though what exactly that work was he couldn't say.

Then one day the Castle came into view. In front of it was a large gate. A notice said: 'No visitors allowed beyond this point'. His friends accompanied him as far as the gate and lingered with him to the very last second. But then his name was called and he disappeared through the gate. Inside everything was so strange. He felt so utterly alone. Ah, if only they had allowed even one of his friends to accompany him, what a difference it would have made. Then he was in the hallway of the Castle. There a man stood waiting for him. For a moment Matthew did not recognise him, as he hadn't the courage to look him straight in the face. But then in a flash he realised who it was. It was none other than the Stranger!

Though the Stranger greeted him with a smile, Matthew bitterly regretted that he hadn't become better acquainted with him during his life. In spite of all the opportunities he had been given he didn't even know his name. His regret became all the greater when he learned that the Stranger was in fact the king's own son.

Death is the loneliest moment of all. Yet for a Christian, death must be seen, not as an encounter with a terrible unknown, but, as happened for the little boy of Naim, an encounter with a caring and compassionate Christ.

Thomas Merton said: 'If death comes to us as an unwelcome stranger, it will be because Christ also has always been an unwelcome stranger. For when death comes, Christ comes, bringing us the everlasting life he has bought for us with his own death.'

What about it if death, when it comes, should interrupt our plans and schemes. Surely we shouldn't mind being interrupted by the unexpected arrival of a friend? What we have to do is to make Christ our constant companion and friend on the road of life, not merely a shadowy figure on the fringes of our life whom we meet on special occasions (such as when we receive the sacraments).

If we have this attitude towards our own death, then we can become a source of great strength and hope for those who have to pass through the castle gates before us. We are called to go along with the dying as far as we are allowed, to accompany them and be with them to the very gate.

'When one's whole life is orientated towards self-giving, at its end one gladly and freely surrenders it back into the hands of God. Then death is transformed into a fulfilment.' (Thomas Merton).

'Everyone's death is the same quality as himself: to the enemy of God an enemy, to the friend of God a friend.' (Rumi).

PRAYER OF THE FAITHFUL

When the people of Naim saw the great deed which Jesus had done, they knew that in him God had visited them. God still visits his people. Let us pray to him through Christ, the Lord of life and death.   *R*. Lord, hear our prayer.

For the Church: that through its voice and its deeds the hope and compassion of Christ may be felt in the world. (Pause).   Let us pray to the Lord.

For all those who work for the sick and the dying: that Christ may give them gentle hands and warm hearts. (Pause).   Let us pray to the Lord.

For all those who have recently suffered a bereavement and who are still in the grip of sorrow: that Christ may comfort them and help them cope with their loss. (Pause).   Let us pray to the Lord.

That God may visit our hearts with his love so that we may be capable of sympathising with others in their sorrow. (Pause).   Let us pray to the Lord.

For local needs.

Let us pray:

Heavenly Father, visit us your people during this Eucharist which we celebrate in memory of Christ your Son. Help us to experience your loving and merciful presence among us. We ask this through the same Christ our Lord.

COMMUNION REFLECTION

What a marvellous power Jesus had —
the power to raise people from the dead.
Yet in a sense we can do the same.

I once met a young man who told me
that as a result of a row
he hadn't spoken to his father for six years,
even though they lived only a few miles apart.
He was an only child;
the mother had deserted the family.
So now the father was living alone.
His world was getting smaller and darker
with each day that passed.
He wasn't yet dead,
but in a sense he was already in the tomb.

'Who will roll the stone away for us?'
asked the women on Easter morning.
That son had the power to roll away
the stone from his father's tomb.
With a word or a gesture
he could set him free from his tomb
of loneliness, bitterness and despair.

What a power we have!
We can call our brother to come forth from his tomb,
or we can leave him languish there.
It is one of the lovely compensations in life,
that we cannot raise our neighbour,
without raising ourselves also.

ELEVENTH SUNDAY OF THE YEAR
Gate-crashing the party

INTRODUCTION AND CONFITEOR

We often use our sins as an excuse for not drawing near Christ, especially in Communion. We say: 'I'm a sinner. I'm not worthy.' But in today's Gospel we see a sinful woman draw close to Christ in love and trust to hear from him the words: 'Your sins are forgiven, go in peace.'

Let us then approach Christ, sins and all, sure that we will find love and acceptance. (Pause).

Lord, you raise the dead to life in the spirit.   Lord, have mercy.

Lord, you bring pardon and peace to the sinner.   Christ, have mercy.

Lord, you bring good news to the poor and the downtrodden.   Lord, have mercy.

HEADINGS FOR READINGS

First Reading (2 Samuel 12:7-10, 13). When challenged with his sin by the prophet Nathan, King David readily admits it and repents. Then the prophet assures him that the Lord has forgiven him.

Second Reading (Gal 2:16, 19-21). St Paul says that Christ has become his life — the Christ who loved him and died for him. All his strength comes from his belief in and union with Christ.

Gospel (Luke 7:36-8:3). This tells of the moving encounter in the house of a Pharisee between Christ and a sinful woman. Here we see 'the friend of sinners' in action.

HOMILY

Jesus was gentle and loving in his approach to sinners. He knew that rejection and judgement never helped to change a person. In fact they have the opposite effect. They tend to confirm a person in his or her present state. So he provided a kind of presence in which people felt accepted and loved, and in this atmosphere they were able to respond and change. It is much easier, far less bothersome, to reject a person than to take the trouble to try and change him.

One night during a sudden blackout a man needed a light very urgently as he wanted to visit a sick friend. He knew that there was an old paraffin lamp down in the cellar. Since he was desperate he dug it out and lit it. But he was very disappointed at the poor light it gave out. This should not have surprised him as it was covered with dust and grime. The globe was not only dirty but also cracked. And the wick smoked badly and gave off a foul smell. It was all too much for the man. You see he liked things to be perfect. That's why he loved new things. He had little time and even less patience for such occupations as cleaning, mending, and polishing.

'This lamp is no use,' he said impatiently to his wife. And with that he extinguished it and threw it into a bag of garbage. 'I'd be ashamed to let my neighbour see me carrying a lamp like that.'

Three weeks later another black-out occurred. This time it was the wife who provided the light. She produced an oil lamp and lit it. Of course the light it gave out could not compare with electric light. Still it was more than adequate to see by, and its rosy glow cast an enchantment over the house.

'What a lovely lamp!' said the husband. 'Where did you get it?'

'That's the same lamp you wanted to throw out,' she replied.

'I don't believe it!' he exclaimed.

With that she took it down and let him examine it at close quarters until he was convinced. Then he said:

'It must have cost a lot of money to get it into this shape?'

'As a matter of fact,' she replied, 'it cost very little money — just a couple of pounds. All I had to buy was a new wick and a tinted globe. But what it did take was quite a lot of time, and a whole lot of care and patience. What a job I had in getting rid of the dirt and grime. It was so deeply embedded in it. And then I had to polish and polish until my hands were sore. But never once did I doubt but that it was worthwhile. Underneath the layers of dirt I could see that it was a beautiful lamp. And don't you think I have been proved right?'

'I couldn't agree more,' was the answer he made.

Now let us look at the meeting between Jesus and the sinful woman. Jesus would have been expected to show his disapproval, not only of her lifestyle, but of herself. After all, he had standards to uphold. Everybody in the room knew the kind of things he stood for, the values he preached and lived by. Even his enemies grudgingly recognised him as a man of God. Simon, the man who had invited him, was a Pharisee. The central dogma of the Pharisee's religion went like this: 'God loves the virtuous, and hates the sinner.'

So now, with the eyes of everybody upon him, what was he going to do? Surely he would show his disapproval by rejecting her? He would of course condemn her. He would put her in her place. Who did she think she was coming in here where she hadn't even been invited? The nerve of her! Jesus would treat her the way the man treated the dust-covered lamp. He would cast her aside.

Simon hadn't even one kind thought for the woman, nor had he as much as a shred of understanding of how she felt. She was a woman who was craving for understanding. If she could find someone to believe in her then maybe she could believe in herself and do something about her sordid life?

But Simon knew nothing either about the approach of Jesus. He hadn't understood the first thing about compassion and mercy. He was a member of the separated ones — the Pharisees. They saw themselves as paragons of virtue. But at the end of the day, what is the value of a virtuous life, if it is a life without mercy and love? Jesus had not come to judge sinners but to befriend them and help them to change their lives.

He understood that side by side with shame and dishonour quite different and holy feelings can exist. He did not see only the woman's dishonour but also her great suffering. He could see that disgrace had touched her only superficially. Not a drop of real vice had penetrated into her heart. He saw that, for nothing in her was hidden from him. Then with the look in his eyes and the touch of his hands he helped her to believe in her goodness and to begin to unfold, just as the spring sun helps a rose to open up, petal by petal, and reveal to the world its hidden beauty.

Even from a human point of view, the approach of Jesus makes a lot of sense. If a child is wet and starving, he needs warmth and food. If a person is in darkness, he needs light. And above all, if a person is down, he does not need someone to put his foot on top of him, but a hand up. As Jean Vanier says so beautifully: 'The person is misery does not need a look that judges and criticises, but a comforting presence that brings peace and hope and life.'

As for the woman, never in her life had she experienced anything like this before. Jesus was the best man she had ever met. She was so unexpectedly happy that she was almost frightened of her happiness. After that beautiful night she began to believe in her own goodness and in God. It was only the beginning of her gradual regeneration, a regeneration that would take her into new places and new worlds.

Jesus understood the weaknesses of people. He knew that if they found love and acceptance they could change. Like in the case of the woman and the lamp, his approach was gentle, but it also called for a special kind of strength. It was much easier to cast the lamp aside than to take the time and the care to clean it up and polish it. It's the same with people. It's much easier to label and pigeonhole them once and for all, and leave them there, than to befriend them and help them up out of their misery. How many people we write-off in this way.

'You'll never improve a man by repelling him.' (Dostoyevsky).

'One can be bent into so many shapes in the course of a lifetime.' (Solzhenitsyn).

PRAYER OF THE FAITHFUL

Let us pray for some of that understanding and compassionate love that Christ showed to all, but especially to those who were rejected and written off.   *R.* Lord, graciously hear us.

For Christians: that they may imitate the patience, tolerance and forgiveness of Christ in all their dealings with others, especially those who are weak and vulnerable. (Pause).   Lord, hear us.

For all those who make our laws or administer them: that they may be both wise and compassionate in their judgements. (Pause).   Lord, hear us.

That the Lord may give strength to the afflicted, and give us the will to do everything we can to help and comfort them. (Pause). Lord, hear us.

For ourselves: that, in his goodness, Christ may turn our hearts to himself and help us do what is right. (Pause).   Lord, hear us.

For local needs.

Let us pray:

Father, our source of life, you know our weakness. May we reach out with joy to grasp your hand and walk more readily in your ways. We ask this through Christ our Lord.

SIGN OF PEACE

Lord Jesus Christ, you looked with compassion on Mary Magdalen, and you said to her: 'Your sins are forgiven. Go in peace.' And Mary Magdalen the sinner became Mary Magdalen the saint. Look not on our sins, but on the faith of your Church, and grant us the peace and unity of your kingdom where you live for ever and ever.

COMMUNION REFLECTION

The story of Jesus' meeting with the sinful woman

shows that he not only sees a person's present state,
but also what a person is capable of becoming.
Simon and the others looked at the woman,
and they saw a sinner who would always be a sinner.
Jesus looked at her and saw a sinner
who was capable of becoming a saint.

One day someone came upon Michelangelo
as he was chipping away with his chisel
at a huge shapeless block of marble.
He was surrounded by dust and fragments of marble.
It was not a pretty sight.
He asked him what he was doing, and he replied:
'I'm releasing the angel imprisoned in this marble.'

Jesus is the one who knows the real and complete me.
He sees my sins, my failures and betrayals.
But he also sees my hidden qualities and talents,
my noble ideals and ardent hopes.
He can help me to bring to birth
the hidden, splendid person that is struggling inside me
to be born and to be free.

TWELFTH SUNDAY OF THE YEAR
Who do people say that I am?

INTRODUCTION AND CONFITEOR

At a crucial point in his public ministry Christ asked the apostles: 'Who do people say that I am?' The ordinary people had all sorts of false ideas. Only Peter gave the correct answer: 'You are the Christ, the Son of the living God.'

Christ asks the same question of you and me. Let us reflect for a moment to ask ourselves what answer we would give. Who is Christ for me? What does he mean to me? (Pause).

We need the light and grace of God to be able to make the same confession of faith as Peter made.

Lord Jesus, you are the Son of God and our Brother. Lord, have mercy.

Lord Jesus, you are the Saviour of the world who takes away all our sins. Christ, have mercy.

Lord Jesus, you are the Light of the world, and our Teacher and Guide. Lord, have mercy.

HEADINGS FOR READINGS

First Reading (Zechariah 12:10-11). This looks forward to a time when a new spirit will be poured out on the people (as happened at Pentecost), and they will mourn over the one they put to death (namely, Christ).

Second Reading (Gal 3:26-29). Paul states that for those who have been baptised there must be no more distinctions. Because of Christ all have equal access to the blessings promised to Abraham.

Gospel (Luke 9:18-24). This tells about Peter's confession of faith in Christ, and how immediately after it Christ told his disciples that he was destined to be rejected and to be put to death. Suffering too awaits all true followers of him.

HOMILY

The tyranny of other people's opinions and expectations! How heavily they can weigh upon us and how unhappy we can be trying to live up to them. Politicians, and others in the public eye a lot, are usually very concerned about their public image. Hence the notice they take of the opinion polls. If the image is not so bright it will be reflected in the polls. This means that it has to be polished up. And frequently it is the image, not the reality, that matters. What matters is how othes see us. As long as they have a favourable image of us, that's all that matters and we are happy.

But even when people get the external facts about us right, how many know the real me behind those facts? Who knows the real person under all the costumes and all the roles? Who knows a person's deepest reality as opposed to his surface appearance? Is there even one person who can see me as I really am? Or who knows what I'm really trying to do? Or who knows me as I really am and who understands me?

Alfred Nobel, from Sweden, invented dynamite. As a result he became rich and famous. One might have expected fame and fortune to have brought him happiness. This was not so. As he neared the end of his life he was extremely unhappy. He had never married and all his life he had been plagued by ill-health. The result was that he had a very pessimistic view of life and of humanity in general.

Then one morning he woke up and read his own obituary in the newspaper. It had been a mistake by a journalist. But he was very disturbed by what he read. Indeed he was deeply shocked. What hurt him most was the false image people seemed to have of him. How, he asked himself, could they have got it so wrong? He discovered that the world saw him merely as the 'dynamite king' and a great industrialist. None of his true aims and ambitions were mentioned in the obituary: his desire to break down barriers of prejudice and misunderstanding, to unite people, to better the human race and the quality of human life, and so on. There wasn't a word about these.

So that was what people thought of him! That was the image they had of him. That's how he would be remembered. He felt they had completely misunderstood him. They had got it all wrong. He wasn't like that. So what did he do? Then and there he made a decision to take immediate action to let the world know what his true ideals and aims were. He left most of his vast fortune in trust to the betterment of the world. He set up five prizes that would be awarded to men and women who had made outstanding contributions to mankind in five areas: physics, chemistry, medicine, literature and peace. This is how he wished to be remembered: not as the man who had invented something capable of blowing the world assunder, but as the man who had the good of humanity deeply at heart. And today, I think it is true to say that he is known more for the prizes than for being the father of dynamite.

In today's Gospel we saw Christ turning to his disciples and asking them: 'Who do people say that I am?' In other words: 'How do people see me? What do they think of me? What sort of image have they got of me?' This is quite a terrifying question to ask. How many of us would have the courage to ask it and relish an honest answer? Naturally we all want to be well thought of. We want to have a good and favourable public image. We want to be popular.

But how wrong people can be is borne out, not only from the case of Nobel, but also from the case of Christ. What crazy ideas people had of him! 'Some say you are John the Baptist (already murdered by Herod). Others say you are one of the ancient prophets come back to life.'

Though the image they had was misguided, it was quite a flattering one. John the Baptist, for instance, had been held in very high esteem by all the people. It was a great compliment to be compared to him. Nothing is easier than flattery. And for ordinary mortals it is well nigh irresistible. But it encourages falseness rather than truth. It is like bread that bloats the eater without nourishing him. Christ, however, did not swallow it. Imagine what might have happened to his mission if he had tried to live up to those images of him!

But Christ did not conform to other people's expectations. They had the idea that the Messiah would be a great political leader who would set up a great kingdom. Jesus did not deny that he was the Messiah — that was the reality, as Peter correctly divined. But he was not to be a glorious Messiah. He was to be a rejected and suffering one. And that was what he was determined to be true to, no matter what the people thought, no matter how it shattered their expectations and illusions. He didn't fulfil the public expectations or project the kind of image the people wanted. No matter what others might think, he knew he had a destiny to fulfil. It was what the Father wanted from him that mattered.

We are in for a life of unhappiness if we play roles so as to keep up a public image and to live up to people's expectations of us. The only thing that we are called to be is *ourselves*. But if we are constantly preoccupied with what others think of us we will never achieve this.

Let us aim at a straightforwardness; at always speaking the truth, and really being truthful. Otherwise we will get entangled in lies, lies from which there may be no way out. They are still lies even if everybody around us accept them as true.

When we find our own true reality we must try to nurture it. And we will not be threatened by the reality of others. We will be able to accept their reality and be enriched by it. But if we never find our own reality we will spend a life pursuing illusions.

'I am beginning to grow out of being concerned about what other people think of me.' (Albert Camus).

'The people can judge me as they like: they are easily deceived, but I cannot deceive myself.' (Tolstoy).

PRAYER OF THE FAITHFUL

Let us pray that our faith in Christ may be both pure and strong, and that we may follow him courageously and generously.   *R*. Lord, graciously hear us.

For all Christians: that they may not only courageously proclaim their faith in Christ before the world but also strive to act accordingly. (Pause).   Lord, hear us.

For all politicians and people who are in the public eye: that they may not seek cheap popularity but strive to speak the truth and to act justly. (Pause).   Lord, hear us.

For all those who suffer for their belief in Christ: that God may sustain them in their trials. (Pause).   Lord, hear us.

That we may always strive to be ourselves and not to be unduly worried either by flattery or criticism. (Pause).   Lord, hear us.

For local needs.

Let us pray:

Father of love, hear our prayers. Help us to know your will and to do it with courage and faith. We ask this through Christ our Lord.

COMMUNION REFLECTION

Lord,
when I was young, I never knew
half of the things that now I do.
I never realised that fame
could prove an empty hollow game.

That wealth, despite all it can do,
rarely beings contentment too.
That beauty, though its power be strong,
cannot hide the emptiness for long.

By the faith
that flowers show when they bloom unbidden;
by the calm of the river's flow to a goal that is hidden;
by the trust of the tree that clings to its deep foundation;
by the courage of wild birds on the long migration;
teach me, good Lord, to do my best;
then I will confide in you and find my rest.

THIRTEENTH SUNDAY OF THE YEAR
On not turning back

INTRODUCTION AND CONFITEOR

We will see in today's Gospel how Jesus headed resolutely for Jerusalem even though he knew that death awaited him there. It's easy to make promises, and to undertake commitments, but it's not always easy to be faithful. It's all too easy, and all too common, to take back or to turn back. Let us think about this. (Pause).

Let us confess our sins of infidelity, asking the Lord to forgive our weakness, selfishness and cowardice.

I confess to almighty God . . . etc.

HEADINGS FOR READINGS

First Reading (1 Kings 19:16, 19-21). This narrates the call of Elisha to succeed the prophet Elijah. Elisha's response is immediate and total.

Second Reading (Gal. 5:1, 13-18). Paul warns the Galatians that, despite their union with Christ and the gift of the Spirit, they still must struggle against the flesh which will do its utmost to lead them into sin and slavery.

Gospel (Luke 9:51-62). This tells how Jesus resolutely took the road to Jerusalem though he knew a shameful death awaited him there. He demands the same kind of unwavering commitment form those who choose to follow him.

HOMILY

In today's Gospel Jesus says to those who want to follow him: 'The person who puts his hand to the plough and who *keeps on looking back,* is not fit for the kingdom of heaven.' In other words, the person who wishes to become a disciple of his must make a complete gift of himself to the task, like the ploughman who must not spend his time looking behind him but give his whole attention to ploughing a straight furrow. This calls for self-discipline, sacrifice and total commitment to the goal.

But of course this is easier said than done, as we all know. It may be easy at the start, and for a while. A doctor beginning to practise loves his patients as if they were his children. But, as the years go by, the difficulties increase. Everyone discovers that the realities of life are nothing like the expectations he had in the first flush of his youthful enthusiasm. The journey from dreaming to laborious doing is a long one. The constant grind of day-to-day living, which can be so humdrum and pedestrian, takes a big toll. We also discover new things about ourselves. All our weaknesses come to light. At an earlier stage we may have been convinced that we were generous. Now we discover that we are egoists.

Given these facts, it's not only easy, but natural, to begin to look back at what we have left or given up. We begin to have second thoughts. Everyone knows the agony of second thoughts and how powerful the counter arguments can be. We can so easily renege in difficult times on what we promised in rosier times. Today it's all too common. No one wants to make a life-long commitment. We live in the age of the 'drop-out'. This has become a new word in our language and is a symptom of the times we live in. Hermann Hess sums it up like this:

'Once in their youth the light shone for them. They saw the light and followed the star. But then came reason and the mockery of the world. Then came faint-heartedness and apparent failure. Then came weariness and disillusionment, and so they lost their way, and became blind once more.'

'They lost their way' in another way of saying they turned back. But fidelity is possible too, as the psychiatrist Viktor Frankl relates. He spent three years in the concentration camps of Auschwitz and Dachau. He tells the following story.

As a doctor he spent a lot of his time tending sick and dying camp inmates. Near the end of the war he and a companion devised a way of escaping. He says he began to collect up his few possessions: a food bowl, a pair of torn mittens, notes for a book he hoped to write. Then he took a last look in on his patients where they lay on rotten planks of wood on either side of a hut. He came to the only man among them who came from his own country. The man was very near to death. Frankl did his best to hide from him the fact that he was escaping. But his comrade somehow guessed it, and in a tired sad voice said: 'So you too are getting out.'

He says he quickly tried to deny it with a lie. But the words cut him and accused him: 'So you too are getting out.' After finishing his rounds he came back to the man. Again he was greeted with a look of despair which went right through him. He felt he was betraying this man. Suddenly he decided to take his fate into his own hands. He ran out of the hut and told his friend to leave without him. He decided to stay with his patients. At once the unhappy feeling of betrayal left him. And he says that even though he had no idea what the days ahead would bring him, he gained an inner peace he had never before experienced. And in fact he also survived the camps.

Today's Gospel begins with the announcement that Jesus turned his face resolutely towards Jerusalem. He knew well what awaited him there: rejection, betrayal, and death. But for him there was no turning back. His Father had given him the task of bringing the Good News of salvation to his brothers and sisters. He would carry out that task, and his Father would help him to be faithful. He was convinced that there was light at the end of the tunnel — his shameful death would lead to the triumph of his resurrection.

What would have happened if Jesus had turned back, if he had opted out when he saw where the path was leading? In his hands he carried all our hopes and dreams. If he had quit then our hopes would have gone up in smoke.

It is the same with us. We carry each other's hopes and dreams in our hands. If I quit then perhaps I shatter the hopes of someone, maybe even many, who are depending on me, who have their hopes pinned to me. But if I persevere, their hopes will be realised, and their dreams will come true. Life's most painful choices are not always between good and evil. If that were so there would be a lot fewer quitters. No, the most painful choices are often between the good and the best. In other words, the things that tempt us to abandon our goal are not always bad. More often than not they are good, and that is what makes it so hard to resist them. We forget what was once precious to us and exchange it for something else that is less good but more immediate. If we wish then to remain faithful, we must be prepared to meet difficulties, especially from inside ourselves. We have to go forward at such times in bare faith, simple hope, and love without sentiment.

The Lord himself will help us to be faithful, to walk resolutely towards the goals to which we have committed ourselves. He will especially help us to follow him. However, it is not enough simply to follow him. There are so many degrees of adhesion. Pilate was merciful until it became risky. Some break down at the first demands of discipleship. We are not his disciples unless we follow him. To follow him means to put our hands in his hands, our steps in his steps. It is to take the same road and to stay on it. It is to let our fears fall away, putting our confidence in him. It's not an easy road. The Master didn't hide this fact from his disciples. But he does promise final victory to those who stick it out.

We need to renew our spirit from time to time, also our belief in, and commitment to, the initial promises made or vows taken.

'When you walk towards the light, the shadow of your burden falls behind you.' (Kahlil Gibran).

'Only God is faithful. Our fidelity lies in the will to be faithful amid all our infidelities.' (Michel Quoist).

PRAYER OF THE FAITHFUL

Let us pray for the grace to be faithful to our promises, commitments and obligations. (Pause).   *R*. Lord, hear our prayer.

For all those who follow Christ: that they may be faithful to their baptismal promises. (Pause).   Let us pray to the Lord.

For our political leaders: that they may be faithful to the promises they make, and persevere in their efforts to secure a society of justice and peace. (Pause).   Let us pray to the Lord.

For married couples: that, when things go wrong, they may not go back on their promises, but go forward to a deeper love and commitment to one another. (Pause).   Let us pray to the Lord.

For ourselves: that at all times we may strive to keep our vision clear and our goal in mind, so that even now we may experience the joy and inner peace that comes from being faithful. (Pause).   Let us pray to the Lord.

For local needs.

Let us pray:

Teach us, good Lord, to serve you as you deserve: to give and not to count the cost; to fight and not to heed the wounds; to toil and not to seek for rest; to labour and not to ask for any reward save that of knowing that we do your will. We ask this through Christ, our Lord.

COMMUNION REFLECTION

Whose woods these are I hardly know,
his house is in the village though;
he will not see me stopping here
to watch his woods fill up with snow.

My little horse must think it queer
to stop without a farmhouse near,
between the woods and frozen lake
the darkest evening of the year.

He gives his harness bells a shake
to ask if there is some mistake;
the only other sound is the sweep
of easy wind and downy flake.

The woods are lovely, dark and deep,
but I have promises to keep;
and miles to go before I sleep,
and miles to go before I sleep.

Robert Frost.

FOURTEENTH SUNDAY OF THE YEAR
The harvest is great but the labourers few

INTRODUCTION AND CONFITEOR

Every Christian is sent by Christ into the world as a messenger of hope and love. The 'world' here means the area in which I live, my places of work, the people I meet every day, and so on. An active concern for the world and for other people is an essential mark of a good Christian.

We are all responsible for some small corner of the Lord's vineyard where it is up to us to reap the harvest. (Pause).

Lord, you send us to bring forgiveness to others as you have forgiven us. Lord, have mercy.

Lord, you send us to befriend the lonely as you have befriended us. Christ, have mercy.

Lord, you send us to bring healing and peace to the sick and the troubled as you have brought healing and peace to us. Lord have mercy.

HEADINGS FOR READINGS

First Reading (Isaiah 66:10-14). Writing after the return from the Babylonian exile, the poet likens Jerusalem to a mother who nurses her children at her breast — a moving image of peace, contentment and love.

Second Reading (Gal 6:14-18). Paul insists that the Christian life is a new existence — it means becoming like Christ. Paul himself, through illness, flogging, and stoning, bears the marks of Christ's passion on his body.

Gospel (Luke 10:1-12, 17-29). This tells how Christ sent out seventy-two disciples in pairs to visit all the towns and places he himself was to visit.

HOMILY

'The harvest is great, but the labourers are few.' This is a very optimistic yet realistic statement. What a lot of good there is that could be done in the world. But, when the chips are down, how few are willing to put themselves out to do it. Catherine de Hueck Doherty says: 'Christians have to preach the Gospel under all sorts of conditions, quietly or loudly, on platforms or in bars.' And she can talk because she has done so. She gives a couple of examples from her own life.

She tells how when she was a young woman she was working as a cocktail waitress in Manhattan bar. One day she announced to a group of GI's and their girlfriends (whom she knew to be Catholics, but of the lukewarm variety) that it was closing time (4.00 am) and that she had to be off.

'Where are you going to, Katie?' they asked.

'It's Sunday, and I'm going to Mass. There's a Mass at 5.00 am in St Paul's Church. That's where I'm headed.'

'That means you're a Catholic then?'

'Yes, I am a Catholic,' she replied.

They couldn't get over the fact that she could be a practising Catholic and work in a place like that. (One of the things that was expected of cocktail waitresses was to go to bed with all VIP customers). Do you know what happened on that occasion? They all trooped off and went to Mass with her. A couple of weeks later a girl from the group returned. She said: 'You've made me think. If you can live a good life while working in a place like this, then maybe I can too. To hell with the GI's and all that! I'm going to Confession.'

She recalls another time she was travelling in the subway in Montreal. She was reading a book when the lady across from her, who was elderly, looked at her and said: 'You have a kind face. Would you mind talking to me for awhile? I have had the flu for the last three weeks and only a nurse visited me for half an hour. The landlady would bring me a tray, but neither of them spoke very much. I am hungry for conversation. I am hungry for companionship. That is the way I feel.'

Catherine tells what happened next: 'We made two trips from end to end of the subway, talking all the time. Then I invited her to a coffee shop and we became good friends. I did not live in Montreal but we corresponded until she died. I know that a lot of her loneliness was dispersed, just because there was someone on the other end.'

So the harvest is indeed rich, for those who have eyes to see it. Most of the time we do see it. It's just that we do not have the kind of heart that Catherine has to respond to it. We make excuses: 'I have no time. I have so much to do,' etc., etc. And so the harvest is not reaped.

When Jesus looked out at the world he saw that the harvest was great, the opportunities many, the need pressing, and the time ripe. This is even truer in the case of the modern world. How much need there is today of the good news of hope and salvation, of peace and healing, of joy and communion. The harvest is there, everywhere, even in the most unlikely places. It is in our institutions: in our hospitals, homes, schools, prisons. It exists among all kinds of groups of people: the sick, the old, the handicapped, prisoners, addicts, the young . . . How many are deeply wounded and in need of healing. How many are without hope. How many without faith. How many without love. Every day is a harvest day, and in every place there is a harvest to be reaped for Christ.

Mother Teresa says: 'Many today are starving for ordinary bread, but that is not the only kind of hunger there is. There is another hunger — the hunger to be wanted, to be loved, to be recognised. Nakedness too is not just the want of clothes. It is also the loss of dignity, loss of purity, loss of respect. And there is homelessness, which is not just want for a house made of bricks, but the homelessness of being rejected, of being unwanted, of being unloved in a throwaway society'.

Christ himself reaped a rich harvest wherever he went, even in the most unpromising places — among sinners and the rejects of society. When he sent his disciples out he knew that they would meet with opposition and failure. He warned them in advance about the 'wolves' they would meet. He himself was no stranger to opposition. Everywhere he went his enemies dogged his steps, but he did not allow them to deflect him from the job of shepherding the flock the Father had entrusted to him.

Every Christian is sent into the world by Christ. But how few of us ever see our faith in this light. We tend to think of faith as something to which we cling for our own sake only, like a lifebelt, instead of seeing it as a call to the service of others. We leave that for the specialists — the priests, nuns, missionaries . . . 'One of the great myths of our civilisation is that of the specialist.' (Jean Vanier). We turn everything over to the specialist. In that way we quieten our consciences and don't have to do anything.

The people Christ sent out were certainly no specialists, at least not in the modern sense of the word. They had no great training. Nor did they have a great education. Yet they became his instruments, co-workers with him in spreading the Kingdom of God. Christ sent them out among the people. We can all do a little. We can't be everywhee, but we can be somewhere. There are things we can do for Christ which will otherwise remain undone. There are places only we can go, situations only we are aware of, doors that will open only to us.

Christ sent out his disciples 'to all the places he himself was to visit.' The messenger doesn't replace Christ. His or her task is to prepare the way for Christ to come to the other person.

'At an early age I learned that the Gospel has to be lived.' (Catherine de Hueck Doherty).

'The daily life of ordinary people is often made up of sacrifices and acts of anonymous heroism.' (Helder Camara).

PRAYER OF THE FAITHFUL

Let us pray that as followers of Christ we may be active in good works so that God's kingdom may come among us. *R.* Lord, graciously hear us.

For the Church: that all its members may realise that they are called by God to work so that the fruits of his Kingdom may become a reality in the world. (Pause). Lord, hear us.

God offers his Kingdom to all, thus showing that in his eyes everybody is important. Let us pray that he may help those in public office to treat all his people with love and respect. (Pause). Lord, hear us.

For all those who are closed and smug and selfish: that the Lord may touch their hearts and make them people who can care. (Pause). Lord, hear us.

God's harvest is abundant because there are so many who are poor or lonely or in pain. That we may be generous towards those in need. (Pause). Lord, hear us.

For local needs.

Let us pray:

Father, the harvest of your love is abundant, but those who work to make this love visible in the world are few. Help us to take part with joy in this splendid task, and to work for the coming of the Kingdom of your Son. We ask this through the same Christ our Lord.

SIGN OF PEACE

Lord Jesus Christ, you said to your disciples: 'When you enter a house say: "Peace to all in this house." If a person of peace lives there, your peace will rest on that person; if not, it will come back to you.' Give us the right disposition of mind and heart so that we may be able to receive the peace others offer us, and thus we will enjoy the peace and unity of your kingdom where you live for ever and ever.

COMMUNION REFLECTION

Christ said: 'The harvst is great,
but the labourers are few.'
Hence what we need is:

More to approve, fewer to disapprove.
More doers, fewer talkers.
More to say: 'It can be done,'
fewer to say: 'It can't be done'.

More to inspire others with confidence,
fewer to throw cold water on everything.
More to take one step in the right direction.
More to get into the thick of things.
More to do something about it,
fewer to sit on the sidelines finding fault.

More to point out what is right,
fewer to keep harping on what is wrong.
More to light a candle,
fewer to curse the darkness.

The labourers are indeed few —
those who are willing to put themselves out
to bring Christ's healing, love and hope to others.
Why can't I become one of those labourers?

FIFTEENTH SUNDAY OF THE YEAR
The Good Samaritan

INTRODUCTION AND CONFITEOR

Today we will hear again Christ's immortal parable about a man lying wounded by the roadside, and how two people passed him by while a third stopped and helped him.

Let us stop for a moment and call to mind the number of times we have passed by someone who needed help. (Pause).

Christ is our Good Samaritan. He does not pass us by. He cares for us, binding up our wounds.

Lord, like the Good Samaritan, you have compassion on us in our sorrows and sufferings.   Lord, have mercy.

Like the Good Samaritan, you bind up our wounds.   Christ, have mercy.

Like the Good Samaritan, you bring us to the Father's inn where we can experience his loving care.   Lord, have mercy.

HEADINGS FOR READINGS

First Reading (Deut. 30:10-14). Moses urges the people to obey God's law, not as something imposed from outside them, but as something that springs up from inside themselves.

Second Reading (Colossians 1:15-20). Paul asserts the absolute supremacy of Christ. He is the beginning and end of creation, the head of the Church, and the universal mediator and redeemer.

Gospel (Luke 10:25-37). This relates Christ's immortal parable of the Good Samaritan.

HOMILY

This is undoubtedly one of the most straightforward of Christ's parables. It doesn't call for a lot of discussion. What it does call for is action: 'Go, and *do the same* yourself.' What is most disturbing in Christ's story is not so much the attack made on an innocent man, but the fact that two people who might be expected to help him pass by without even showing compassion for him, not that compassion by itself would have done any good. How could their feelings be so dulled, and their sympathies so atrophied? This indifference to the pain and sufferings of others is so widespread today. The defiant cry of Cain rises on all sides: 'I am not my brother's keeper.'

Philip Toynbee (son of the famous historian, Arnold Toynbee) relates a strange and shocking incident that happened to him. He had gone to a meeting near Cambridge, and had parked his car in a pub car park. When he got back to the car he found three police cars outside the pub, their blue lights winking on top of them.

He looked for the cause of the police presence and saw a wrecked motorbike against the wall. Then he saw a lot of blood on the road, and noticed a dented crash helmet lying some ten yards away. On enquiring what had happened he was told that about half an hour previously a young man on the bike had hit the side of a van and ricocheted into the corner of the porch. His body had just been taken away and the police were now busy taking photos with flash bulbs in the rainy darkness.

He went into the pub. Inside it would have been impossible to guess that anything unusual had happened. There was loud jukebox music, loud laughter, rattling tills — that peculiar kind of hectic din which is heard in pubs late on a week-end evening. Nobody was talking about the young man who had just been killed on the other side of the very wall where the jukebox was beating and blaring.

He asked himself the cause of this? Was it shock at what had happened? Was it that they were putting on a stiff upper lip? Or were they just determined that nothing should spoil their fun? He couldn't decide which of these had produced that astonishing appearance of total indifference, but it looked as if it was the last reason more than the others. It was this indifference that shocked him more than the incident itself. After all, accidents like this are, unfortunately, all too common today.

Why did the priest and the levite not stop? Because the first question that came to their mind was: 'What will happen to me if I stop?' Whereas the first question that came to the Samaritan's mind was: 'What will happen to the wounded man if I don't stop?' He makes it all sound so simple, because he is not thinking of what will be the result for himself — he is not even interested in that — but only of what he ought to do.

People today are very cautious about getting involved. Getting involved is a messy business. It disrupts your life. You never know the amount of trouble you are letting yourself in for if you decide to answer a cry for help. It is much safer, and far easier, to close your heart and go quietly by on the other side of the road.

'The most widespread form of betrayal was not to do anything bad directly, but just not to notice the doomed person next to one, not to help him, to turn away one's face, to shrink back. They [the KGB] arrested a neighbour, your comrade at work, or even a close friend. But you kept silent. You acted as if you had seen nothing.' (Solzhenistyn). Yet how often we unthinkingly define a good neighbour as 'one who always minds his own business.'

The strong point in Christ's story is that it involved a Samaritan helping a Jew. It is the most unlikely peson who emerges as the hero. The man who helped was not even a religious man. And he too could have conjured up several good reasons for not getting involved. Why hadn't the priest and the levite helped? After all, it was their job, so to speak. Besides, it was a dangerous road on which to hang about. Then, to cap it all, the wounded man was a Jew, and they hated the Samaritans. Yet the Samaritan brushed all these reasons aside and opened his heart to the wounded man. His reaction was instinctive. Why? Because he was that kind of man. He could not find it in him to pass by a fellow human being who was wounded and crying out for help. He was immediately 'moved with compassion.' But he didn't leave it at that. He stopped to help.

At one time or another we've all acted like the priest and the levite. We have passed by someone who needed our help. We refused to get involved. No doubt in each case we could come up with highly plausible excuses. But when all is said and done, the real reason we did not help is that we lack concern for a fellow human being. We were simply too preoccupied with ourselves.

The parable of Christ is more relevant today than ever before. How many people today lie wounded by the roadside of life. Their wounds are not always visible. Many of today's deepest wounds are invisible. They are not physical and do not therefore show up on the outside. People can be wounded in spirit. Perhaps there are such people on my own street, if not in my own house: a depressed man who has lost his wife, a man who has worked all his life and is now suddenly redundant, a deserted wife and mother, lonely kids, forgotten old people . . . all waiting, lying quietly there maybe not having the courage to call out, waiting for the coming of a Good Samaritan.

Is my heart big enough to embrace even some of these? Ah, Good Samaritan, in a world of indifference and preoccupation with self, you shine out like a light in the dark. You are like water in the desert.

'A drop of help is worth an ocean of pity.' (Proverb).

'Speeding by go the buses without stopping, signalling what I must never signal: FULL.' (Helder Camara).

PRAYER OF THE FAITHFUL

Let us pray that we may learn the lesson of Christ's great parable and put it into practice in our daily lives. *R.* Lord, hear us in your love.

For all Christians: that they may not follow the example of the priest and levite, who put their own safety first, ignoring the cries of the wounded man. (Pause). We pray in faith.

For all those in public office: that they may show special care for the weak, wounded and vulnerable members of society. (Pause). We pray in faith.

For all those in the caring professions: doctors, nurses, firemen, ambulance personnel . . . that they may carry out their tasks with Christlike compassion. (Pause). We pray in faith.

That we may be aware of what is happening around us, keeping our eyes and hearts open so that we may respond at once to any cry for help. (Pause). We pray in faith.

For local needs.

Let us pray:

Lord, you taught us to care for one another, and you set us an example. You got involved so deeply with us that it cost you your life. You may not demand as much from us, but we ask your grace to respond to whatever calls your love makes on us. We make all our prayers through Christ our Lord.

COMMUNION REFLECTION

Often we never know exactly who it is
we are meeting in the person of our neighbour.

In the year 1880 in Paris
a rather poorly dressed priest showed up at a presbytery,
looking for a night's lodgings.
He had come from Turin,
and was trying to raise funds to build a church.

The visitor's name was John Bosco.
The resident priest put him in the attic.
Many years later when John Bosco was canonised,
the priest said: 'Had I known who it was,
I would not have put him in the attic.
I would have given him the best room in the house.'

Often we know even less of the true identity
of those we come across who are in need of help.
But it shouldn't matter.

All that matters is
that we see in each of them a wounded human being,
and that we do our best to bind up their wounds.

SIXTEENTH SUNDAY OF THE YEAR
Putting first things first

INTRODUCTION AND CONFITEOR

When we come to celebrate the Eucharist we are sometimes told that we should leave behind us our cares and concerns. Rather, what we should do is bring them with us and lay them at the feet of Christ. This is what a woman called Mary does in the Gospel of today. Let us do that. (Pause).

Let us now confess our sins to God and to each other.

I confess to almighty God . . .

HEADINGS FOR READINGS

First Reading (Genesis 18:1-10). When Abraham gave hospitality to three strangers he did not know that he was entertaining God himself. The strangers reward him with the good news that his wife is to bear him a child.

Second Reading (Colossians 1:24-28). Paul suffers for his converts. He is a minister of 'that mystery hidden for generations,' namely the calling of the Gentiles to salvation.

Gospel (Luke 10:38-42). The sisters, Martha and Mary, welcome Jesus into their home in Bethany, though each does so in a different way.

HOMILY

It's the easiest thing in the world to get one's priorities wrong. It happened to Martha. It's amazing how the trivia jump to the forefront and clamour for immediate attention, whereas the important things are left to later, perhaps forgotten and remain undone, or if they are done they are rushed and consequently badly done.

Two women went to Lourdes on a pilgrimage. Why did they go there? They wanted to bring their pains and sufferings, cares and anxieties, to God, and to lay their lives before him. That in essence was why each of them went there. But this is what happened when they got there.

The first woman immediately forgot the main purpose of her visit. She started to rush around to see the sights. Everywhere she went there were fast-moving crowds. Without noticing it she simply got swept along by the current, pausing only to take the ritual photos. In her rounds she saw lots of glittering souvenirs. She might as well buy them now in case there might not be time later or she might run short of money. It took a lot of time and energy to choose the ones she liked and to make sure that no one back home was forgotten. Then she took them back to the hotel where she wrapped them up and put them away carefully.

Now that she had started down that particular path she felt she might as well go to the end. What about all those cards she had promised to send? No time like the present. So off she went and bought a whole bunch of cards. It took several hours to get them written. Again she had to be careful not to forget anyone or she would never hear the end of it when she got back. Now that she had written them she might as well post them. She walked to the post office and was happy to see the end of them.

She heaved a huge sigh of relief and said to herself: 'Now I must go and say some prayers.' But by now she was just about ready to drop from exhaustion. When she got to the grotto she had neither the will nor the energy to pray. One has to be in good form to pray. It's not an easy exercise. We need to be fresh. Hence it has to get the best time of the day. But she had given it the worst time — the end of the day when she was worn out. She decided to leave it until tomorrow and headed for bed. She didn't realise that the organisers had a very busy day planned for tomorrow.

What about her friend? As soon as she arrived at Lourdes, she took a little nap in the hotel after booking in. Then refreshed she headed for the shrine. On the way she passed by souvenir and card shops. They could wait. She remembered why she had come. She made her way to the grotto where she recollected herself, and in a spirit of love and trust, sought to assemble the fragments of her scattered life and lay them before her God. It was such a beautiful place. There was something in the atmosphere that made it easy to pray. She had to tear herself away from it eventually, but when she returned to her hotel she felt refreshed in body as well as in spirit. She looked forward to deepening this experience during the days ahead.

Martha and Mary welcomed the Lord to their house. The first thing Martha thought about was to prepare a good meal for him — a very kind and hospitable thought. Being a very practical woman she got down to work at once. There was a lot of work involved because as far as she was concerned only the very best was good enough for Jesus. We can easily sympathise with her. We can even admire her. But she has her priorities wrong. There is something more important that she is neglecting. And that is to listen to his words.

Mary, on the other hand, gets her priorities right. First things first. Here is a priceless opportunity to hear the words of the man who claimed to have the very words of eternal life itself. Afterwards she will be able to see to the other things. She remembers that he once said: 'I did not come to have service done to me but to serve.' So she sits at his feet and drinks in his words.

Poor Martha! It's not simply that she is busy, but that she is *too busy,* so much so that she has time for nothing else. She is anxious, distracted, troubled and agitated. She has become a slave of her duties. Her work has swallowed her whole. But Mary has got it right. 'Mary has chosen the better part.' The better part means the more important part, and this is the person of Jesus and his word. Wasn't that the very reason why he had come — to speak his word?

Most of us should be able to identify with Martha. We rush about, busy with many things, yet constantly short of time. We neglect people. We don't have time to listen to them. It's very difficult to drink from a fast-flowing stream, but so easy to drink from a calm deep pool. Neither have we time to reflect on our lives, to listen to the word of God and to pray. Yet without the word of God we are blind and our activities are rendered barren, or at least they leave us drained and empty. We end up as the slaves of our jobs and duties.

But God's word 'is a lamp for my steps and a light for my path.' We have to listen to his word so that we may do his will, and surely to do his will is the whole purpose of our lives. What a lot of words we listen to in the course of a week — gossip, conversation, radio, television . . . Yet we may end the week without having even one minute for the word of God. Is it any wonder that sometimes we are like a man lost in a forest, beating his way through the undergrowth, sweating and straining, constantly exhausted yet going nowhere? Whereas with a little time for thought and reflection we might be like a person who has found a sure path through the woods, and who walks that path calmly and resolutely. We go to Mass and receive Communion, but often just out of routine. Or it is just a shortcut, or a slight detour, on our way to more important business.

No matter how busy we are we must take time to listen to another voice, the one near us who is forever chiding us with 'You never listen to me'. We have to live and eat and work. But we must try to stop worrying and fretting. From time to time we must stop, if only for a few minutes. God is saying: 'Be still. I, your God, want to speak to you. I have something important to say to you.' I hope we can learn from the example of Mary.

'There are a hundred Marthas in the world for every one Mary.' (Philip Toynbee).

'Spiritual awakening is the most essential thing in a man's life, and it is the sole purpose of his being.' (Kahlil Gibran).

PRAYER OF THE FAITHFUL

Let us pray that we may welcome Jesus into our hearts and into our lives as Mary did, and that like her, we may choose the better part. *R.* Lord, hear our prayer.

For the followers of Jesus: that like Mary they may always be conscious of their need of his peace, healing and forgiveness. (Pause). Let pray to the Lord.

For all our leaders: that they may listen to Christ and be guided by his teaching in all the difficult decisions they have to make. (Pause). Let us pray to the Lord.

For people who feel abandoned, left out and rejected: that they may meet with acceptance and be brought in from the cold. (Pause). Let us pray to the Lord.

That we may be open people, ready to share with others, ready to accept them and make them welcome, since we know that the Lord has made us welcome. (Pause). Let us pray to the Lord.

For local needs.

Let us pray:

God our Father, you sent your Son among us to seek out and to save the lost, to welcome back into your family all those who are despised and rejected, and to offer to all a place at the banquet of your kingdom. Help us to be open to him and to the gifts he wants to bring us in your name. We ask this through the same Christ our Lord.

COMMUNION REFLECTION

Placing ourselves in the presence of God.
The first thing we have to do is to be still physically.
Next we have to halt the mind,
something which is far more difficult to do.
We have to empty it of our cares, anxieties and plans.
Then we make a surprising discovery —
the world turns without us.
This means that neither we nor our schemes,
which may appear to us to be of the utmost importance,
and which are devouring all our energies,
are as important as we imagine.

Then our projects lose their power over us.
A healing process begins.
Far from the strain and turmoil of life,
our fragmented self is reassembled.
We slowly become whole again.
We rest quietly in the presence of God,

like a little boat which has been tossed by the sea,
and buffetted by the wind,
rests secure in a sheltered harbour.

In his presence we experience our true worth,
which consists, not in doing, but in being.
We surrender ourselves into his hands.
We are at peace.
Even our dreams have been put to sleep.

SEVENTEENTH SUNDAY OF THE YEAR
How to pray

INTRODUCTION AND CONFITEOR

The Mass is above all a great opportunity to pray. The Mass is
a prayer — the greatest of all prayers. So let us make sure that we
do pray it. The word of God will tell us the kind of things for which
a Christian ought to pray. At the same time we have to open our
hearts and make the prayers and needs of others our own.
(Pause).

Let us begin by asking for forgiveness for our sins.

I confess to almighty God . . . etc.

HEADINGS FOR READINGS

First Reading (Genesis 18:20-32). Abraham intercedes with God
on behalf of Sodom, a city full of evil. We catch the flavour of the
bargaining that might go on in an oriental bazaar with prices being
ruthlessly slashed.

Second Reading (Colossians 2:12-14). Through Baptism a Christian is inserted into Christ's death and resurrection; he dies to the
old sinful way of life, and rises to live a new life.

Gospel (Luke 11:1-13). The apostles ask Christ to teach them
how to pray. In reply Christ urges them to come to the Father, and
with childlike trust, to pray to him for all their spiritual and
temporal needs.

HOMILY

(Note: there are two separate topics in what follows).

(1) I have always been fascinated by the picture of Abraham
pleading with God to save Sodom and Gomorrah provided he
could find in them a handful of just people. The idea coming across
is that a handful of just people will not be punished even for the

sake of punishing a multitude of wicked people. Yet how often this happens in our world. Indeed, we even go to the opposite extreme — we are quite willing to punish a multitude of innocent people as long as there are a few guilty people among them. Let us take a few examples.

When governments are fighting against guerrillas, it often happens that they think nothing of wiping out a whole batch of men, women and children, provided that in doing so they can get rid of a few guerrillas. It happened in Derry, in Vietnam, in Argentina, and many other places. It should be pointed out that guerrillas tend to use the same tactics.

It happens in the classroom. The teacher goes out for a while. When she returns to the classroom something has happened, say a chair has been broken. No matter how she pleads or threatens she cannot find out the culprit. He won't own up and the others won't give his name. So what does the teacher do? She punishes the whole class. Detention for all!

The same thing happens at home. A valuable cup from a set gets broken when the mother has her back turned. Nobody owns up. So all the children are punished: 'No TV for the rest of the evening! You'll all go straight to bed when you have your homework done.'

It happens so often that you would think it part of our mentality. But it's wrong. God will never resort to it. He will not pull up a bunch of weeds in case he might uproot even one stalk of wheat while doing so. It's terrible to be punished for something you did not do. It leaves you with a terrible feeling of bitterness. It's so unfair. Solzhenitsyn says: 'Neither our education, nor our upbringing, nor our experience prepares us in the slightest for the greatest trial of our lives: being arrested for nothing and being interrogated for nothing.'

Yet we often resort to it as the first resort, as the most natural and just way of solving our problem. We are quite willing to punish ninety nine innocent people provided we are thereby sure of also punishing the one guilty person. But God's ways are not our ways, as the first reading tells us. God will not punish a hundred people, though ninety nine of them are guilty, as long as there is even one just person among them.

Philip Toynbee tells how he was once hitch-hiking in France. He stood for forty minutes hailing cars and lorries without success. He noticed the coldly dismissive glances of the drivers with sadness but without anger. But finally one man stopped and gave him and his wife a lift. The amiability of the man more than made up for the almost violent indifference of the others. As he said: 'One just man can save a whole city.'

(2) Both readings (the Gospel in particular) are about prayer, especially prayer of petition. But often we don't even know what we want, much less what is truly good for us. Today we want one thing, tomorrow we want something else.

A man was so pestering God that one day God decided to give him three wishes in the hope of getting rid of him! Straightaway the man made his first wish. Regretfully he asked that his wife might die so that he could marry a more suitable woman. His wish was granted.

But at the funeral he was flabbergasted at the number of people who praised his deceased wife. He never realised she had so many admirable qualities. He realised that he had made a mistake. So he asked God to bring her back to life. This left him with only one wish.

He found it very hard to make up his mind, as he couldn't afford another mistake. Should he ask for immortality, or for money, or for good health? Unable to decide he asked God for advice. God laughed at him and said: 'Just ask to be contented no matter what life brings you.'

In the Gospel we are given the great prayer of Jesus — the Our Father. It is a prayer for all times and for every occasion. It embraces in its short and simple phrases every relation between us and our heavenly Father. It is at once the most simple of prayers and the most profound. If one lived it, by putting each of its phrases into practice in daily life, then he would indeed be perfect as his heavenly Father dearly wishes him to be. The Our Father is the beginning and end of all prayers. An interesting thing to note about it is that everything is in the plural.

But even the Our Father can become a prayer we say simply by rote. Rote formulas, in and of themselves, are no more prayers than the barkings of a dog are truly speech. God may hear and understand, as we may hear and feed a barking dog. Real prayer is when we place ourselves in the presence of God. Then even our thoughts become prayers, so that words are often superfluous.

Consider some of the things Jesus said we should pray for: for our daily bread — for what we need just for today, not for tomorrow; that we might be able to forgive so that we may be forgiven; that we might be able to overcome our temptations, and that we might be delivered from evil.

But Christ also gives us the climate in which we should pray. This climate is one of love and trust. We are praying to our heavenly Father who loves us and cares about us. He alone knows what is truly good for us. In a nutshell: we are invited to pray that we may do his will rather than our own will. We should ask, seek and knock so that we may discover what God's will is for us, and then ask for the courage and the strength to do it.

'God is not someone who grants our wishes; he is someone who fulfils our hopes'. (Antony Padovano).

'The word of the Gospel is understood only when it is obeyed.' (Thomas Merton).

PRAYER OF THE FAITHFUL

Let us pray in the spirit of the Our Father: with unlimited confidence in God, in his love for us and presence with us. *R.* Lord, hear our prayer.

For the followers of Jesus: that they may seek to know the will of the Father and have the grace and strength to do it in their daily lives. (Pause).   Let us pray to the Lord.

For all those responsible for public order: that they may work for the coming of the Kingdom of God: a kingdom of holiness and truth, a kingdom of justice, love and peace. (Pause).   Let us pray to the Lord.

For those in special need: the sick, the troubled, the lonely, the despairing . . . (Pause).   Let us pray to the Lord.

That we may have the 'bread' to meet our daily needs: the greatness of heart to be able to forgive; the courage to love even our enemies; the strength to overcome our temptations and all evil. (Pause).   Let us pray to the Lord.

For local needs.

Let us pray:

Lord, teach us to pray: to go on confidently asking, to go on joyfully seeking, to go on hopefully knocking at the door, so that the good things you want to give us may be ours. We make all our prayer through your Son, our Lord Jesus Christ, who lives and reigns with you and the Holy Spirit, one God, for ever and ever.

COMMUNION REFLECTION
Asking, seeking, and knocking.

Christ said that the person who asked would receive;
the person who searched would find;
and the person who knocked would have the door opened to him.

But if a person asks in a half-hearted way,
then he will not receive.
And if he fears to lose the pleasures of the old world,
then he will not find the joys of a new world.
And if he knocks half fearing that the door will open,

so that he will go in and be shut off
from the comforts of the world,
then the door will not open to him.

There are some people who are unwilling
to renounce a single one of their former values
in order to gain a new one.
Such people will never be unified or free,
and they make it very difficult for themselves
to enter the kingdom of God.

EIGHTEENTH SUNDAY OF THE YEAR
How much is enough?

INTRODUCTION AND CONFITEOR

Possessions exercise a big hold over the human heart. But when we are preoccupied with material possessions we forget the more important things in life. Jesus said our main concern should be to 'make ourselves rich in the sight of God.'

Let us examine ourselvs briefly on our attitude to possessions. (Pause).

Lord Jesus, you help us to trust in the heavenly Father rather than in money and possessions.   Lord, have mercy.

Lord Jesus, you help us to share rather than to hoard.   Christ, have mercy.

Lord Jesus, you help us to serve others rather than wait for them to serve us.   Lord, have mercy.

HEADINGS FOR READINGS

First Reading (Ecclesiastes 1:2; 2:21-23). The writer points out that the things that are supposed to satisfy human beings do not satisfy them. Look at all the toil and effort a person puts into acquiring wealth. To what purpose? — to leave it to his heir.

Second Reading (Col 3:1-5, 9-11). One consequence of death and resurrection with Christ (through Baptism) is that the Christian's true home is now in heaven. Therefore, he must seek the things that are above by leading a good life in this world.

Gospel (Luke 12:13-21). This contains a warning against greed. We are urged to make ourselves rich, not in the goods of this world, but in the sight of God.

HOMILY

A certain amount of money and material possessions are necessary if we are to live up to our dignity as human beings and children of God. Christ was aware of this. His parable is not then about *need*. It is about *greed* pure and simple. The man in the story was rich to begin with, but he still wasn't satisfied. Greed is like a fire — the more wood you pile on it, the hungrier it gets. For the greedy person there is no such thing as enough.

Tolstoy tells a story about a peasant called Pakhom. Pakhom had only one grievance. He had no land. 'Only give me land, and I will fear no man,' he said. Then some land became available. This was his big chance. By scraping together every penny he had, he put down a deposit, and lo! he was a landowner. He had forty acres. He was overjoyed. The very grass seemed to grow greener, the flowers bloomed sweeter there than anywhere else. So it appeared to Pakhom.

For a time he was happy. But then he began to feel cramped. He heard that in another region better land was available. So he sold out, moved there, and bought eighty acres. And excellent land it was. Only thing there wasn't enough of it. If he had more he could produce more. So once again he felt cramped. Still, he stayed there for five years and made a lot of money.

Then one evening a stranger arrived at his house. Pakhom gave him hospitality for the night. He told the stranger about his desire for more land. Then the stranger told him that away to the south, beyond the mountains, there lived a tribe of people who had an endless amount of land, all excellent grassland. 'The people there are as simple as sheep,' said the stranger. 'You can get anything out of them for next to nothing.'

Off he went and found everything exactly as his visitor had described. The people and their chieftain gave him a warm welcome and were most appreciative of the gifts he brought with him. They told him he could have as much land as he wanted and wherever he wanted it. There was only one condition: 'We sell by the day,' said the chieftain. 'As much land as you can walk round in a day, that much is yours for only a thousand roubles. You must, however, return to the spot from whence you start on the same day, otherwise your money is forfeited.'

Pakhom thought this was an excellent bargain. He couldn't sleep all that night, thinking of the land that would soon be his. He arose before sunrise and did not even wait for breakfast. 'I have no time to lose,' he kept saying. As soon as the sun peeped above the horizon a marker was put in the ground on top of a knoll, and he was off. Men followed him on horseback and drove stakes into the ground to mark the path he traced out.

He walked fast and made excellent progress. The farther he went the better the land became. Dinner time came and he was getting weaker. He grabbed a bite but continued walking. He began to veer to his left. But it was difficult to close the circle. Time flew. In his eagerness to encompass as much as he could, he lost track of time. Then to his horror he saw the sun beginning to sink in the western sky. Even though the knoll lay a long way off he headed for it as fast as he could. Only now he was worn out from hunger and walking. Ah, if only the sun would wait for him! But it wouldn't. Now he was delirious and had lost all thought of land. If only he could make it to the top of the knoll before the sun went down. And he did. He just made it to the top as the sun vanished. Once there, however, he collapsed face downwards on the ground.

'Ah,' said the chieftain, 'I congratulate you. You have earned much land, more than any man I can remember.'

But Pakhom made no reply. They turned him over. He was dead. They buried him where he fell.

So how much is enough? When we have obtained those things which are necessary to live (food, clothes, shelter, warmth . . .) where do we go from there? Do we go on to stockpile more of them, or do we go in pursuit of superfluities? Some people are rich, but only in superfluous items. They neglect themselves. They neglect the quality of their lives. They end up as impoverished human beings. 'People have come to such a pass that they frequently starve, not for want of necessities, but for want of luxuries.' (Thoreau). It was Thoreau who also said that after we have acquired the necessities there is an alternative to seeking more and more of the same. We can then *really live*. We can go for depth and quality. He also said: 'Money is not required to buy one necessity of the soul.'

Christ's parable is not directed only at the rich. It is directed at each of us, for anyone can be bitten by bug of greed. A poor person can be just as greedy as a wealthy person, maybe even more greedy. It is not how much you possess that does the damage, but your attitude towards what you possess. Happiness is not having what you want, but wanting what you have.

Acquisitiveness is the most foolish of all vices. No amount of possessions can make our lives on earth secure. We enrich ourselves not by grabbing all we can from life, but by giving, as any fruit tree shows us. By all means let us work to improve our lot for ourselves and our families. But let us heed Christ's words: 'Make yourself rich in the sight of God.' Let this be our priority.

Goodness of life is the real treasure. A good person is a rich person. An empty heart is the only poverty we should fear, that is, a heart which is devoid of love, and peace, and serenity. It is not what we carry in our purses or in our bank accounts that makes us rich. It is what we carry in our hearts. To live well and happily a person actually needs very little. If you want a fire to burn brightly, you don't have to put a mountain of firewood on it. A little will do, provided it is dry and seasoned.

Even though the man in Christ's story was wise after an earthly fashion Christ called him a 'fool'. Why? Because he neglected the three most important factors: (a) he forgot God; (b) he forgot eternal life — his wealth gave him a bogus immortality; (c) he forgot his obligations to the poor.

When all is said and done, is there even one person who works as hard at his personal life as he does at his professional life?

'The poor person is the one with many needs: the rich person is the one with few needs.' (Plato).

'We prove our greatness, not by the amount of our possessions, but by the grandeur of our actions.' (Solzhenitsyn).

PRAYER OF THE FAITHFUL

Often in life we don't know what we want or what is truly important. Let us, therefore, pray for the gift of wisdom that we may get our priorities in tune with those of the Gospel. *R.* Lord, graciously hear us.

For the followers of Christ: that they may not judge success in life by the amount of money they earn or the amount of possessions they manage to acquire. (Pause). Lord, hear us.

For our political leaders: that they may work untiringly to ensure a fair distribution of the wealth of the country. (Pause). Lord, hear us.

For the poor and the dispossessed: that they may experience the closeness of Christ to them in their poverty. (Pause). Lord, hear us.

That we may realise that the most valuable things in life are things which no amount of money can buy — things such as health, friendships, peace of mind, and goodness of heart. (Pause). Lord, hear us.

For local needs.

Let us pray.

Lord, deliver us from the demon of greed for material things, so that we may seek to grow in favour with our heavenly Father and with our fellow-man. We ask this of you who live and reign for ever and ever.

COMMUNION REFLECTION
Elvis Presley owned eight cars, six motorbikes,
two planes, and a vast mansion as a home.
In that mansion he had sixteen tv sets.
He had several bank accounts,
one of which contained a million dollars.
Yet he died at forty-two of drug abuse,
a sad and pathetic figure.
What did it profit him?

'People,' said the Little Prince,
'rush about in express trains,
but they do not know what they are looking for.
They raise five thousand roses in the same garden,
and they still do not find what they are looking for.
Yet what they are looking for
could be found in a single rose.'

Lord Jesus, teach us wisdom of heart.
Help us to live lives that are worthy
of sons and daughters of the heavenly Father,
and thus we will make ourselves rich in his sight.

NINETEENTH SUNDAY OF THE YEAR
Watchful servants

INTRODUCTION AND CONFITEOR
   Today's Gospel says that both Jesus and the thief come to us 'at
an hour we least expect'. But there the similarity ends. The thief
comes to rob us. Jesus comes to surprise us with his gifts. Like
faithful servants we must be always on the alert for his coming. But
are we? Do we not often live carelessly and foolishly, as if we were
not accountable to God for our lives? (Pause).
   Let us ask forgiveness for our sins of sloth and carelessness.
   I confess to almighty God . . . etc.

HEADINGS FOR READINGS
   First Reading (Wisdom 18:6-9). This reading realls that, when
the Jews suffered in Egypt, God came to their rescue. Those who
put their trust in the Lord will not be disappointed.
   Second Reading (Hebrews 11:1-2, 8-19). This recalls the
magnificent faith that Abraham had in God. Little wonder that in

one of the eucharistic prayers we refer to him as 'our father in faith'.

Gospel (Luke 12:32-48). Shorter form recommended). This contains among other things the parable of the waiting servants. It urges a constant watchfulness and faithfulness.

HOMILY

The hardest thing of all to achieve is to serve another person freely and out of love. But if we achieve it, we not only make the work a lot lighter, but we remove all fear and compulsion from it. We will not spend our time looking over our shoulder to see if 'the boss' is watching us. We will do what has to be done whether he is absent or present. This is the ideal today's Gospel puts before us regarding our service of Christ, our Master.

There was a king who had a number of servants working for him. He placed great trust in them and allowed them a lot of freedom. He was a kind-hearted and open man, yet no simpleton. And though he was not one to intrude, he knew the games servants sometimes get up to.

There was a hierarchy of jobs to be done in and around the palace. Some of these were highly coveted and keenly sought after: jobs such as that of valet, butler, chauffeur, gardener, groundsman, and so on. Besides providing a clean and comfortable work place, one full of pleasant sights and scents, these jobs kept you in the limelight. You were working right under the gaze of the king. He couldn't fail to notice you.

If you got one of these jobs you were made. Not only were you assured of an easy life, but if you played your cards right and availed of every opportunity to ingratiate yourself with the king, then higher jobs were almost sure to come your way. You might, for instance, be made an ambassador. To impress the king then become the name of the game for many of the servants. They were full of eyes and ears. They watched each other as well as every move the king made. When the king was present their manners were impeccable, their work perfect, and their attitude one of total subserviance. But when the king was absent these same servants were the first to speak disparagingly about him, and they sat about doing as little as possible, sometimes even drinking and playing cards late into the night. Of course they claimed to love their king, but theirs was a mercenary love. There was no true love in their service, and no respect either.

Now down at the other end were those who worked at menial jobs, done in near total obscurity. Indeed some of these jobs bordered on the degrading and the humiliating, like working in joyless sculleries and dank cellars. Now those who worked in these lowly and obscure places were by no means paragons of virtue. Indeed many of them saw their work as a life-long, grim, painful and unrelenting duty. Their service was poisoned with a mixture of aversion and loathing. They looked on their work as a curse and a burden, without any redeeming features. Only a handful did their work in a way that fostered their dignity and worth as persons.

I now want to introduce you to the hero of this little story. His name was Patrick, and he did the lowest job of all — disposing of the royal refuse and taking care of the dump. The dump was hidden behind a tall hedge at the far end of the gardens. It was an ugly place. When he was not working on it Patrick was going back and forth transporting foul-smelling refuse bins in his wheelbarrow. As the gardener would not allow him to go through his neat garden, Patrick had to go all the way round on the outside of the perimeter hedge. In this way he went back and forth completely unnoticed. The smoke rising from the incinerator was about the only visible sign of his service and of his existence.

Yet, strange as it may seem, Patrick didn't perish in this obscurity. Though a man of little education, he was a rare man, and brought an astonishing purity of attitude to his lowly task. While most of those in high positions served the king either out of fear of losing their privileges or in the hope of winning further rewards, Patrick served his king out of love. Even though he was very conscious that he was a 'mere binman', as the others referred to him, Patrick knew who he really was. He was a servant of a very worthy king. As far as he was concerned it was a privilege to be in his service. This attitude of his added a very special dimension to his life. Without it the work, which was tedious and tiring, dull and dirty, would undoubtedly have got him down. Whether the king was present or absent made no difference. He had a very necessary job to do and he did it. As a consequence he enjoyed a deep serenity of mind that baffled those above him.

On one occasion the king returned unexpectedly from a trip abroad. On his arrival he walked right through the house and out into the gardens. He noticed things lying about, and no trace of the servants. They were having a siesta. Though he observed everything he made no comment. Then he headed for the dump. There he found Patrick at his job. On seeing his king Patrick was mortified.

'I'm sorry, your Majesty,' he said. 'If I had known you were coming I'd have cleaned myself up.'

'Don't worry,' said the king. 'Patrick, I have good news for you. You may have thought that your work was going unnoticed. It wasn't. I saw everything you did. Now I want you to come to the palace tonight. Bring your wife and family with you. I am giving a dinner in your honour. Then I'll tell you about a very important job I want you to do for me.'

Patrick protested that he wasn't worthy of such an honour but the king would have none of it. When the other servants heard this they were green with envy. They were not invited to the dinner, and were told that on the next day their positions would be reviewed!

I hope this little story captures some of the flavour and the spirit of today's Gospel which contains the warning Jesus gave to his disciples, when he urged them to be like good and faithful servants, ever-watchful for the return of their master. I don't think it is necessary to refer this 'return' to death, but if we do, then the story brings out a very important lesson.

For most people it's just not possible to be ready for death, in the sense of having one's work done and all the loose ends neatly tied up. Death frequently comes as the great intruder and disrupter of a person's life and plans. It comes when least expected. But death means an encounter with the Master, namely, Christ. It doesn't matter whether or not we have done everything we would like to have done. All that matters is the spirit of our service: the quality and depth, the warmth and love of the relationship we have built up with Christ.

Alas, many people are much more ready for the coming of the thief than for the coming of Christ.

'Stay awake, because you do not know the day nor the hour of your master's return . . . These words shake me like the wind shakes a tree.' (Catherine de Hueck Doherty).

'We always pay dearly for chasing after what is cheap.' (Solzhenitsyn).

PRAYER OF THE FAITHFUL

Let us pray for the grace to follow the warning of the Gospel, so that when Christ comes to us in life or in death we may be ready for him and welcome him with joy.   R. Lord, hear us in your love.

Christ says: 'Fear not!': that Christians may follow him out of love and never out of fear. (Pause).   We ask this in faith.

Christ says: 'Keep your belts fastened': that our leaders may lead not just by word but also by example. (Pause).   We ask this in faith.

Christ says: 'Keep your lamps burning': for those who live foolishly and recklessly as if they were accountable to no one for their conduct. (Pause).   We ask this in faith.

Christ says: 'Stay awake!': that we may be saved from laziness

and all forms of apathy so that we may not squander life's opportunities. (Pause).   We ask this in faith.
   For local needs.
   Let us pray:
   Heavenly Father, help us, the followers of your Son, to walk the
road of life as pilgrims of faith, messengers of hope, and sources
of love. We ask this through Christ, our Lord.

SIGN OF PEACE
   Lord Jesus Christ, you said to your disciples: 'If you are bringing
your gift to the altar, and there remember that someone has
something against you, leave your gift there before the altar, go
and be reconciled with that person first, and then come back and
present your offering.' By this you wanted us to know that we cannot be reconciled with our heavenly Father if we are not reconciled
with one another. Help us to seek reconciliation with one another,
so that we may enjoy the peace and unity of your kingdom where
you live for ever and ever.

COMMUNION REFLECTION
The trouble with Christ is
that he often comes at the wrong time,
and often wearing the wrong kind of clothes.

The other day he came to my door.
He couldn't have come at a worse time.
I had a hundred and one things to do.
He just stood there,
a faint smile on his face.

I didn't ask him to come in,
in case he might decide to stay all day.
Eventually I said: 'What do you want?'
'Nothing, I was just passing by,
so I thought I'd drop in and say "hello",' he replied.
Sensing my mood, he excused himself and went away.

When he was gone I was mad with myself.
Though he said he didn't want anything,
I'm sure he did want something.
He just wanted a little companionship.
But I refused him with the excuse that I was too busy.

Ah, if only he had come at a more suitable time.

TWENTIETH SUNDAY OF THE YEAR
Fire upon the earth

INTRODUCTION AND CONFITEOR

Does the teaching of Christ ever disturb me? Does it cause me to question the way I'm living? Does it ever bring me into conflict with those who do not live by the Gospel?

If it does not do so, it can only mean that I'm not really hearing it. Christ's teaching is like a sword that separates good from evil. It is like a fire that burns off the weeds but leaves the wheat. Let us reflect on this to see where we stand — with Christ or against him? (Pause).

Let us ask his forgiveness for our cowardice.

Lord Jesus, your teaching is like a sword that separates the true from the false.   Lord, have mercy.

Lord Jesus, your teaching is like a fire that separates the wheat from the chaff.   Christ, have mercy.

Lord Jesus, your teaching is like a great light that scatters the darkness of injustice and evil.   Lord, have mercy.

HEADINGS FOR READINGS

First Reading (Jeremiah 38:4-6, 8-10). This describes how the prophet Jeremiah was charged with treason and set upon by his enemies. Christians have always seen him as a figure of Christ.

Second Reading (Hebrews 12:1-4). The author exhorts his readers to persevere in their faith, regardless of cost. They must model themselves on Christ.

Gospel (Luke 12:49-53). The coming of Christ marks a time of division. People will be called on to declare their loyalties. This will result in disruption and dissension.

HOMILY

'I came to cast fire on the earth . . . I came, not to bring peace, but the sword.' *Fire* and *sword* — strange words to hear coming from Christ! Traditional weapons of torture, which unfortunately down the ages his followers haven't hesitated to use against their enemies. But we wouldn't expect Christ to use them. Nor did he. When James and John wanted him to call down fire and brimstone on a Samaritan village that refused them admittance, he told them they didn't know what they were talking about. And when Peter drew his sword in the garden Christ told him to put it away.

Obviously, then, these words are not meant to be taken literally but metaphorically. Yet they stand for something real and very strong in Christ. It is wrong to see Christ just as an exceptionally meek and gentle person. He was gentle but not weak. Think how the armed gang fell back in the garden when he came forward and identified himself. Not only do the terms 'fire' and 'sword' stand for something in himself, they also stand for something about his message. It caused disruption. It brought division. How could this be? There is no greater disrupter of the 'peace' than the man who preaches justice and truth. We have an outstanding example in Jeremiah. But let us take another example.

There was a village in northern India. Water was vital. But the people were lucky to have a good well. Only thing it was a long distance from the village. It was no joke for the women whose task it was to carry full pots on their heads from the well to their huts. The well was for those born into a caste. It was a gift from God to his faithful servants. Hence it was called 'God's well'. It was forbidden to the outcasts, those who belonged to no caste — the 'untouchables' as they were called. These had to make do with water scooped from drains and mud holes which caused all kinds of illnesses among their children. It was a peaceful and orderly village. Everybody knew their place: high caste, low caste, and no caste.

But one day a bright young idealistic engineer arrived in the village. He seemed a gentle, peace-loving chap. The villagers took to him at once. They also liked the idea he came up with. He noticed the long trek the women were forced to make daily to the well. He noticed the untouchables drinking out of mud holes. Moved with compassion he showed them plans he had drawn up for sinking a well right in the heart of the village. They would be spared the long and tiresome journey to the well. Clean and pure water would be available on tap in the village square. The women looked on the news as an answer to their prayers. The blueprint was produced and all were excited about it.

But the night before the drilling was due to start the young engineer let slip a remark: 'Of course the water will be available to everyone, even the untouchables.' He didn't know what he was letting himself in for. He stirred up a hornet's nest. No way would the villagers agree to share the water with the untouchables.

However, after some persuasion some did agree. Then the village was split in two. For a while the two factions faced each other and things threatened to turn nasty. But in the end those who were against sharing it prevailed. They turned on the young man and let him have it. 'Look!' they said. 'This used to be a quiet and peaceful village. Everything was normal until you came along.'

'Normal, did you say?' the engineer remarked, fighting back. 'Is it normal that some human beings should drink out of mud holes while others drink out of clear wells?'

But they wouldn't listen to him. They chased him out of the village, calling him a 'trouble-maker' and a 'disrupter of the peace'.

So you can see how the bringer of justice, without which peace has no meaning, can cause scandal and division. In much the same way Christ's message caused scandal and division, so that in that sense he brought a 'sword'. What he was saying was that God's mercy and forgiveness was being offered on equal terms to everybody, sinners and just alike. He said that the Kingdom of God was like a tree in whose branches all the birds of the air could find food and shelter. This meant that all of God's children are dear to him. All are equal in dignity. If any are special to him it is not the great ones but the little ones, the 'untouchables' — the poor, the weak, the vulnerable — these are special to him, special because they have greater need of his love and care.

This was a terrible blow to those who believed that they were superior — the scribes and Pharisees. It had the effect of an atomic bomb on their smug and enclosed world. They resisted, but Christ did not back down. He did not go for a softer option. This meant open conflict with the religious establishment of his day. He called them 'hypocrites', 'blind guides', and 'white-washd tombs'. Pretty strong language, I think you'll agree. They in their turn called him a 'trouble-maker', a 'man possessed', a 'breaker of the law', and so on. Hence we can see that Christ did not exactly bring peace. He brought disruption. He caused division. He forced people to declare where they stood — for or against the truth, for or against the light.

Ah, if he had said only 'nice' things! But he insisted on saying truthful things too, even when they were unwelcome. Hence the division caused. His words not only shocked but infuriated some. The words he spoke to the poor were different from those he spoke to the rich. The words he spoke to sinners were different from those he spoke to the smug Pharisees. We betray the Gospel if we reduce it to bland tidings to all in the same tone that blissfully ignores the differences between rich and poor, between the privileged and the dispossessed. Such an insipid Gospel would not be a leaven in the world.

As followers of Christ we should not be afraid to rock the boat if needs be. The true Christian is a threat, a source of division, a light that shows up the darkness, and is resented by those who want to remain in the darkness. Because of his sense of justice, the Christian will oppose those who exploit the weak and the poor. By his transparency he will come into conflict with those who trade in lies and dishonesty. By his dedication to others he will expose the selfishness of those who look after Number One. By his openness and tolerance he will come into conflict with the narrow-minded and bigoted. He shouldn't be surprised if he has to suffer. He is in very good company. Christ foresaw this: 'A servant is not greater than his master. If they persecuted me, they will persecute you too.' (John 15:20).

'When I give bread to the poor, they call me a saint. But when I ask why the poor have no bread, they call me a communist.' (Helder Camara).

'No man's praise can cheat me into thinking that to be good which is really evil.' (Thoreau).

PRAYER OF THE FAITHFUL

Let us pray that the fire Jesus came to kindle may burn brightly in our lives and that we may enkindle it in the world. *R.* Lord, hear our prayer.

That the Lord may purify all that is good in his followers, thus enabling them to be generous and courageous people. (Pause). Let us pray to the Lord.

For all those leaders who are genuinely working for peace and for a more just world: that the Lord may uphold them when they suffer because of this. (Pause). Let us pray to the Lord.

For all those who are neither hot nor cold, who always play it safe, never getting involved in issues of justice and truth. (Pause). Let us pray to the Lord.

That the Lord may help to separate us from all that is false and phoney, all that is shallow and unworthy, so that we may be better witnesses to him in the world. (Pause). Let us pray to the Lord.

For local needs.

Let us pray:

Lord, you came to set people's hearts on fire. You brought the warmth of the Father's love to those who lived in the coldness of rejection. You brought the sword of division wherever falsity reigned. Help us your followers to come out of the shadows and live in the sunshine of your Kingdom. For you live and reign for ever and ever.

SIGN OF PEACE

Lord Jesus Christ, you said to your disciples: 'Blessed are the peace-makers, they shall be called the children of God.' We are better at making war than making peace. Help us to put an end to all fighting and quarrelling, so that we may enjoy the peace and unity of your kingdom where you live for ever and ever.

COMMUNION REFLECTION

There are two kinds of silence.
There is the silence of the graveyard.
Here silence speaks of one thing — death.
This silence tends to frighten and repel.

Then there is the silence of a spring evening.
Not a leaf stirs,
Not a sound is heard except the music of the birds.
Yet all things are awake,
all things are growing.
This silence is mysterious and enchanting.

So there are two kinds of peace.
There is the peace of the swamp:
things look normal on the surface,
but its depths are full of rotten things.
Peace that is based on injustice is like that.
It is a false peace and Christ came to disrupt it.

But then there is true peace —
a peace in which all of God's children
have their basic rights respected,
and are able to live in freedom and dignity.
This is the peace Christ came to bring.
But peace like this doesn't happen.
It has to be made.
Sometimes the makers of it will be branded as troublemakers.
But Christ had another name for them.
He called them 'children of God'.

TWENTY-FIRST SUNDAY OF THE YEAR
The narrow gate

INTRODUCTION AND CONFITEOR

Christ warned his contemporaries not to pin their hopes of salvation on the mere fact that they were members of God's Chosen
People. He urged them to make their way in 'by the narrow gate'.
By this he meant they should deny themselves and strive, by the
grace of God, to live good lives.

We should rely on nothing but God's gratuitous love for us, and our whole aim should be concentrated on returning that love. Let us reflect on this for a moment. (Pause).

Let us ask his forgiveness and the grace to emend our lives.

I confess to almighty God . . .

HEADINGS FOR READINGS

First Reading (Isaiah 66:18-21). The author describes Jews making their way back from the ends of the earth to worship in the restored city of Jerusalem. With them they bring non-Jews who join them in worshipping the one God.

Second Reading (Hebrews 12:5-7, 11-13). As a father shows his concern for his son by seeing to it that he receives training in discipline, so God trains his children through suffering so that they may grow to maturity and reach their goal.

Gospel (Luke 13:22-30). The Kingdom of God is offered not just to the Jews but to people from the four corners of the world. However, only those who follow the path of Jesus will gain access to it.

HOMILY

It's amazing how easily people begin to take you for granted. You begin by doing a favour for another person out of the sheer goodness of your heart. For example, you volunteer to drive a neighbour's child to school. In a few short months the neighbour forgets that you are doing her a favour and begins to think that her child has exclusive rights to your car. When you confront her with the facts you find her not very receptive. There's a story to illustrate this.

A certain country had an old and beautiful custom. When the harvest had been gathered in, the people held a festival. The festival was held in the grounds of the royal palace. Now while most of the 'goodies' consumed at the festival were provided by the king, each guest was expected to make a small contribution. The country was famous for its wines. There wasn't a single household that did not produce its own vintage. The idea was that each guest would bring along a bottle of white wine to the festival. The wine was emptied into a large vat and all were free to drink from it.

Now while in theory the festival was open to all the people of the realm, in practice it came to be limited to those who lived in the immediate environs of the palace. Naturally, after the passage of time, the latter came to believe that they had exclusive rights to it. They resented the presence of outsiders. Indeed, they went so far as to refer to it as '*our* festival'. And the king, who was very old, appeared to go along with this. At least he never interfered.

But then the old king died and his son ascended the throne. He immediately introduced a number of much-needed reforms. The people rejoiced at having such an enlightened and progressive king. But when he decided to introduce changes into the festival, ah, that was another matter! He decided to throw it open to all his subjects. Rich and poor, outsiders and insiders, those from far away and those from nearby — all were welcome.

Those who believed that they had exclusive rights to the festival took a dim view of this. They thought the young king had lost his head. How could he treat everybody the same? Did he not owe something to those who had been loyal to his father? Some of them felt so strongly about this that they decided to boycott the festival. Those who did attend were in for a couple of shocks.

Now the castle had two gates; a wide main gate, and a narrow side gate. In the old days the main gate was always wide open on the day of the festival, though a guard was placed on it to see that no 'undesirables' got in. The first shock our friends got was to discover that the main gate was closed. A nearby sign read: 'Enter by the narrow gate'. When they got to the side gate another shock lay in store for them. They were made to enter one at a time, and servants posted there insisted not only on checking to see if they had brought a bottle of wine with them, but also in tasting it. The cheek of them! Who did they think they were anyway?

'What's this?' they exclaimed. 'A search? It was never like this in the old days. We object.'

'Sorry', the servants replied. 'but we have orders from the king. No one gets in who has not brought a bottle of wine.'

There was panic among their ranks. The reason was this. Some of them, relying on the fact that they had always been admitted as a matter of course, had been careless and neglected to bring a bottle of wine with them. Others, on hearing that outsiders had been invited, had decided to cheat. Unwilling to share their wine with strangers, who in their view were unworthy of being present, they had brought along water in dark bottles! When this was discovered they blushed and were humiliated in front of their neighbours. They were refused admittance. Naturally they protested vigorously:

'How come all those strangers have been admitted while we, who are the king's immediate neighbours, are being excluded? Why, the king has walked our streets, and we ate and drank with his late father! This never happened in his time. We all entered freely through the main gate, not through this narrow gate.'

The young king overheard this and replied: 'My father was a kind man. He allowed you to enter the festival freely. The festival was meant for everybody, but you turned it into an exclusive club. You were no loyal subjects of my late father. You were only interested in yourselves. But from now on things are going to be different. The festival is open to everyone on equal terms. That's the way I want it, and that's the way it's going to be.'

They complained and fumed. But in the end they had to go away. They felt hard done by but had no one to blame but themselves.

This story should help us to understand the scene in today's Gospel. Jesus came to announce the good news of the Kingdom of God. The Jews were the first people he invited to the banquet of the Kingdom. But they refused to obey his call to repentance. They thought they could enter the Kingdom as a matter of course. After all, were they not members of God's Chosen People? But Jesus told them that this fact alone was not enough. They must enter by 'the narrow gate'. That is, they must strive by means of effort and sacrifice to produce the fruits of repentance. They must traffic in good, not in evil. Then they could enter the Kingdom. Otherwise their privileged position would benefit them nothing. And if they refused to enter, then the Kingdom would be offered to outsiders, namely, the Gentiles. These would accept it and gladly produce the required fruits. Thus 'the first would be last and the last first.'

All this is highly relevant for us. Through our Baptism we are members of the new Chosen People. We are in a privileged position. We are the 'insiders'. But we must not rely on that fact alone. Nor should we rely on other bogus credentials — things which in the eyes of Christ count for nothing — such as money, rank, status, etc. We can count on nothing but on God's love and mercy. Therefore, let us be happy to make our way in by the 'narrow gate'. Our bottle of wine consists of our efforts at returning God's love.

'In our times a lot of Catholics only profess to believe, but their deeds are opposed to their beliefs.' (Catherine de Hueck Doherty).

'The concept of God should make us larger, freer and more loving.' (James Baldwin).

PRAYER OF THE FAITHFUL

Let us pray that we may traffic in goodness and not in evil, and thus enter the Kingdom through the narrow gate. *R*. Lord, graciously hear us.

For all the followers of Jesus: that the faith they proclaim in words may be borne out in their deeds. (Pause). Lord, hear us.

For all government leaders: that they may strive to promote the well-being of all their people and not just that of a privileged few. (Pause). Lord, hear us.

For the Jewish people: that they may receive Christ as their Saviour and forgive what Christians have done to them. (Pause). Lord, hear us.

That we may strive to follow Christ in our daily lives by practising justice and charity towards all we meet. (Pause). Lord, hear us.

For local needs.

Let us pray:

Merciful Father, fill our hearts with your love and keep us faithful to the Gospel of Christ. Give us the grace to rise above our human weaknesses. Grant this through our Lord Jesus Christ, your Son, who lives and reigns with you and the Holy Spirit, one God, for ever and ever.

COMMUNION REFLECTION

Christ said there are two roads we can follow.
The first is wide and easy to travel.
All you have to do is yield yourself to the current
and you'll be carried along.
In other words — follow the crowd.
It is downhill most of the way.
It is the way of comfort and ease.
It is well lit with glittering neon lights
which offer the traveller all kinds of enjoyments.
Many are fooled and travel down this road.
But in the long run it leads them nowhere.
They die in the desert.

The second road is narrow and difficult.
You will often have to go it alone.
It is uphill most of the way.
It is the way of sacrifice and struggle.
At times you will have no light to guide you
save that of the stars.
Few take this road.
But they are the lucky ones.
For eventually the desert sands run out
and the traveller enters with joy into the Promised Land.

TWENTY-SECOND SUNDAY OF THE YEAR
Giving without hope of return

INTRODUCTION AND CONFITEOR

In today's Gospel Jesus says to us: 'If you are invited to a party take the lowest place.' How often we put ourselves first, grabbing the limelight.

Again he says to us: 'Give to those from whom you have nothing to receive.' How often we give in order to win the praise of others, and only to those who will return the compliment.

We know that these attitudes are unworthy of a follower of Christ. (Pause).   Let us ask pardon for them and for all our other failings.

I confess to almighty God . . .

HEADINGS FOR READINGS

First Reading (Sirach 3:17-20, 28-29). This praises the person who is humble. A humble person is open to God and never rejects wisdom, no matter where it comes from.

Second Reading (Hebrews 12:18-19, 22-24). This contrasts Mount Sinai and Mount Zion. Sinai is the place where the old covenant was made. Zion stands for the heavenly Jerusalem — the goal of the Christian's pilgrimage.

Gospel (Luke 14:1, 7-14). Jesus urges his followers not to covet places of honour, and always to act out of unselfish motives.

HOMILY

(Note: The theme of the first part of the Gospel — 'He who humbles himself will be exalted' — is dealt with on the Thirtieth Sunday).

Quite rightly, giving or generosity has a very high rating among Christians. In fact you can tell a true Christian from a mere pretender by the presence or absence of giving. But we rarely look at *the quality* of our giving. Giving of itself is not enough. It has to have a certain quality to it. It is *the way we give,* and *the spirit in which we give,* that is all important. In today's Gospel Christ sets us a very high standard. Real giving, he says, has no trace of self-interest in it.

There was a man called Oliver who had a great reputation for generosity. He died and went up, post haste, to the gate of heaven. Back on earth people who knew him were saying: 'Oliver will be let straight in and get a very high place up above.' But it didn't work out quite like that.

When he got to the gate he was met by the fisherman, Peter who, as we know, has charge of the keys. He took Oliver aside and showed him two piles of gold, one small and one large, each made up of nuggets of varying sizes and shapes.

'What are these?' asked Oliver.

'These are the acts of giving you performed while on earth — one nugget for each act.'

Oliver looked again at them. How they glittered! His heart filled with pride and joy. But then Peter began to speak again:

'Alas, not all giving is true giving,' he said. 'A lot of it is tainted with self-interest, and that makes it worthless in the eyes of God. So I'm afraid we'll have to test your acts of giving.'

On hearing this Oliver grew alarmed. 'But that's demanding the impossible,' he said. 'After all, it is only natural that people look to their own interests.'

But Peter insisted on the test. He got a sieve which had large meshes in it, and he began to place all the gold from the smaller pile in it. 'But why not begin with those in the larger pile?' said Oliver.

'Those don't count,' Peter replied. 'They represent all the gifts you gave to your friends, relatives, cronies, and so on.'

'That means that things like Christmas gifts and cards don't count?'

'That's correct. They are gone in one fell swoop.' With that the nuggets in the larger pile turned into dust before his eyes. Then a sudden wind blew up and the dust disappeared. Oliver turned pale. With that Peter began to shake the sieve. When he had finished he had all the biggest nuggets in the sieve, the others having slipped through. 'What are you doing now?' asked Oliver.

'I'm removing those gifts that you gave only to get something in return.'

'Does that include gratitude?'

'Yes. Such giving was a kind of investment.' With that he tossed the nuggets aside. As soon as they hit the ground they turned to dust and were blown away by the wind. He then adjusted the meshes of the sieve so that they became smaller, and he put the remaining nuggets into it. He shook it and once again tossed aside those that remained in it, which were naturally the biggest ones. 'What was that for?' Oliver asked.

'That removed the gifts you gave for the sake of showing off, when you gave to win the praise and recognition of others. In a word — when you gave for the sake of inflating your own ego.' Oliver shuddered.

Once again Peter adjusted the sieve so that the meshes became even finer, putting the remaining nuggets in. 'Now we shall remove all those things you gave only out of a sense of duty, or merely to quieten your conscience,' he said. 'Such giving has a coldness and lack of spontaneity about it. We'd rather we didn't have to give, but we have to if we wish to avoid embarrassment or something worse.' With that he shook the sieve. The nuggets that remained in the sieve he tossed aside, and they suffered the same fate as the others.

And once again he gathered up the remaining ones, few though they were, putting them into the sieve, the meshes of which he had made even smaller. 'What now?' asked Oliver, dejectedly. 'Now we will remove the gifts you gave merely because giving made you feel good. Your self-image dazzled. You glowed inwardly and went on a spree of self-congratulation.' He shook the sieve, tossed aside what had got trapped in it, and they crumbled and disappeared.

'Stop! Please stop!' Oliver cried, seeing how small the pile that remained was. 'But we really should go on,' said Peter. 'We should look at the cost of your giving. For instance, if we removed those things you gave but which you never missed, how much would disappear? And what if we removed those gifts you gave merely because the receiver was a person of importance, or was someone you felt deserved your gift?' But poor Oliver wasn't listening anymore. 'I've no hope then,' he moaned.

But with that Peter said: 'And now, Oliver, I've got some good news for you.' On hearing the words 'good news' Oliver perked up and asked: 'What good news?'

'There is still hope for you', said Peter. 'You came here bringing all those good deeds with you. With them you hoped to buy your way into heaven. But heaven can't be bought, not even with all the good deeds in the world. But the Lord is not like we are. He is the greatest giver of all. He gives even to those who are completely undeserving of his gifts. Let us now go and meet him. You'll soon see how generous he is.'

'But I'm empty-handed,' Oliver protested.

'That means you are poor. He gives most generously to those who are poor and who know it. So cheer up!'

How many of our good deeds would pass this test? How many deeds of giving of real quality have we performed, deeds that are pure gold as opposed to fool's gold? But disinterested giving is not easy to achieve. To sacrifice our own interest for the sake of others goes clean against the modern mentality. Rather are not most people out to benefit themselves at the expense of others?

If we look through the Gospel we will see how Christ practised this unselfish giving. He mingled with, and bestowed himself on, those who had nothing to give him in return. Nor did he ask for anything. The Good Shepherd is happy when he has found the lost sheep, no matter what hardships he suffered in searching for it. He is happy when, as a result of his loving care, the sheep are thriving. He does not think of himself.

Happy are we if we reach the stage where giving has become part of our nature. To give is not a luxury for the Christian. It is our first and fundamental duty as followers of Christ. It is something so obvious that we shouldn't even talk about it. The true Christian loves his brother without expecting any reward for it.

'If you want to be happy, give, without counting or regrets.' (Michel Quoist).

'The ideal giving is when the giver doesn't know to whom he is giving, and when the receiver doesn't know from whom he is receiving.' (Saying of the Rabbis).

PRAYER OF THE FAITHFUL

Let us pray to our heavenly Father for the attitudes of mind and heart that Jesus wanted to see in his followers. *R*. Lord, hear our prayer.

For Christians: that they may seek to correct their own faults before considering those of others. (Pause). Let us pray to the Lord.

For all those in high places: that they may not seek their own glory but devote themselves generously to serving those under them. (Pause). Let us pray to the Lord.

For those in our society who are always left out or who have to be content with the lowest place . . . the poor, the lonely, the unfortunate . . . (Pause). Let us pray to the Lord.

For true generosity of heart, so that we may be able to give as Christ gave, without expecting anything in return. (Pause). Let us pray to the Lord.

For local needs.

Let us pray:

Teach us, good Lord, to serve you as you deserve: to give and not to count the cost; to fight and not to heed the wounds: to toil and not to seek for rest; to labour and not to ask for any reward save that of knowing that we do your holy will. We ask this through Christ our Lord.

COMMUNION REFLECTION

In telling of his experiences as a prisoner in Auschwitz,
Viktor Frankl gives a magnificent example
of the kind of giving Christ praised,
namely, giving without any hope of return.

On returning from work in the evening,
with soup bowl in hand, you lined up
for your meagre ration of food.
Frankl was always happy when he was assigned to the line
in which prisoner-cook F was giving out the soup.

Why?
Because he was the only cook who did not look

at the faces of the men whose bowls he was filling.
He was the only one who dealt out the soup equally,
regardless of who the recipient was.

In other words, he did not make favourites
out of his personal friends or fellow countrymen,
picking out the potatoes for them,
while others got watery soup skimmed from the top.

How difficult it is to find someone to do this
even in so-called normal circumstances.
Yet here was a man who did it in the hell that was Auschwitz
where everyday one was faced with decisions of life and death.
How did he manage to do it?
From where did he get his inspiration?

TWENTY-THIRD SUNDAY OF THE YEAR
Counting the cost and paying the price

INTRODUCTION AND CONFITEOR

You can measure a person's commitment to a cause by what he
or she is prepared to pay for it. We cannot hope to be genuine
followers of Christ without making sacrifices and paying a price.

What does it mean for me to be a Christian? How does it affect
my life? What does it cost me? (Pause).

Lord Jesus, you help us to shun what is false and follow the way
of truth.   Lord, have mercy.

Lord Jesus, you help us to do what is right even when we have
to suffer for it.   Christ, have mercy.

Lord Jesus, you help us to keep our eyes fixed on eternal life
which is the goal of our earthly pilgrimage. Christ, have mercy.

HEADINGS FOR READINGS

First Reading (Wisdom 9:13-18). Faced with the mysteries of the
universe, the meaning of history, and the mind of God, we are
ignorant. But God has not left us in our ignorance. He has given
us the gift of knowledge.

Second Reading (Philemon 9-10, 12-17). Philemon was a Colos-
sian, converted by Paul. His slave Onesimus ran away and
somehow reached Paul in prison, where he was converted. Paul
urges Philemon to take him back, not as a slave, but as a brother.

Gospel (Luke 14:25-33). This contains two very short parables dealing with the theme of self-renunciation or the cost of discipleship. (Note: the word 'hate' is a Semitic expression. 'Love less' would be nearer to what Christ had in mind).

HOMILY

When people believe in something and want it very much, they are generally not afraid to pay the price. Life is full of examples: climbers, joggers, football fans . . . Their name is legion — those who count the cost and pay it down to the very last penny. The tragedy, however, is that often the goals people set themselves, and the projects into which they pour so much energy and sacrifice, are frequently not really worth it. Many people pursue shadows, or sweat to obtain not the real thing, but a cheap imitation.

Matilda was a charming and pretty girl. Her only problem was she had been born into a very poor family. Yet she wanted to be rich more than anything else in the world. Her only hope then was to marry a man of wealth and distinction. But the best she could do was to marry a civil servant. He did his best to make her happy, but he could not afford the things she dreamed of — pretty dresses, jewellery, a well-furnished home, and so on. She refused to go out to work. Instead she spent her days in tears of regret, despair, and misery.

She complained that they never went anywhere. At last her husband got an invitation to a state banquet. But she now complained that she had nothing suitable to wear. So he took some of his modest savings from the bank. With these Matilda bought a lovely dress. But now she had no jewellery to go with it. In a moment of inspiration, however, she thought of a rich school friend of hers called Marie. She went to Marie and asked her if she would give her a loan of some jewellery. Marie was only too happy to oblige. She gave her a loan of a very beautiful necklace.

Matilda went to the banquet. All smiles and graciousness, in her exquisite dress and necklace, she was the prettiest woman in the room. She lapped up the attention that was heaped on her like a hungry cat at a saucer of milk. When she finally got home in the early hours of the morning she decided to take a last look at herself in the mirror, just to see herself in all her glory one more time. It was then she discovered, to her horror, that the necklace was missing.

Though they searched for it all next day and the following days they did not find it. They were forced to give up. Matilda hadn't the courage to tell Marie the truth. So what did they do? They bought a new one, one that looked exactly like the one she had lost. It cost 40,000 francs. Where did the money come from? Half of it came from the last of her husband's savings. The other half they borrowed at enormous interest rates. When they returned the necklace to Marie she never noticed the change. In fact she didn't even open the box but put it into a drawer and thought no more about it.

Now Matilda began to know what real poverty was all about. But she was determined to play her part in getting the money back, and play her part she did. They gave up their flat and moved into a basement room. They got rid of their maid and Matilda did the housework herself. She also did the washing. Dressed like a poor woman she went with her basket on her arm to the greengrocer, and the butcher, bargaining, wrangling, and fighting over every penny. Her husband took an evening job. And this went on for ten whole years.

At the end of that time they had paid back everything they owed, including all the interest on the loans. But Matilda now looked an old woman. One day, quite by accident, she ran into her old friend Marie.

'O my poor Matilda, how you've aged!' said Marie.

'Ah, I've been through very hard times since we last met, and all because of you.'

'Because of me? I don't understand.'

Then she told her about losing the necklace and how they had worked all those years to recover the money. On hearing this Marie stopped dead. Then she said:

'You mean you bought a diamond necklace to replace mine?'.

'Yes,' said Matilda, 'and you never noticed it, they were so much alike.' She smiled with pride and satisfaction as she said this. Then Marie took her by the hand and in great distress said:

'Oh, my poor Matilda! Why, my necklace was only imitation. At the most it was worth 500 francs.'

Ah, as Solzhenitsyn says, 'we pay dearly for chasing after what is cheap.' If only Matilda had been able from the very beginning to put even half of that effort into what she wanted from life, it could have been hers, and she would not have wasted all those precious years.

But we most also expect to pay dearly for what is worthwhile in life. Christ said that there is a price to be paid by all those who wish to follow him, a high price at that. He said one should sit down, reckon it up, and see if one was ready to pay it. Following him is a serious business and should be undertaken with both eyes open.

The Church must be careful lest it betray the Gospel. It should beware of offering people cheap grace and cheap therapy. People are very vulnerable. As Gandhi said: 'We all want to obtain a thing of inestimable value dirt-cheap and in double-quick time.' But of course this cannot be. One wonders if many of our novenas do not fall into this trap.

In some circumstances to follow Christ might mean sacrificing the dearest things in life. Thus, if one is a Christian in Russia, one has to say goodbye to advancement in one's job. And you cannot afford to be ambitious for your children, or be too fussy about the kind of flat you live in.

But there is a price to be paid in the free world too. One might have to give up a good job. Some doctors in England emigrated rather than take part in abortions. To seek reconciliation with another person might mean losing face and sacrificing one's pride. We could go on. Philip Toynbee wrote: 'Those who are trying to live Christian lives today are faced, not with martyrdom, not even with hostility, not even with contempt. They are faced with the deadly indifference of their fellow countrymen, lightened only by occasional bursts of amused curiosity.'

The goal Christ sets us is immensely worthwhile. It is the only one which, in the long run, does full justice to us — the goal of an authentic way of life with one's eyes set on the eternal life to come. Even here on earth there are rewards. By striving to live as an authentic Christian we achieve an integrated and liberated personality, as well as an undreamed-of happiness and inner peace. It's not easy. But Christ knows our frailty. He lavishes his grace on those who strive sincerely to follow him.

'Often the success we prefer in life is not the success we are seeking.' (Anthony Padovano).

'If you have built castles in the air, your work need not be lost; that is where castles should be. Now put the foundations under them.' (Thoreau).

PRAYER OF THE FAITHFUL

Let us pray that we may see Christ more clearly, follow him more nearly, and love him more dearly, day by day. *R*. Lord, graciously hear us.

For all Church leaders: that they may preach the Gospel in an attractive and authentic way. (Pause). Lord, hear us.

For all government leaders: that they may carry out their responsibilities with wisdom and integrity. (Pause). Lord, hear us.

For all those who suffer because of their living of the Gospel: that Christ may sustain them with his grace and hope. (Pause). Lord, hear us.

That amid an uncertain and changing world we may keep our eyes fixed on Christ and follow him with unwavering commitment. (Pause). Lord, hear us.

For local needs.

Let us pray:

Father, our source of life, you know our weakness. May we reach out with joy to grasp your hand and walk more readily in your ways. We ask this through Christ our Lord.

SIGN OF PEACE

Lord Jesus Christ, you said to your disciples: 'Come to me all you who labour and are overburdened, and I will give you rest. Learn from me, for I am gentle and humble of heart, and you will find rest for our souls.' Lord, teach us gentleness and humility of heart so that we may enjoy the peace and unity of your kingdom where you live for ever and ever.

COMMUNION REFLECTION

(Solzhenitsyn gives the following example of fidelity to Christ).

It concerns a ten year old girl whose whole family
had been scattered to distant labour camps
because of their belief in God.

The girl was first taken to an orphanage.
But she refused to give up the cross
her mother had hung around her neck before leaving.
She tied a knot so that they could not
take it from her during sleep.
The struggle went on and on,
but it was no good.
She would not give up the cross.
'You can strangle me and take it from a corpse
if you like,' she said to them.

She also refused to submit herself to retraining,
that is, to the propaganda of the Party.
In the orphanage she was forced to live with children
who were the very dregs of Russian society.
Yet she refused to steal or to curse.

They never broke her.
She ended up doing ten years in a labour camp.

TWENTY-FOURTH SUNDAY OF THE YEAR
The lost sheep

INTRODUCTION AND CONFITEOR

In today's Gospel we have the lovely story about the lost sheep and how happy the shepherd was when he found it. Christ said that there is great joy in heaven when even one sinner comes back to God.

When we sin we stray from God. Which of us can say that we have never strayed from God? But Christ is the Good Shepherd who comes looking for us, and how happy he is if he finds us and we agree to return to the Father with him. Let us pause for a moment to call to mind the sins that separate us from God. (Pause).

Lord Jesus, you are concerned about us when we stray into the paths of sin.   Lord, have mercy.

Lord Jesus, you come looking for us with the love of a good shepherd.   Christ, have mercy.

Lord Jesus, you rejoice when you find us and bring us back to the Father's love.   Lord, have mercy.

HEADINGS FOR READINGS

First Reading (Exodus 32:7-11, 13-14). The people have strayed from the path God marked out for them. They have turned their backs on the God who brought them out of Egypt and have fallen into idolatry, but Moses intercedes for them.

Second Reading (1 Tim 1:12-17). Paul says that Christ came into the world to save sinners. In his conversion he himself experienced the saving mercy of God.

Gospel (Luke 15:1-32. Shorter form recommended in order to concentrate on the parable of the lost sheep.) The Pharisees complain because Jesus has been mixing with sinners. Jesus justifies his actions in three parables: the parable of the lost sheep, the lost coin, and the lost son.

HOMILY

(Note: this might be more effective if presented as a dialogue. The first part could be spoken by two adults; the second by two children).

Amos and Abel began to round up their scattered sheep. Evening was coming on. Time to start heading for the fold. Amos had a hundred sheep. They were his own, and he really took good care of them. Abel had several hundred sheep but did not own them. In fact he had only been hired a few months ago. The real owner of the sheep was a large landowner who was a very busy man. When they had rounded up the sheep Amos wore a worried look.

'What's the matter?' asked his companion.

'I can count only ninety-nine sheep. One is missing. Curley is missing.'

'You mean you can actually tell which one is missing?' said Abel.

'Sure. I know every single one of those sheep. I have watched them grow from the time they were lambs.'

'Do you know something', said Abel again. 'I don't even know exactly how many sheep are supposed to be in the flock. So if one went missing I'd have no way of telling. But if the owner doesn't care, why should I? What are you going to do?'

'I'm going looking for the lost sheep of course,' said Amos.

'You mean you're going to leave the ninety-nine here and go looking for the good-for-nothing one that got herself lost?'

'Yes. I've often done so before.'

'You're mad. It's only one. Haven't you still got ninety-nine others? Forget about the stupid thing. You'll find it tomorrow.'

'Tomorrow might be too late. Besides I can't forget her. I tell you I not only know each of these sheep by name, but I love each one of them. I just wouldn't be able to sleep peacefully tonight if I abandoned the lost one. I'd never forgive myself if a wolf attacked her and killed her. I am responsible for my sheep.'

'Maybe she will come back on her own?'

'A lost sheep must not be left to come looking for the shepherd. It is up to the shepherd to go looking for it.'

'I still say you're crazy. In any case, can't you see it will be dark soon. Let's go home.'

But Amos would not relent. With long, fast strides he set off in an easterly direction. From long experience he knew the places where Curley was likely to be. As for Abel, he headed for home with his master's sheep. He was working no overtime because he wasn't paid for it.

In fact one of Abel's sheep was missing also. He and Curley were now sheltering in a ravine to the east. Whereas Curley was a rather scraggly creature, he was a really fine specimen. (We'll call him the Fair One). By this time they both realised they were lost. It was a pretty awful feeling. When you're lost you've no moorings. Everything with which you are familiar has disappeared. It is scary and unnerving. Though inwardly the Fair One was suffering terrible pangs of loneliness and desperation, outwardly Curley appeared to be the more worried.

'How come you don't appear too worried?' she asked.

'The truth is I didn't get lost. I ran away. But of course I'm lost now.'

'You ran away? Why would you do something like that?'

'Neither the shepherd who looks after us, nor the man who owns us, cares one way or another. I'll bet you that I haven't even been missed. Outwardly I may not appear to be worried. But inwardly I feel terrible. You see, when I ran away I was being defiant. It was my way of hitting back at them. But I never knew I'd feel like this. It's terrible to be lost and realise that nobody is looking for you. Nobody is looking for me because nobody cares about me. I don't matter to them. I'm not precious to anyone. I don't even have a name. They've already forgotten about me. I don't even have a home to do to.'

'I don't understand. Haven't you got the fold like I have?'

'I don't call that home. Home is where you're loved.'

'Ah, now I can see that you really are lost,' said Curley sympathetically. 'When you've no real home you're lost no matter where you go. You're lost all the time. To be honest, if I was in that situation I'd just lie down and wait for the wolf to come. But it's different for me.'

'In what way?' asked the Fair One sadly.

'You see, I know my shepherd knows me and loves me. Right now he is worried sick and is searching for me. All I have to do is wait right here and he will find me. You'll see.'

'Ah, if only I had someone who cared about me like that I'd never have run away.'

They waited. Then in the distance a strong, clear voice was heard calling.

'There!' Curley exclaimed. 'Why did I tell you? That's the shepherd's voice. I knew he wouldn't abandon me.'

'But will he not beat you, or at least scold you severely for running away?'

'Beat me? He won't beat me. He may scold me a little, but I believe I deserve it. It was careless and selfish of me to wander off and get lost as I did.'

With that Curley began to run towards the shepherd. As soon as Amos saw her he too ran. When they met he took her into his arms and hugged her. Then he put her on his shoulder and, with a smile on his weather-beaten face, he headed for home. Meanwhile the Fair One had been watching all this from behind a rock where he had run for cover. The sight brought tears to his eyes and made him feel his lostness all the more keenly. He wandered off aimlessly into the gathering gloom. He was never seen again.

What a picture of Christ emerges from this simple parable. He showed his concern for the 'lost sheep' (tax collectors, sinners and such like) who had been abandoned by the official shepherds. The official shepherds were shocked at what he was doing. But he replied by saying that he was merely doing what any shepherd worthy of the name would do.

We all have had some experience of being 'lost'. To be in sin is to be lost, to be away from the Father's house. But we also have had some experience of being 'found' by Christ, the Good Shepherd. And if we should stray again, how lovely it is to know that Someone will come looking for us, that we are precious to Someone, namely Christ.

In our world today there are a lot of lost people — lost morally, spiritually, and in all sorts of other ways. They are lost because they have no guides, no one to take an interest in them, no one to make them feel that they are worthwhile. Every Christian who has had the experience of being found by the Good Shepherd will show an active concern for those who are lost. He will in his or her turn become a shepherd like Amos.

'Life needs delicate hands.' (Jean Vanier).

'I do not agree with the big ways of doing things. To us what matters is an individual.' (Mother Teresa).

PRAYER OF THE FAITHFUL

Let us pray that having experienced the love and care of Christ, the Good Shepherd, we may try to be loving and caring towards others. *R.* Lord, graciously hear us.

For all the shepherds of the Church: that they may faithfully watch over the flock of Christ, showing special care for the lost sheep. (Pause). Lord, hear us.

For those in charge of civil affairs: that they may be caring in their jobs; for all parents, that they may create homes where their children will know they are loved. (Pause). Lord, hear us.

For all those who are lost, and who have no one to take an interest in them. (Pause). Lord, hear us.

That we may realise how precious we are as individuals to the Lord, and that we may try to be loving towards all those we come into contact with each day. (Pause). Lord, hear us.

For local needs.

Let us pray:

Father, guide us in your gentle mercy for, left to ourselves, we cannot please you. We ask this through Christ our Lord.

SIGN OF PEACE

Lord Jesus Christ, you said to your disciples: 'I am the vine, you are the branches; separated from me you can do nothing; united with me you will bear much fruit.' Strengthen the bonds that unite

us with you and with one another, so that we may enjoy the peace
and unity of your kingdom where you live for ever and ever.

COMMUNION REFLECTION
We all need to anchor our lives
to true values and enduring truths.
Unfortunately many people form the flimsiest of ties.
They anchor their boats to things that are weak.
They pin their hopes on values that are false.
When the strain is put on, the tie snaps,
and they are wrenched from their moorings.
Their old certainties vanish,
and they are alone —
lost on the limitless sea of life.

But we need anchors other than faith and principles.
People who have never known a close relationship
with another human being are anchorless.
They are at the mercy of the cold winds
of anguish, loneliness and frustration.
They have never had that anchor in life
that gives them the feeling that they are worthwhile,
and that thereby gives them stability and security.

Without such an anchor,
their hearts will always be restless,
and in a sense they will always be lost.

TWENTY-FIFTH SUNDAY OF THE YEAR
Choosing between God and money

INTRODUCTION AND CONFITEOR
There is no doubt but that the so-called 'good life' (money, comfort, success, pleasure . . .) exercises an enormous pull on us all.
We want to serve God but we do not want our service of him to
interfere with our habits, our impulses, our way of life . . .

Today's Gospel tells us that we cannot serve God and money at
the same time. Let us examine ourselves for a moment to see where
our loyalties lie. (Pause).

Lord Jesus, you help us to put the Kingdom of God first in our lives. Lord, have mercy.

Lord Jesus, you help us to discover the joy and freedom there is in doing the Father's will rather than our own. Christ, have mercy.

Lord Jesus, you help us to live as children of the light rather than as children of the darkness. Lord, have mercy.

HEADINGS FOR READINGS

First Reading (Amos 8:4-7). Amos was a great champion of social justice. In this short reading he depicts the 'religious' employers waiting impatiently for the sabbath to end so that they can get on with their lucrative but dishonest trading.

Second Reading (1 Tim 2:1-8). Paul urges Christians to pray for everyone, especially those who hold public office, because God wants everyone to be saved.

Gospel (Luke 16:1-13. Longer form recommended). This contains the parable of the astute steward who used his ill-gotten money to gain admittance into people's homes. Christ says we can learn something from him.

HOMILY

Christ's parables are far from being pious little stories with nice morals to them. To begin with they are very secular. Then the things that happened in them, and the characters that appear in them, are by no means always edifying. I suppose of all the parables, that of the Dishonest Steward is the least edifying. Let us look at it more closely in the hope of finding out what it is saying to us. Given the kind of grasping world we live in, it is a highly relevant parable.

Saul worked for Jacob. Jacob owned a lot of property and a vast estate. He charged high rents from his tenants and lived like a lord on the profits. As he liked to spend a lot of time abroad he needed a servant to run the estate in his absence. He was looking for someone who could be relied on to get the tenants to pay their rent on time. What he needed, therefore, was an unscrupulous man who would tolerate no nonsense from the tenants and who would not hesitate to put the boot in if necessary. He found the man he was looking for in Saul — or thought he did.

Saul was a man of the world, who was immediately attracted by the perks the job offered — an easy life, supplementary pay, rewards, and so on. He saw that he was on to a good thing. If he played his cards right, a life of comfort, pleasure and ease was assured.

But the wise old Jacob had made a mistake. While Saul had most of the qualities he desired in his head steward — intelligence, obedience, efficiency, ruthlessness — he lacked the most important one of all, namely, honesty. Saul was dishonest, but for the moment he played his cards very carefully. How did he manage to get the job before a lot of others? He greased palms and pulled strings.

But once he had got the job, and his boss had gone away, he showed himself in his true colours. He had to handle a lot of money. Even an honest person finds it hard to be indifferent to money. But for Saul it was a bait he simply couldn't refuse. Saul had always been dishonest, even in small things. So now that big things were involved he was not going to change. He began to appropriate some of the money for himself and his own use. The first thing he did was to increase the rents, the extra money going into his own pocket. Naturally the tenants kicked up but he quickly silenced them. Once he gave greed a free hand money soon became his god.

He knew the kind of man Jacob was, so he decided to grab what he could for himself while the going was good. 'Who knows how long the job will last?' he said to himself. 'Old Jacob is having a good time off the sweat of the tenants, so why shouldn't I do the same?' So he began to live it up. He embarked on a smart lifestyle, and gave free rein to all his baser instincts. He lived a life of total selfishness and sensuality. He never did anything which didn't have some clear advantage for himself. The word honour had no meaning for him.

He was a nominal believer, though it was years since he had prayed. In effect he was a heathen at heart. He didn't care if heaven existed, or judgement or eternity. All this had long been hazy in his mind. He wanted nothing but the passing, uncertain life of this earth. He never suffered a pang of conscience. Rather, he prided himself on his smart way of life.

And the amazing thing is this. He was such a cute operator that for several years he got away with it. When Jacob would come back to check up on him, Saul put on such a display of deception and fawning that he was taken in. But eventually of course he was found out. First of all the tenants reported him, though Jacob was reluctant to believe them, knowing how adept tenants are at complaining. And secondly his lifestyle betrayed him. Thoreau says: 'Any nobility begins at once to refine a man's features, and any meanness or sensuality to imbrute them.' So it was with Saul. His coarse and base life was reflected on his features and Jacob noticed it. He called him in and asked him to give an account of his stewardship.

Naturally it was a moment of acute embarrassment and humiliation for Saul. But it could have been a great moment of truth for him. It could have been a turning point in his life. But by now he had grown so accustomed to his smart and selfish lifestyle that he was incapable of breaking out of it. And so, now that his master was about to sack him, he tried to ingratiate himself with the tenants, yes, with those very tenants who up to now he had cruelly oppressed. He relied on his old weapon — dishonesty. And he discovered that they too were vulnerable. Thus he eased his way out of one world into another, and continued to live dishonestly off the earnings of other people. He had grown so fat that he could not now deny himself anything.

He sure is a strange character for Christ to hold up as a model for us! In plain language he was a scoundrel. Yet Christ said we could learn something from him. Here was a typical man of the world, who dedicated all his energy to achieving a smart way of life based on money and what it could buy. He was like a foxhound, who, once he falls on the scent of a fox forsakes all else and follows it. So it is with the 'children of darkness'. If only the 'children of light' would show the same dedication and resolve in their pursuit of goodness! How few people work even half as hard on their personal lives as they do on their professional lives.

Even though we are dealing with a thorough scoundrel we should all be able to see something of ourselves in him. As we said earlier, it is hard to remain indifferent to money, given the kind of world we live in. How money talks! How many doors open to it. In reality it is the only god worshipped by all, and whose voice is always listened to. It has been said that where money is concerned there are only two measures: no money and not enough money. We have to use it, but it doesn't have to become our god.

But how easily it takes a grip on us. Even a decent person can be drawn in without noticing it. A person starts off with a sharp eye for business, and gradually becomes acquisitive, avaricious and cunning. It's easy to fool oneself. We like to think that we are religious people, but often we live like heathens while lifting our cap to God on Sunday. Are we not, to some extent, all victims of what Philip Toynbee calls 'that many-symptomed modern disease'? By this he means 'futile haste, activity for its own sake, unthinking greed, cruel and grasping indifference to the pain of others, refusal of honest self-examination . . .'

One of the most urgent needs of today is to remove the partition between religion and the rest of life. Too often we confine our religion to church. As one teenager put it: 'You go to Mass without thinking and afterwards do as you like.' But it doesn't have to be like this. We have a choice. We can choose to be children of the light, and be just as dedicated in the pursuit of goodness as the children of darkness are in their pursuit of evil.

'Honest toil makes a person's bread taste sweet.' (Thoreau).

'If you do not know the difference between pleasure and spiritual joy you have not begun to live.' (Thomas Merton).

PRAYER OF THE FAITHFUL

As children of the light let us pray that we may be as resourceful and dedicated in our pursuit of goodness as the children of darkness are in the pursuit of evil. *R*. Lord, graciously hear us.

For Christians: that God and his Kingdom may have first place in their lives. (Pause). Lord, hear us.

For all those in positions of responsibility: that they may not use their position for their own selfish advantage but for the good of all those under them. (Pause). Lord, hear us.

For all those who have made a god out of money and who neither seek nor desire anything beyond the pleasures of this world. (Pause). Lord, hear us.

That we may always treat others the way we would like them to treat us. (Pause). Lord, hear us.

For local needs.

Let us pray:

Father, Christ, your Son, told us that if we sought your Kingdom first, then all the other things that we need would be given to us. Help us to take him at his word, so that we can live lives worthy of your sons and daughters. We ask this through the same Christ our Lord.

COMMUNION REFLECTION

A man who had lived a life of selfish luxury
died and went up to heaven.
An angel was sent to show him to his house.
They passed many lovely mansions,
and each time the rich man thought:
'This must be mine.'
But not so.
They passed through the main street
and arrived at the outskirts
where the houses were very small.
Finally they came to a miserable hut.
'This is yours,' said the angel.
'This is my house? There must be a mistake,'
the rich man exclaimed.
'No,' the angel answered,
'there is no mistake'.
This was the best we could do
with the materials you sent up.

TWENTY-SIXTH SUNDAY OF THE YEAR
Rich man, poor man

INTRODUCTION AND CONFITEOR

In today's Gospel we have a story about a rich man who feasted sumptuously every day and refused to share even the crumbs from his table with a starving beggar at his gate. Try to picture the scene. (Pause).

We are all tainted with selfishness. We don't find it easy to share our possessions with others. We find it even harder to share ourselves with them. But we are all beggars before God. We need his forgivenes especially for our refusal to share. Let us ask for this forgiveness.

I confess to almighty God . . .

HEADINGS FOR READINGS

First Reading (Amos 6:1, 4-7). Amos speaks to the wealthy of both Judah and Israel. Their crime is that they could not care less for the plight of the poor. Besides, their conduct will bring ruin on the whole nation.

Second Reading (1 Tim 6:11-16). As Jesus was faithful to his call in face of an hostility that led to his death, so Christians facing persecution should be faithful to God's call.

Gospel (Luke 16:19-31). This contains Jesus' famous parable of the rich man and the beggarman.

HOMILY

No human being, much less a follower of Christ, can say that he is responsible only for himself, and that his neighbour's plight is none of his business. Otherwise he speaks like Cain who said: 'I am not my brother's keeper,' and he acts like Dives who was so cushioned by his lavish lifestyle that he was totally oblivious to the presence of the beggar at his gate and treated him as if he were less than nothing.

Lazarus was a very poor man. He was dressed in rags, full of sores, and hadn't even a crumb of bread to eat. He had no friends except the dogs of the street. He was in misery, and the misery of a person without a friend. Dives, on the other hand, was a very well-off man. He lived in a mansion, wore the most expensive clothes, and ate like a king. Yet, in the biblical sense, that is in the eyes of God, Dives was the poorer of the two. How could that be? The rich are wounded by their riches, just as the poor are wounded by their poverty. A little story will illustrate this.

A businessman in San Antonio, Texas, parked his brand-new car on the street and went off to do some business. When he got back to it he found a poor little boy of about eleven years of age examining it with eyes full of wonder and envy. Here is his own account of what happened then.

'When I put the key in the car door the boy asked: "Is that your car, mister?"

' "Sure," I replied.

' "It's beautiful. How much did you pay for it?"

' "To be honest, Sonny, I haven't got a clue."

' "You mean you bought it and you can't remember what you paid for it?"

' "Sonny, I didn't buy it. I got a present of it."

' "From whom did you get it?"

' "My brother."

' "You mean your brother gave it to you and it didn't cost you a penny?"

' "That's right."

' "I wish that I . . ."

'I thought I knew exactly what he was going to say: "I wish that I *had a brother* like that." But when he finished the sentence I was jarred to the soles of my feet. For he didn't say that at all. What he said was quite different. He said: "I wish that I could *be a brother* like that."

'There was I in my fancy suit and with the keys of a brand-new car in my hand. And there was he in rags, empty-handed. Yet he had more in his heart than I had. He was far richer than I was. When I recovered I asked him to come for a drive in the car with me. But he declined saying that his old clothes were too dirty and would ruin the seat of the new car. But after I insisted he got in and we began to drive around. After going a mile or so he asked if I would drive past his house — a flat on the fourth floor. He got out and ran upstairs. In a flash he was down again carrying his little brother in his arms. The little brother was crippled with infantile paralysis. Pointing to the new car he said:

' "You see that car, Bud. One day I'm going to buy you a car like that. We'll go for a trip and you'll be able to see the sights for yourself."

'Deeply moved I said: "Sonny, he is going to see the sights right now. Both of you sit in."

'They did so. We drove downtown to the biggest toy store I could find. The next few hours were the happiest of my life.'

To get back to Christ's story. In point of fact Dives was suffering from the worst kind of poverty of all — poverty of the heart. His heart was empty. It was devoid of love and compassion. Why, even the dogs of the street showed more compassion in their own way than he did. Looked at from that point of view Dives was a very poor specimen of humanity.

Wealth can make a person very blind. When we are well-off we forget (if we ever knew) what it is like to be poor. When we come across poor people why is that we want to look the other way? The reason is that, if we have any conscience at all, they disturb us. So we pretend not to see them. The poor do not often cry out, but they have a way of speaking with their eyes. 'The protests of the poor are the voice of God.' (Helder Camara).

By the way, there is no suggestion in the Gospel that Dives' wealth was ill-gotten or that Lazarus was a victim of oppression. The sin of Dives consisted, not in what he did, but rather in what he did not do, that is, share some of his riches with the poor man. 'The biggest disease in the world today,' says Mother Teresa, 'is the feeling of being unwanted (like Lazarus at the gate). And the greatest evil in the world today is lack of love — the terrible indifference towards one's neighbour which is so widespread.'

The gap between Dives and Lazarus is growing into a gigantic abyss. If the Church doesn't address itself to this problem it runs the risk of becoming dangerously irrelevant. We must not only look at the gap itself but at the causes of the gap. Christians must be a voice for those who have no voice, namely, the poor. And not just the poor of the Third World, but the poor in our midst. But our concern must go beyond words. We must share with them. Otherwise we are no better than Dives.

The frightening thing about Christ's parable is this: Dives was obviously a believer. He had heard what the Bible had to say, but clearly its message hadn't penetrated beyond his ears. It hadn't converted him. His heart remained like a stone. And there is no place in the Kingdom of heaven for a person like that. He would be as out of place as a blind man in a cinema.

Some might still think that this parable is not addressed to people like you and me. They might protest: 'I'm not rich.' But it's not just about money. Even though we may not be rich in material things we still have something that we can share with someone in need. Hence the question we might ask is: 'Who is sitting outside my "gate" . . . begging, not necessarily for bread, but maybe for a word of recognition, or a bit of companionship, or a little love, or forgiveness . . .' And the time to share is *now*. As for material things, if we realise that riches are the one thing that prevent us from being rich, then we will stop hankering after them.

'Poverty makes a person subhuman; excess of wealth makes a person inhuman.' (Helder Camara).

'A man's wealth consists, not in what he keeps, but in what he gives away.' (Rabbinical saying).

PRAYER OF THE FAITHFUL

Let us pray to the Lord that he may teach us what real poverty and real riches are in his eyes. *R*. Lord, hear our prayer.

For all the followers of Jesus: that they may see that it is a very great poverty not to be able to share with others. (Pause). Let us pray to the Lord.

For all the rich and the powerful: that God may touch their hearts, changing them from stones into flesh and blood. (Pause). Let us pray to the Lord.

For all the poor who sit patiently at the closed door of life's banquet, waiting for someone to invite them inside. (Pause). Let us pray to the Lord.

That we may realise that we are truly rich in the eyes of God when we are able to show mercy and compassion, understanding and forgiveness to others. (Pause). Let us pray to the Lord.

For local needs.

Let us pray:

Lord, you said that whatever we do to the least of our brothers and sisters we do to you, and whatever we refuse to do to them we refuse to do to you. Help us never to forget this, and to put it into practice in all our dealings with others. We ask this of you who live and reign for ever and ever.

COMMUNION REFLECTION

It's not easy to convert the rich.
It's like this.

The more people have,
the more they have to lose.
The more they have to lose,
the more fearful they become.
The more fearful they become,
the more defensive they get.
The more defensive they get,
the more they cut themselves off.
The more they cut themselves off,
the more closed they get.
The result is that they end up with a withered heart.
And it's impossible to breathe life into a withered heart.

To close one's heart is to begin to die.
To open one's heart is to begin to live.

At the end of the day it's not what we carry
in our purses or bank accounts that matters.
It's what we carry in our hearts.
That is where the rich man was found wanting.

Poverty of heart is the worst form of poverty.

TWENTY-SEVENTH SUNDAY OF THE YEAR
Still only mere servants

INTRODUCTION AND CONFITEOR

Some people think that they are doing God a favour when they keep his laws and worship him. But to serve God is not a duty. It, is a privilege. The quality which, above all others, we should bring to our service is that of love. Even when we've done all we are supposed to do we still have only done our duty.

What sort of spirit do we being to our worship and service of God? (Pause).

Lord Jesus, you help us to give and not to count the cost.   Lord, have mercy.

Lord Jesus, you help us to toil and not to seek for rest.   Christ, have mercy.

Lord Jesus, you help us to seek no reward except that of knowing that we do the will of the Father. Lord, have mercy.

HEADINGS FOR READINGS

First Reading (Habakkuk 1:2-3; 2:2-4). The prophet complains to God about the prevalence of injustice. God responds by promising to save those who trust in him.

Second Reading (2 Tim 1:6-8, 13-14). Timothy is urged to accept his share of suffering for the Gospel, and, with the help of the Holy Spirit, to bear these sufferings cheerfully as Paul did.

Gospel (Luke 17:5-10). A little faith, provided it be authentic, can do great things. The disciples are urged to serve God without any claim on a reward.

HOMILY

I think it is true to say that the most generous and heroic deeds in life are those which are performed, not in the line of duty or in the hope of monetary or other rewards, but out of pure love. In one way this is very surprising as it goes clean contrary to the spirit of the age in which we live — people have to be paid for everything they do. Yet in another way it is not at all surprising, for as soon as the concept of reward enters the scene, far from acting as a spur to generosity, it often acts as a blight on it. Consider the following two contrasting examples.

People are working in a car factory. The cost of living is rising at an alarming annual rate. Yet the wages of the workers have remained the same for several years. Each year the workers see that the company records enormous profits. Discontent spreads among them. So they go on strike. Eventually after a bitter struggle negotiations are entered into and a deal hammered out. The company agrees to meet their demands in exchange for 'increased productivity.' (How often we hear that phrase today). Now if you were to ask one of the workers for his reaction, he would probably say something like this: 'I'm not prepared to work unless I'm paid a decent wage.' And who could blame him? Now for the second example.

It is late afternoon on a raw day on the edge of winter. Everybody is in a hurry to get home as they battle their way through the city traffic. Suddenly a cry arises: 'There's a man in the river!' People rush to the wall and look down into the muddy and uninviting water. Sure enough — there is a man down there trashing about in the dark water. His desperate cries for help reach the on-lookers above the din of the traffic. Then, with a screech of brakes, a car swings out of the line of traffic, and comes to a halt close to the kerb. A youngish man jumps out, throwing off his coat and shoes as he does so. He gets up on the wall, takes a quick look down, and then dives into the murky waters. After a couple of unsuccessful dives he eventually grabs the drowning man and hauls him to safety. Out on the roadside a crowd gathers around the rescued man as they wait for an ambulance to come. Presently it arrives and takes the man to hospital from where he is later released, none the worse for his ordeal. A reporter comes by, and seeing the possibility of a good story, begins to fish for information. But, far from seeking the limelight or the plaudits of the people, the rescuer has vanished. If you asked him why he did it he would probably say something like this: 'I do no more than my duty. It was nothing special. In any case, it is a privilege to be able to save a man from drowning.'

What a difference there is between these two situations. You are in two different worlds. If we were to bring the employer-worker relationship into our service of God it would lead to a pitiable religion and result in a terrible impoverishment of spirit. If we wish to be true to the spirit of the Gospel, the attitude that we must bring to our service of God must be like that of the rescuer.

It is surprising how many people think that God owes them something. This is especially true of sincere people who take their religion seriously, and who try as best they can to live by God's commandments. What they think, even though they may never say so, is something like this: 'I've kept my side of the bargain; now it's up to God to keep his side of it.'

They imagine God as being like the typical employer. If you do the work then as a matter of justice your employer owes you your wages. But this introduces a mercenary attitude into something that is essentially supposed to be a love affair beween God and us. In a way it is hard to blame such people, considering the kind of world we live in. People are willing to work but they want to be paid, and paid at once. They want to be praised and paid with love for love. Otherwise they are incapable of love or service.

But this attitude reduces the service of God to a bargain or a contract — something for something. A reward in heaven in exchange for faithful service on earth. Seen like this, religion becomes a cold, formal and businesslike affair — not very attractive, to say the least.

But in the Gospel Jesus said that even when we have done all we are expected to do (and which of us would be so bold as to make that claim?), we still can't make any demands on God. He was hitting at the mercenary attitude which was so prevalent in his day, especially among the Pharisees. Judaism was dominated by the idea of merit. According to the Pharisees' way of thinking, God 'owed' salvation to those who kept the Law of Moses. But Jesus said that salvation cannot be earned. It is a gift from God. We can never, therefore, put God in our debt, and we can never have any claim on him. When we have done our best to live by his commandments, when we have fulfilled all our duties, we are still no better than slaves before their master. A slave has no claim on his master. He cannot demand either wages or thanks, quite independently of what he may have done for his master. So it is between God and us. It goes without saying, however, that there is no place either in our service of God for the 'something for nothing' mentality.

But there the comparison with the slave ends. After all, God is not a slave owner. He is our Father. We are his children. Children do not do the will of their father for the sake of rewards. They do it because they want to try to return his love for them. Hence the Good News might be summed up like this: A generous Lord, who wants his disciples to serve him out of love, not out of duty.

'Even if I had done some good works to trust in, I would not want to trust in them.' (Thomas Merton).

'Let us never try to sweeten Christ's teaching.' (Catherine de Hueck Doherty).

PRAYER OF THE FAITHFUL

Even if we have faith strong enough to move mountains, it will benefit us nothing if we have no love. With this in mind let us make our prayers known to the Father. *R*. Lord, grant us a loving faith.

That the Lord may sustain the Church in the faith of the apostles, helping us to encourage each other and share our gifts. (Pause). Let us pray to the Lord.

For employers: that they may pay decent wages and treat their employees in a way that enhances their human dignity. (Pause) Let us pray to the lord.

For all those who are assailed by doubts or weighed down by uncertainties; for all the unemployed: that the Lord may sustain their hope. (Pause). Let us pray to the Lord.

That the Lord may help us to serve him, not out of a sense of duty like slaves, but out of love, as befits his sons and daughters. (Pause). Let us pray to the Lord.

For local needs.

Let us pray:

Father, let your people's prayers come into your loving presence. Forgive them their sins, so that by your grace they may serve you in a spirit of love. We ask this through Christ our Lord.

COMMUNION REFLECTION

Walter Ciszek SJ spent fifteen years
in forced-labour camps in Siberia.
Through all those years he belonged
to the lowest brigades doing the dirtiest work —
digging foundations by hand,
carving out with pick and shovel
long sewer trenches through the frozen ground,
loading and unloading with bare hands
the heavy construction materials,
crawling in damp, dark mines,
where death was always only one careless step away.

What kept him going?
He says:
'Men died in the camp,
especially when they gave up hope.
But I trusted in God,
and so I never felt abandoned or without hope.
I owe my survival to my faith in God.'

Of all the things we can give another person
the greatest is trust.

Lord, increase our faith in you,
so that we may trust you more fully
in all the happenings of our lives,
great and small, bitter and sweet.

TWENTY-EIGHTH SUNDAY OF THE YEAR
The ten lepers

INTRODUCTION AND CONFITEOR

Ten desperate people came to Christ and were cured by him. Yet only one of them came back to thank him. Christ has touched us in many ways and we too are frequently ungrateful.

We still need Christ. We may not be as desperate as the lepers were but we are all tainted with the leprosy of sin. Let us not be afraid to admit this. (Pause).

Let us ask God to rid us of the leprosy of our sins.

I confess to almighty God . . . etc.

HEADINGS FOR READINGS

First Reading (2 Kings 5:14-17). Naaman, general of the Syrian army, is cured of leprosy. As a result he comes to believe in the true God, and is lavish in his gratitude towards the prophet Elisha.

Second Reading (2 Tim 2:8-13). Paul reminds Timothy that the work of preaching the Gospel will not be easy; it will result in hardship, opposition and persecution.

Gospel (Luke 17:11-19). The story of ten men who were cured of leprosy by Christ, only one of whom returned to thank him.

HOMILY

In some ways this is one of the most incredible stores in the entire Gospel. Here were ten extremely fortunate people. They had been cured of the most dreaded disease of all — leprosy. Leprosy was the ultimate uncleanness which cut off its victim from the community. Would you not think, then, that having been cured, the very first thing they would have done would be to rush back and thank the man who had cured them? Yet only one of the ten did so. How could this be? Using a little imagination, let us see if we can answer this puzzling question. All ten of them went home, showed themselves to their priest, and got a clean bill of health. This is what happened afterwards.

The first was MARY, the wife of a shopkeeper. On returning home she found the house in a mess. It wasn't her husband's fault. It wasn't easy to run a business and look after a house. He was worn out. He needed help at once. Going back was out of the question — at least for the moment.

The second was AARON, a farmer. The summer had been a very bad one. He got back to discover that the harvest was in danger of being lost. At that very moment a change was imminent. Good weather had been forecast. There wasn't a minute to be lost. There would be plenty of rainy days when he could go back.

The third was SAUL. He went home to a very loving family. He got the warmest of receptions. They threw a big party in his honour, during which he was smothered in welcomes. They wouldn't hear of him going anywhere. Hadn't he been away long enough! It was *they* who prevented him from going back.

MARTHA was the fourth. When she got home her all-time favourite TV programme was on, something she had been starved of during her isolation. She soon lost herself in the programme. She would go back tomorrow. But tomorrow never came, there was so much to catch up on.'

The fifth was DANIEL. He saw that his business was very run-down. Prior to his illness he had been very ambitious, a 'get rich quick' merchant. He had so much lost time to make up for. Going back was very low in his list of priorities. Soon he forgot about it altogether.

AMOS, the sixth, had no home to go to. He was feeling very bitter about his leprosy and about his whole life. He blamed God and everyone else. When he got cured he collected some money that was owed to him, went out on the town, and got drunk. Going back never entered his head.

PETER was the seventh. When he got back he had no job. But just then someone told him about an interview for a very good job. He went off for the interview. Going back was not on at the moment. It would depend on whether or not he got the job.

ANNA was the eighth. She was actually on her way back in the car when she saw a filling station giving out petrol. (There was a petrol strike on just then). She queued for three hours and got a fill-up. She went straight home then. Her husband needed the car for work. It would be a shame to waste petrol on a journey that wasn't really necessary.

Ninth came JOSEPH. As soon as he got cured he got a bright idea. Why not sell his story to one of the sensational tabloids? Leprosy from the inside! That should make a great story. No time to waste. One of the others might get the same idea and beat him to it. Going back had no place in his plans.

Finally, there was SIMON. He also had a number of reasons for not going back, and each of those reasons clamoured for attention. Among those reasons was one really compelling one — he was a Samaritan, and the man who had cured him was a Jew. There was no love lost between the two races. It wasn't going to be easy for a Samaritan to thank a Jew. However, being the kind of man he was, he set this and all the other reasons aside, and did what he felt he had to do. He went back to render thanks.

Ah, excuses, excuses, excuses! Some reasonable and most plausible; others shallow and petty; still others shabby and unworthy. And yet, in nine cases out of ten, they were effective. They prevented those people from doing the one thing that cried out to heaven to be done.

We can imagine Jesus saying something like this to Simon:

'My dear Simon, so you came back. The only one to do so. The other nine have been declared clean by the priests, but I assure you their cure is only skin-deep. While it's true that their sores, pimples and whiteness of skin are gone, nothing else about them has changed. After the bitter and hurtful experience they have returned to their old selves. They have not benefitted in the slightest from what they have been through. They are the same old people, with the same hard attitudes, mean ways, selfish habits, worldly concerns, shallowness and superficiality of life. They never suspect that a person can have inner leprosy as well as outer leprosy. By inner leprosy I mean leprosy of the mind and heart. They are still suffering from that, and it is unlikely that they will ever be cured of it. For they are not even aware of it. And who will have the courage to point it out to them?

'But you, Simon, are a new man. Your cure is not just skin-deep. It has reached into your mind and heart. Stay like that and you'll never forget this day. Go in peace now, and by the way — thank you for thanking me.'

We all have been touched by Jesus. We all have encountered him, especially in the sacraments. Otherwise we wouldn't be here this morning. What has changed in our lives as a result of our encounter with Jesus? If there has been a change, how deep has it gone? How has it affected our values, our concerns, our lifestyle? Are we perhaps like the nine — changed only superficially? Interiorly, we go our own sweet way, pursuing goals that are anti-Gospel. Should we not try to imitate the Samaritan, who allowed himself to be changed utterly as a result of that one encounter with Jesus? Then we too will know some of the joy he felt on that unforgettable day.

'You cannot cure or be cured unless you love.' (Catherine de Hueck Doherty).

'We write in the sand the benefits we receive, but the injuries we write on marble.' (Thomas More).

PRAYER OF THE FAITHFUL

Let us pray to God for the gift of being grateful for all his benefits to us. *R*. Lord, graciously hear us.

That as followers of Christ we may be grateful for the gift of faith by which we know him and his purpose for us. (Pause). Lord, hear us.

For all the human family: that people may see their lives as a gift from God, and show their gratitude by living a good life. (Pause). Lord, hear us.

For all the sick and those who are handicapped in any way: that they may experience the healing touch of Christ. (Pause). Lord, hear us.

That we may be able to see the hand of God in our crosses, pain and failures, because they help us to grow and to discover who we are. (Pause). Lord, hear us.

For local needs.

Let us pray:

God our Father, you are the source of all we have and are. Teach us to be always grateful for the many good things you have given us. We ask this through Christ our Lord.

SIGN OF PEACE

Lord Jesus Christ, you heard the cries of the lepers, and in your compassion brought them in from the cold. Help us to reach out a warm hand towards those we are rejecting, so that we may enjoy the peace and unity of your kingdom where you live for ever and ever.

COMMUNION REFLECTION

Thank you, Lord, that I can see;
so many are blind.
Thank you, Lord, that I can hear;
so many are deaf.
Thank you, Lord, that I can walk;
so many are crippled.

Thank you, Lord, that I have food;
so many are hungry.
Thank you, Lord, that I have shelter;
so many are homeless.
Thank you, Lord, for the touch of a friendly hand;
so many are lonely.

Thank you, Lord, for sharing your cross with me;
it helps me to grow and discover who I am.
Thank you, Lord, for all your blessings;
so many deserve them better than I do.
Help me always to be grateful.
Amen.

TWENTY-NINTH SUNDAY OF THE YEAR
Pray without ceasing

INTRODUCTION AND CONFITEOR

Prayer is a good test of our commitment to Christ. How often do we pray? (Pause). What kind of things do we pray for? Do we pray only for material things or when we are in trouble? (Pause).

We pray too seldom. Everything else tends to come before prayer. And even when we do pray often our hearts are empty and our minds distracted by other things.

Let us now pray for the Lord's forgiveness.

I confess to almighty God . . .

HEADINGS FOR READINGS

First Reading (Exodus 17:8-13). This relates the first battle fought by the Israelites after their deliverance from Egypt. They are victorious, not through their own power, but through the power of God which comes to them as a result of the prayer of Moses.

Second Reading (2 Tim 3:14-4:2). Paul instructs Timothy to abide in the sound doctrine which he has been taught since childhood, and to be zealous in preaching the message of Jesus.

Gospel (Luke 18:1-8). Jesus exhorts his disciples to pray continually and never to grow discouraged.

HOMILY

Just as no one can run a marathon without training, so no one can live a proper Christian life without prayer. But we have to have a proper understanding of what prayer is and what it does. Here is a parable about prayer. In it we find two wrong attitudes, and one right one.

Three men found themselves in a dark cellar which had no doors or windows, in fact no exit whatever. They were trapped there and their prospects of getting out were very slim. Let me introduce you to the three men.

The first was George, a writer. He had long given up the practice of his faith. Not only had he no faith but he was poisoned by cynicism. How did he react to his predicament? He did nothing except sit there cursing both the darkness and God. 'I'm not a very practical man, I'm afraid,' he said, trying to excuse himself. His only contribution was to spread gloom and despair. 'It's no use. There's nothing we can do. We're doomed. We might as well resign ourselves to our fate.'

The second man was a very religious man by the name of Peter. He immediately began to argue with George. 'You mustn't talk like that,' he said. 'You mustn't blame God. What you should do is get down on your knees and pray to God for deliverance.' This only produced scoffs from George. How did Peter spend his time? He got out his rosary beads and began to pray. But then he sat back and waited for a miracle.

The third man was a bricklayer by the name of Ivan. He was quite a religious man in his own way, though he would never boast about it. But he was also a very practical man. So what did he do? He looked around, and with the light of a match found a small chisel and a hammer. With these he began to chip away at the solid wall.

The plaster was very hard and the darkness was a terrible handicap. Hence the work was slow, monotonous and extremely tiring. After two hours he succeeded in making a small dent in the wall. The dust got into his eyes, nose and mouth. Blisters appeared on is hands. Neither of the other two showed any desire to help him. George sat in one corner smoking and keeping up an endless and silly chatter. Peter sat in another corner saying his beads. From time to time Ivan paused to pray. His prayer went like this: 'Dear God, I believe that with your help we can make it out of here. So help us now.'

Then he went back to his work. At one point he felt absolutely alone. He could no longer hear the prayers of Peter, and George had lapsed into silence or fallen asleep. But still, somehow, he forced himself to go on chipping at the wall. And slowly he was making an impression on it. Finally, after hours of painful work, a big stone disloged itself and light streamed in from next door. He began to shout for joy. His two companions helped him to widen the hole, and eventually they crawled through and were free.

'Thanks be to God!' said Peter, and went off to the nearest church to thank God for his deliverance. He forgot to thank Ivan. When he had gone George remarked: 'See that man! There he goes to tell everyone that God worked a miracle for him.'

'Perhaps he's right', said Ivan quietly.

'Now surely a practical man like you don't believe that nonsense?' said George.

'All I know,' Ivan replied, 'is that without God's help I would never have been able to do what I did. Peter's prayers were a big help to me, unlike your idle chatter.'

Here you have three different attitudes towards prayer. You have that of George: prayer is a waste of time. Which is logical enough if one has no faith. Then you have Peter's attitude: you want something badly so you pray for it. But having prayed you sit back and wait for God to deliver it into your lap. A lot of our prayer is like that, especially our prayer on behalf of others. We pray for them but we leave it at that. Our prayer doesn't commit us to do anything. We leave the rest to God. Finally, there is Ivan's attitude. He believes in prayer, but he doesn't look on it as a substitute for action. Rather, having prayed, he immediately does something. And his prayer serves the purpose of keeping up his courage and above all his hope. Prayer for him is no easy way out. He realises that we haven't prayed fully until we have done what we can to make our wish come true.

If you look at the first reading you will see Ivan's view of prayer in action. The Israelites relied on the prayer of Moses, not as an excuse for doing nothing but as a spur to action. And Jesus urges us in the Gospel not to grow weary but to keep on praying. We may not always get what we want from God, but then do we always know what we want or even what is good for us? Remember what St James says: 'When you pray and don't get what you ask for, it is because you haven't prayed properly, you have prayed for something to indulge your own desires.' (4:3). Perhaps, then, we should pray, not for what we *want,* but for what we *need.* Our prayer will sustain our faith. It will help us to persevere in our struggles.

Walter Ciszek SJ spent in all twenty-three years in Russia, most of them in the slave labour camps of Siberia. It was his faith that helped him to survive. And it was prayer that helped him to keep that faith alive. He says: 'I learned soon enough that prayer does not take away bodily or mental anguish. Nevertheless, it does provide a certain moral strength to bear the burden patiently. Prayer helped me through every crisis. But I had to purify my prayer and remove from it all elements of self-seeking. I learned even to pray for my interrogators.'

And Henri Nouwen says: 'Nobody has to prove to me that prayer makes a difference. I become irritable, tired, heavy of heart, without prayer. Besides, prayer puts me in touch with the Holy Spirit who directs my attention to the needs of others instead of my own.'

Prayer gives us insight as well as strength. It supports those who go beyond human hopes and human reasons. It helps us to do things we could not have done if we hadn't prayed. Sometimes we excuse ourselves by saying that we haven't time to pray. No matter how busy we are we find time to eat and to read the paper. Yet we say we haven't time to nourish our souls with prayer! If we starve our souls, we will deprive our lives of their fruitfulness, no matter how full they may be of activity.

But prayer is a lonely business and, from a worldly point of view, often apparently totally unproductive. Hence we need support in our prayer. Even Moses needed support. This is where prayer groups come into their own. Often we tell our small children to say their prayers, but how often do we support them with encouragement and example? How often do we bother to pray with them?

Finally, we might try to end all our prayers with the perfect prayer: 'Thy will be done.' Let us continue to pray, but leave the result to God.

'Prayer is the oil that keeps the lamp of faith burning brightly.' (Mother Teresa).

'When things are going badly we are not ashamed of our God. We are only ashamed of him when things go well.' (Solzhenitsyn).

PRAYER OF THE FAITHFUL

Jesus told his disciples about the need to pray continually and never lose heart. In obedience to his instruction let us pray now for our own needs, for the needs of the Church, and those of all the world. *R*. Lord, hear our prayer.

That Christians may have unlimited confidence in God's unfailing love for them and in his presence with them in all their trials. (Pause). Let us pray to the Lord.

For all the leaders of the human community: that they may seek to know the will of God and get the grace to do it. (Pause). Let us pray to the Lord.

Let us pray for the world's poor: that they may have the bread to meet each day's need through the generosity of others. (Pause). Let us pray to the Lord.

That we may be convinced of the value of prayer and make room for it in our daily lives. (Pause). Let us pray to the Lord.

For local needs.

Let us pray:

Father, grant that what we have said with our lips, we may believe in our hearts, and practise in our lives. We ask this through Christ our Lord.

COMMUNION REFLECTION

Prayer is not a stratagem for occasional use,
a refuge to resort to now and then,
especially when things are bad.

It is rather like an established residence
for the innermost self.

All things have a home:
the bird has a nest,
the fox a den.
the bees a hive.
A soul without prayer is a soul without a home.

To pray is to open the door of my innermost self
so that God and the soul may enter.

Prayer is not asking things of God,
but receiving what he wants to give you.

It is not offering yourself to God,
but welcoming God offering himself to you.

THIRTIETH SUNDAY OF THE YEAR
The Pharisee and the tax collector

INTRODUCTION AND CONFITEOR

The Pharisee in Christ's story boasted that he was not like the rest of men. By this he meant that he was not a sinner.

At the start of the Mass we confess in no uncertain terms that we *are* sinners. We admit that we offend in our thoughts and in our words, in what we do and in what we fail to do. Furthermore, we make no excuses. (Pause).

I confess to almighty God . . .

HEADINGS FOR READINGS

First Reading (Sirach 35:12-14, 16-19). God is no respecter of persons. He shows no partiality for the rich and the powerful, but listens to the humble prayer of the just and the lowly.

Second Reading (2 Tim 4:6-8, 16-18). Paul, a prisoner in Rome, feels that his death is drawing near. But his confidence is unshaken and his hope of the 'crown of glory' is bright.

Gospel (Luke 18:9-14). This contains the great parable of Christ about the Pharisee and the tax collector.

HOMILY

A good lady, having heard this parable and the sermon on it, when leaving church was heard to say: 'Thank God, I'm not like that Pharisee!' If we are honest we have to admit that most of us in fact are like him. We do exactly the same as he did. We parade our good deeds before God and use them as a justification for looking down on others. We may not do so in so many words, but we think it. A number of people went into a church to pray. Here is how they prayed. (Different voices could be used).

(1) The first (a man) prayed like this: 'Thank you, Lord, that I have a good job. Mind you, I worked hard to get it, and even harder to keep it. I think I can say that I've proved myself worthy of it. I thank you that I've never had to live off the dole. Every penny I possess I've earned by the sweat of my brow. I'm not like those dossers and lay-abouts who are forever sponging on society. They should be put to work instead of getting constant handouts . . .'

(2) The second (a woman) prayed like this: 'Thank you, Lord, that my kids are clean and well-behaved. I'm not saying that they're angels, but you won't find them going around wrecking telephone kiosks or terrifying old people. Nor will you hear them using bad language. Unlike those gurriers down the street, who are let run wild and do whatever they like. The language out of them! Why, Lord, even you would be shocked if you heard it. These are the criminals of tomorrow. I make sure that my kids stay well clear of them . . .'

(3) The third (a woman) prayed like this: 'Thank you, Lord, that my marriage is working out. Of course Jim and I have had our problems, but we've stuck together. We've worked things out. Not like those others whose marriages are breaking up within a year or two of starting. The first sign of a problem and one or both of them make a dash for freedom. It happened to some of my own neighbours, the very ones who seemed to have everything going for them. But obviously they couldn't take the rough with smooth. It's society that will pay for their fickleness, when all those kids from broken homes are let loose on it . . .'

(4) The fourth (a man) prayed like this: 'Thank you, Lord, that I can take a drink and leave it at that. I'm not like those others who don't know when to stop. They live in the pub and only surface for fresh air. Like your man next door who comes home footless every night. I can hear the wife giving out and the kids screaming. It's locked up the likes of him should be if he can't drink in moderation . . .'

(5) The fifth (a woman) prayed like this: 'Thank you, Lord, that I have been able to stick to the religion I was brought up in, unlike a lot of my neighbours. Some of them are like the ox and the ass of the crib — they appear in church only once a year. Maybe I'm a bit of a traditionalist. For instance I don't go for Communion in the hand. I don't think I'm worthy of touching the Host. But when I see Mrs So-and-so coming up with her hand out it sends a shudder down my spine. You'd think by her holy attitude that she was the Blessed Virgin Mary herself. Next thing she'll be putting herself forward as a minister of the Eucharist . . .'

(6) The sixth (a man) didn't even go inside the church. He said this prayer as he passed by: 'Lord, I thank you that I am not like the crowd who go in there every Sunday to worship you. They're nothing but a bunch of hypocrites, if you ask me. Inside there they give each other a handshake as a sign of friendship by the way, and I know for a fact that when they come out some of them won't even talk to one another. They say they worship you but I know different. They worship money. At least I'm being honest. I know I'm no saint, but then I don't pretend to be one . . .'

The point that is being made is that there is a Pharisee lurking in each of us. All of the above people were sincere people. They were not lying. They did the things they said they did. The same was true of Christ's Pharisee. He was scrupulously honest, a faithful family man, and a meticulous observer of the Law. He did even more than the Law required of him. It required only one fast a year, but he fasted twice a year! That's zeal for you. And again, the Law only required tithes of certain commodities, but he paid tithes on all of them.

Where then did he go wrong? First of all his attitude to God was wrong. He believed that he had run up a formidable credit-balance with God. Therefore he had got God in his debt. God owes him salvation. It is easy to fall into this trap. We've talked about it before. (See twenty-seventh Sunday). Secondly, his attitude towards his neighbour was all wrong. He felt that his good and upright life put him above others. It not only gave him a warm inner glow (nothing particularly wrong with that), but greatly inflated his ego. He put himself up on a pedestal. From his lofty pedestal he looked down on others, especially on tax collectors and sinners. No, he didn't just look down on them, he actually despised them.

He was oozing with pride. This pride poisoned him at the core and infected all his good deeds. There wasn't a shred of humility in him. Humility consists in being precisely the person you actually are before God. And humility is the soil in which all other virtues flourish. Without it they either go to seed or never flower.

The Pharisee serves as a warning to the righteous. It's easy to deceive oneself. You look around you and you see so much crime and corruption in the world and, though you may never say it aloud, you think: 'Thank God, I'm not like all those others who rob and steal . . . etc.' Ah, the pride and selfishness that can exist among good and devout people. It is impossible to weigh the sins of others without putting one's own fingers on the scales.

The tax collector said: 'Lord, be merciful to me I am a sinner.' In saying this he was simply being realistic. He was only telling the truth. 'I know I am a sinner.' If we can say this with conviction and humility, we are very close to God, and it gives us a great sense of freedom. We no longer have to pretend that we are holy. Being virtuous doesn't preclude slipping and falling, once in a while. Being virtuous means getting up and trying again.

'There is no odour as bad as that which arises from tainted goodness.' (Thoreau).

'I am old enough to know that I am no better than others.' (Carlo Carretto).

PRAYER OF THE FAITHFUL

Let us pray for the grace that we may imitate the humility of the tax collector and shun the pride of the Pharisee. *R.* Lord, be merciful to me a sinner.

For all members of the Church: that we may never parade our good deeds before God or look down on other people. (Pause). Let us pray.

For all in authority: that they may have the humility to acknowledge their faults, and resolve to correct them. (Pause). Let us pray.

For all the fault-finders and begrudgers: that they may realise that it is not necessary to put out the other person's light in order to let one's own shine. (Pause). Let us pray.

That we may come before God as we are, with all our sins and wounds, so that we may enjoy the benefits of his forgiveness and healing. (Pause). Let us pray.

For local needs.

Let us pray:

Heavenly Father, may we so pray during this Mass, that, like the tax collector, we may go away from here right with you and with our fellowmen. We make all our prayers through Christ our Lord.

COMMUNION REFLECTION

William Barclay told the following story.

Once he was on a train journey from Scotland to England.

As he was passing through the Yorkshire moors

he spotted a little whitewashed cottage.
How its radiant whiteness shone out
against the drab and bleak moors!

A few days later he passed that way again
on the return journey.
Snow had fallen and was lying deep on the ground.
He came again to the little whitewashed cottage.
But now its whiteness actually seemed drab
against the virgin whiteness of the snow.

So if we should be tempted
to compare ourselves with others,
let us compare ourselves with none other
than Christ himself.
When we lay our imperfect lives beside his sinless life,
all we will be able to say is:
'Lord, be merciful to me, I am a sinner.'

This is the most moving of all prayers,
and one that God cannot fail to hear.

THIRTY-FIRST SUNDAY OF THE YEAR
Zacchaeus: the man out on a limb

INTRODUCTION AND CONFITEOR

Today's Gospel is a shocking one, at least it shocked the people of Christ's time. What caused the shock was the fact that he went to stay with the most hated man in the community. He did this because he was thinking, not of himself, but of the other person's need.

How often we do what will make us popular, rather than what is right. We go where we will be most welcome, rather than where we are most needed. We befriend those who are kind of us, and ignore those we don't like. In many ways we turn the Gospel upside down. (Pause).

Let us confess our sins and ask forgiveness with humility and confidence.

I confess to almighty God . . .

HEADINGS FOR READINGS

First Reading (Wisdom 11:22-12:2). It was out of love that God created the world in the first place. Therefore he does not desire the destruction or death of the human family, but is always ready to pardon the sins of those who repent and return to him.

Second Reading (2 Thess 1:11-2:2). Paul urges the Thessalonians to be worthy of their call and assures them that God will help them to be true to it. At the same time he tells them that the Second Coming of Christ has not yet taken place.

Gospel (Luke 19:1-10). This relates the conversion of a rich tax collector by the name of Zacchaeus.

HOMILY

One of the most Christlike men of this century, or perhaps any century, was not even a professed Christian. Indeed it can be said that he took the teaching of Christ far more seriously than the vast majority of Christians. I'm referring to Mahatma Gandhi, of whom Albert Einstein said: 'Generations to come will find it hard to believe that such a man as he ever walked upon this earth'.

It was March 1931, and Gandhi, accompanied by some eight of his close disciples, had set out to walk two hundred miles to the sea in order to defy a government ban which prevented the people from taking salt from the sea. It was a symbolic act of defiance, and Gandhi was prepared to take the consequences. It was one of the strangest marches ever witnessed and soon got very wide press coverage, not only in India, but throughout the world.

Following winding dirt roads from village to village, Gandhi led his disciples forward. Of course by this time he was the most talked-about and respected man in India. The procession soon became a triumphant march. The villages through which the marchers passed were festooned in Gandhi's honour. Between the villages, peasants sprinkled water on the road to keep the dust down, and they threw leaves and flower petals on them to make the going easier on the feet. In every settlement hundreds of workers abandoned their work and joined them for at least part of the way to show solidarity with them.

Gandhi was well known to be a staunch opponent of the iniquitous caste system. He especially abhorred the treatment meted out to the untouchables, that is, those who belong to no caste, and who were the rejects of Indian society. He referred to the treatment of the untouchables as 'a blot on the soul of India'. He was determined to do all he could to eliminate this blot.

One evening he and his followers arrived at a large and prosperous village. Gandhi knew that a lot of untouchables lived there. The villagers gave him a great welcome. The head of the village then approached him and invited him to stay in his house for the night, where he would be able to have a bath, good food, and a decent night's rest. Gandhi thanked him but refused the offer. He said: 'Where are your untouchables? I will stay with them.' And he did, even though his action shocked the village leaders and many of its respectable citizens. Gandhi went among the untouchables in their hovels on the outskirts of the village. And they welcomed him with open arms. He touched them. He ate with them and played with their children. He called them 'the children of God.'

Next morning they had tears in their eyes as he left them. By his presence among them Gandhi had not only given them much-needed hope, but also a sense of their own dignity and worth. As a result of his action the village fathers bade him a frosty farewell. But this didn't bother Gandhi, who said: 'I have no wish to be reborn. But if this should happen, then I want to be reborn among the untouchables, so that I might succeed in liberating them and myself from their wretched condition.'

Gandhi's action in that village reminds us of Christ's action in Jericho. I know that there is one big difference. Zacchaeus was not poor like the untouchables. He was rich. But in another sense he too was an untouchable. And he was also poor because he was lost in his riches and in desperate need of salvation. And that is why Christ went to stay with him, even though by doing so he shocked and scandalised the villagers and their leaders.

It would have been so fitting, so entirely appropriate, for Christ to go where he would have been assured of a great welcome; where he would have been dined, wined and honoured; where he would have been surrounded by well-wishers and admirers, and treated like a hero. But he turned his back on all this, and went instead to the house of an outcast.

Christ did this because, like Gandhi, he was not thinking of himself but of others. He said: 'I did not come to have service rendered to me, I came to serve. I came to seek out and to save those who are lost.' In other words, he goes, not where they will make the biggest fuss over him, but where he is most needed. The Churches, I fear, have made Christ very respectable. We all know categories of people whose company we feel would be inappropriate for him. We, the respectable people, feel that he belongs among us, Witness what happens to the pope wherever he goes. All the undesirables, the very people who have most need of him, are kept carefully out of sight.

The amazing thing is that Christ succeeded in converting Zacchaeus. Christ knew that Zacchaeus, like every person, had goodness in him, but that goodness needed to be evoked. Zacchaeus had for years been living a selfish, cruel and complacent life. But a veil concealed the full reality of his state from him. Yet he hadn't forgotten beyond recall that he was a man, that he carried the divine spark within him, and that he was capable of higher things. His conscience hadn't been completely numbed. It still whispered to him, making him feel uneasy about his life. But he didn't realise that this uneasiness and shame were the voice of the finest qualities of his soul begging for recognition.

What Christ did was gently draw back the veil, giving Zacchaeus a glimpse of what lay behind it. But then he pointed him in a new direction. He gave him a new vision. He led him into a whole new world he never knew existed — the world of sharing. He did this, not by threats, but by showing concern for him. He proved his concern by facing the wrath of the villagers. This concern touched the heart of Zacchaeus, a heart long dead and frozen. Jesus spoke to his heart and turned it upside down. For Zacchaeus that encounter with Christ was a great and dazzling moment in his life. Afterwards he was like a man who had risen from the dead.

If only we the followers of Christ had a little of Christ's Spirit. If as a teacher I could give most attention, not to the bright kids, but to the weak ones. If as a parent I could give most care to the troublesome child rather than to the obedient one. If as a neighbour I could reach out to that neighbour everyone finds difficult and who is cut off, rather than to all those nice ones. If as a doctor I could give my best to the poor who cannot reward me adequately, rather than to the rich. If we are not careful we can easily turn the Gospel upside down. We do this when we give more attention to the person who has done most to deserve it, rather than to the person wo has most need of it.

Finally, in a very real sense, each of us could say: I am like Zacchaeus. I need Christ to come to me with his salvation. I need his love to help me to overcome my selfishness and reach out to others in love.

'What impresses me about Christ is that there is no difference between what he says and what he does.' (Perez Esquivel).

'It is not a mark of prestige for the Church to be in good standing with the rich and the powerful.' (Oscar Romero).

PRAYER OF THE FAITHFUL

Let us pray for some of that spirit of open and generous love Christ showed to Zacchaeus. *R*. Lord, hear us in your love.

For the Church: that like Christ it may see its primary mission as that of 'seeking out and saving those who are lost.' (Pause). Let us pray to the Lord.

For the rich, the powerful, and all those who exploit the poor and the weak of the earth: that they may be converted to the Gospel. (Pause). Let us pray to the Lord.

For all the outcasts of society: that like Christ we may have the courage and the generosity to befriend them. (Pause).   Let us pray to the Lord.

That we may learn from the example of Zacchaeus, who after one encounter with Christ changed his life completely. (Pause). Let us pray to the Lord.

For local needs.

Let us pray:

Lord, you have given us a wonderful example. You never write off anybody. For you there is always hope of turning over a new leaf. May this give us hope for our own lives, and serve as a model for us in our dealings with others. We make all our prayers to the Father, through you, Christ our Lord.

SIGN OF PEACE

Lord Jesus Christ, the night before you died, you prayed for your apostles in these words: 'Father, may they be one as we are one.' May we be one in mind and heart so that we may enjoy the peace and unity of your kingdom where you live for ever and ever.

COMMUNION REFLECTION

It was coming towards the end of October,
and in spite of days of gusting wind,
the trees refused to give up their leaves.
But then one morning the ground was covered with frost.
It was a perfectly calm morning.
There wasn't even a breath of wind.

As the sun rose an amazing thing happened —
the leaves began to fall in droves.
It was as if the trees were surrendering them voluntarily
under the gentle influence of the sun.
Long before noon the trees were bare.

We are all selfish by nature.
We cling to our comforts.
We do not give up things easily.
Love alone has the power to disarm us,
causing us to drop our defences,
whereas force only causes us to close up.

Through his gentle and loving approach
Christ disarmed Zacchaeus,
getting him to open up
and share his ill-gotten goods with the poor.

People are essentially good,
but this good has to be awakened and called forth.

THIRTY-SECOND SUNDAY OF THE YEAR
Travelling in hope

INTRODUCTION AND CONFITEOR
The liturgy of today is dominated by the idea of an afterlife. This belief should light up our lives with meaning and hope. Often, however, it is but a pale and shadowy thing, shedding no more light than a crescent moon. Besides, we are so concerned with this life that we do not really desire or seek the life that is to come. (Pause). Our hope of a better life to come rests, not on anything human, but on the word and the power of Christ.

Lord Jesus, you have gone ahead of us to prepare a place for us in the Father's house. Lord, have mercy.

Lord Jesus, you banish the darkness of our doubts with the light of faith. Christ, have mercy.

Lord Jesus, you bind us together as the new People of God, journeying towards the promised land of eternal life. Lord, have mercy.

HEADINGS FOR READINGS
First Reading (2 Maccabees 7:1-2, 9-14). This tells (in part) the story of the martyrdom of a mother and her seven sons. They drew their strength and their hope from their faith in the resurrection of the just.

Second Reading (2 Thessalonians 2:16-3:5). Paul prays for the Thessalonians that God will comfort and strengthen them so that they may remain steadfast in the pursuit of goodness.

Gospel (Luke 20:27-38. Longer form recommended). The Sadducees, who didn't believe in an afterlife, ask Jesus a question. The aim of the question is to ridicule the idea of bodily resurrection from the dead.

HOMILY
Belief in an afterlife is surely one of the most important of our beliefs as Christians. But how seriously do we take it, and what part does it play in our lives? Of course we say we believe it. Do we not end the Creed each Sunday with these words: 'We look for the resurrection of the dead, and the life of the world to come.' But

often these tremendous words can just roll so glibly off our tongues. The test is how much would we be prepared to lose or suffer for our belief in this life to come?

Nicholas was a political prisoner in Russia. He was also a convinced Christian. Together with tens of thousands of his fellow countrymen and women he was swept up in one of Stalin's numerous purges of 'undesirables'. These were plucked, often in the dead of night and without even a moment's warning, from their places of work or from the bosom of their families, and taken off for long and searching weeks, perhaps months, of interrogation sessions. At the end of those sessions, most of them, confused in mind and crushed in spirit, signed documents confessing to crimes they never committed. Their only 'crime' was that they didn't fit in; they wouldn't consent to be silent, obedient cogs in the godless machine called 'the State'.

After this they were dispersed to remote regions of Siberia and made work like slaves. But some were not even that lucky as to get this thin chance of survival. They were marked down for liquidation. They were considered to be too dangerous. Their way of thinking was likely to pollute the minds of the unthinking masses. Nicholas was one of those due for execution. He was temporarily dispatched to a remote northern island. There his guards informed him that he was to be executed on the following Friday. But when Friday came he received an unexpected visit from his wife, Clara. He begged a favour from his jailors — to postpone his execution until Monday so as not to spoil his wife's visit. They could shoot him after she left. They agreed to his request which shows that there was some goodness still left in them.

He made an immediate decision. He would not tell his beloved Clara of his imminent death. Nothing, just nothing must be allowed to spoil for her the joy of this their last weekend together. But this was easier said than done. For three whole days he never left his wife's side. And all that time he hid from her the news of his execution. It took enormous sensitivity and self-control on his part to do this. He had to watch every word he said. He could not allow his spirits to drop, not even for a second. He could not allow his eyes to darken. Just once as they were walking along a woodland path she turned around unexpectedly and saw him bent over double, clutching his head in his hands.

'What's wrong?' she asked.

'It's nothing,' he lied. 'It's just a passing headache.'

At the end of the three days Clara left him. For her they had been days of immense happiness. The boat carrying her back to the mainland pulled away. It had only just gone out of sight when Nicholas turned himself over to his jailors, saying: 'You can shoot me now. I'm ready.'

They were flabbergasted at his apparent indifference to his fate. They said to him: 'How can you be so calm, so indifferent to death?' Nicholas answered: 'I'm not indifferent to death. Like everyone else I love life and want to go on living. But if in order to live I must deny my faith in Christ and in all I hold dear and sacred, then I would rather die. In any case, I do not look on death as the end of everything. I see it rather as a gateway to the real life, that life for which our years on earth are but a preparation. I mean the life Christ promised to those who believe in him and who follow his way.'

If there was no life to come then our lives on earth would be ultimately meaningless. They would constitute a road to nowhere, a stream that flows into the desert and disappears. George Orwell put it very forcefully: 'There is no possible substitute for faith, no pagan acceptance of life as sufficient to itself, no pantheistic cheer-up stuff, no pseudo-religion of Progress with glittering Utopias and ant-heaps of steel and concrete. Either life on earth is a preparation for something greater and more lasting, or it is meaningless, dark and dreadful.'

Above all else, belief in an afterlife gives us hope — that most precious of all spiritual commodities. Without hope there is no future. What a light the hope of that eternal life promised by Christ to his followers sheds on our lowly lives, on our work, and on all our struggles and sacrifices. At present we are pilgrims, pilgrims of hope. But we are not travelling in the dark. We are following the map left us by Christ.

Moses led God's People out of the slavery of Egypt on their great journey to liberation towards the promised land, a land 'flowing with milk and honey', yet he himself never set foot in that land. He died in the desert. In a very real sense, we also die in the 'desert'. We cannot reach the final promised land without passing over the Jordan of death. But we do not die in despair. Like the brothers we read about in the first reading, we die 'relying on God's promise that we shall be raised up by him.' We do not place our hopes on anything human. We place them on God and on his word. He is a God, not of the dead, but of the living. He made us not for eternal death but for eternal life.

From time to time we are all assailed by doubts. What if, after I've been a believer all my life, when I die it suddenly turns out that there's nothing at all, nothing but wild grass growing on my grave? We shouldn't be afraid to admit out doubts. We have to confront them. Much is hidden from us on earth. Nevertheless, from time to time we are given a mysterious, sacred sense of a living bond with another world, with a lofty and superior world. 'Though nothing can be proved, one can become convinced.' (Dostoyevsky).

Our belief in an afterlife should spur us on to live a better and a more worthwhile life. It should rescue us from meanness and shallowness. But let us not forget that we do not make the pilgrimage to the promised land of eternal life all alone. We make it with others — with the members of God's People. With faith in the word of Christ let us go forward together in joyful hope.

'Sunset is a promise of the dawn to come.' (Thoreau).

'While on earth, we grope almost as though in the dark and, but for the precious image of Christ before us, we would lose our way completely and perish.' (Dostoyevesky).

PRAYER OF THE FAITHFUL

Let us pray that God may help us, not only to be firm in our belief in eternal life, but to desire it ardently as the goal that will fulfil all our hopes and longings. *R.* Lord, graciously hear us.

For the Church: that through the faith of its members it may be a beacon of hope for all the world. (Pause). Lord, hear us.

For all of mankind: that those who live without hope and who do not know Christ may come to believe in the eternal life he promised. (Pause). Lord, hear us.

Christ dried the tears of Martha and Mary by raising their brother Lazarus from the dead: may he comfort all those who mourn the death of a loved one. (Pause). Lord, hear us.

That we may grow in the knowledge and love of Christ during our life on earth, so that we may come to see our death for what it is — a joyful encounter with him. (Pause). Lord, hear us.

For local needs.

Let us pray.

Heavenly Father, your only-begotten Son overcame death and gave us the hope of eternal life. Grant that all who believe in him may triumph over death and come to share in his glory. We ask this through the same Christ our Lord.

COMMUNION REFLECTION

Do not pursue what is illusory — property and position.
Live with a steady superiority over life.
Don't be afraid of misfortne,
and do not yearn after happiness;
it is, after all, all the same:
the bitter doesn't last for ever,
and the sweet never fills the cup to overflowing.

It is enough that you don't freeze in the cold,
and if thirst and hunger don't claw at your insides.

If your back isn't broken,
if your feet can walk,
if both arms can bend,
if both eyes can see,
and if both ears can hear, then whom should you envy?
And why?
Our envy of others devours us most of all.

Rub your eyes and purify your heart —
and prize above all else in the world
those who love you and who wish you well.
Do not hurt them or scold them,
and never part from any of them in anger;
after all, you simply do not know
but it might be your last act,
and that will be how you are imprinted in their memory.

Alexander Solzhenitsyn, *Gulag Archipelgo,* Vol. I, p. 591.

THIRTY-THIRD SUNDAY OF THE YEAR
Witnessing to Christ in a world of confusion

INTRODUCTION AND CONFITEOR
As Christians we do not live in a special world. We live in the real world, a world which is full of confusion and trouble of every kind. It is in the midst of this world that we are expected to be witnesses to Christ.

Are we? Could I honestly say that even in a small way I let the light of Christ's truth or goodness shine in the world? (Pause). Let us ask pardon for our cowardice.

I confess to almighty God . . .

HEADINGS FOR READINGS
First Reading (Malachi 3:19-20). For evil doers the Day of the Lord will be a day of judgement; but for the upright it will be a day of salvation.

Second Reading (2 Thessalonians 3:7-12). As far as possible, each person must try to earn the food that he eats.

Gospel (Luke 21:5-19). This foretells the destruction of the temple in Jerusalem. The disciples are warned to beware of false prophets and to be ready to face persecutions of every kind.

HOMILY

Christ did not tell his disciples to live in a world apart, a safe, secure, comfortable world of their own. He sent them out into the real world. They were to be witnesses to his Gospel 'before men', that is, in the midst of people and in the hurly-burly of life. Yet in spite of this Christians have always been tempted to isolate themselves so as to keep themselves free from the contamination of evil.

For several years now little David has been living in a world of his own. In fact ever since the day of his birth he hasn't lived in the real world. During all that time he has literally been 'untouched by human hands.' David suffers from a very rare ailment. He is one in ten thousand. His problem is that he has no resistance to disease. A minor illness, such as a common cold, which a normal person would shrug off in a day or two, could kill David. That is why he has to live in a plastic bubble.

In his little bubble world he lives a germ-free existence. Everything he eats and drinks and uses has to be thoroughly sterilised. And thanks to his highly protected environment he is healthy and even thriving. Now he has been given a specially designed space suit which means he can leave his bubble and walk around among ordinary people. But he can never quite be one with them. He is still cut off.

The truth he must accept is that he cannot live in the real world. That is his fate and his cross. He gets a lot of attention, since most things have to be done for him. Though everybody admires his fortitude, most people pity him in his isolation. He can never feel the wind in his face, or let water run through his fingers, or splash through mud like ordinary children. There is so much that he can never experience. But the world he lives in is a safe world. Outside of it he could not survive.

The Pharisees, with whom Christ clashed on numerous occasions, were very sincere and very religious people. But they lived in a world of their own. It was a very sheltered and protected world. Unlike David who had no choice, they entered that world of their own choice. They cut themselves off because they firmly believed that the world was not fit for them. They might inhale the fatal germs of sin and human evil.

So what did they do? They constructed a 'bubble world' of their own. They called themselves the 'separated ones'. They regarded themselves as God's favourites, God's chosen few. 'Thank God we are not grasping, unjust, adulterous like the rest of mankind.' This was their daily prayer. They must not have any contact with the ordinary riff-raff.

They didn't expect to be pitied in their isolation. They expected to be admired. They put themselves on display to make it easier for this to happen. As far as they were concerned, it was those who lived in the contaminated world outside who were to be pitied. Even though their lives were hemmed in by all kinds of disciplines, they didn't mind. It was a small price to pay for the privilege of being special.

We all face the temptation to create 'bubble worlds' of our own . . . worlds of privilege, wealth, comfort, religion . . . But by doing this we are not acting according to the mind of Christ. Consider today's Gospel. Christ knew well what the world was like, and how rough it can be at times. He told his disciples in advance about the trials and tribulations they would encounter. Even though they were his very disciples, precious to the heavenly Father, they would be spared nothing. If anything, the 'powers of darkness' would single them out for special treatment — they would be 'hated by all on account of his name.'

He foretold that the temple, the very centre of Jewish worship and the focus of all their pilgrimages, would be utterly destroyed. What a blow that must have been to them. He told them they would meet all kinds of false prophets speaking in his name. He urged them not to be taken in. He told them that there would be terrible wars and revolutions that would tear the world apart. He urged them not to be afraid. He told them there would be great earthquakes, plagues and famines. Finally he told them that they themselves would suffer all kinds of persecutions — betrayal even by members of their own families, imprisonment, trial and death.

He hid nothing from them. Paradoxically, the time they should be most on their guard was when people spoke well of them. 'Beware when people speak well of you, for that is how they treated the false prophets.' They were not to depend on privilege. They were, as Paul urged, to earn their bread by the sweat of their brow. But Christ gave them the assurance that in the end his power would see them through all these trials. What a tremendous assurance. They were not to rely on their own cleverness or strength, but only on his help.

The kind of world Christ described sounds awfully familiar — exactly like the one we live in! Wars, revolutions, persecution of Christians . . . It is surely comforting to know that Christ foresaw all this. We should not get dismayed then by it all. Let us never forget or be ashamed of what we are — his disciples. Of all the tragedies that could happen to us, betrayal of Christ would be the most serious. But perhaps the greatest threat is not that we might become victims of real evil, as that we might simply vanish into the crowd, and so lose our identity and sense of mission as Christians. Then the salt would have lost its saltiness. 'The greatest temptation of modern man is escape into the great formless sea of irresponsibility which is the crowd.' (Thomas Merton).

We are not to think that we are better than others or superior to them. We are exposed to the same germs of evil as all others. But if we are genuine followers of Christ we must in some way be different. We must be 'in the world but not of the world.' We are followers of Christ. We must try to be true to that. Then in the midst of a chaotic world we will be messengers of hope and bearers of light. Above all, we will be witnesses to his truth.

'Beware lest you be held in honour by men in the marketplace, while inside yourselves you are full of darkness.' (Alan Paton).

'All situations in the world are good places in which to make saints, so long as the persons in them show that they are not in agreement with sin.' (Oscar Romero).

PRAYER OF THE FAITHFUL

Let us pray that we may be courageous witnesses to Christ and his Gospel in the midst of a confused and chaotic world.   *R.* Lord, hear our prayer.

For the followers of Christ: that they may not be deceived by false prophets, even when they claim to speak in his name; and that they may not lose heart in times of trial and persecution. (Pause). Let us pray to the Lord.

For all world leaders: that in spite of innumerable setbacks they may persevere in their efforts to bring about a just and peaceful world. (Pause).   Let us pray to the Lord.

For all those who are lost or confused and who are easy prey for false prophets. (Pause).   Let us pray to the Lord.

That we may bear witness to Christ by lives of truth, honesty and goodness. (Pause).   Let us pray to the Lord.

For local needs.

Let us pray:

God our Father, you are the same yesterday, today and for ever. Help us to have confidence in your unchanging love and goodness, so that when things go wrong we may have the hope and strength to persevere in goodness. We ask this through Christ our Lord.

COMMUNION REFLECTION

Everything God made was a consolation to me,
even grief itself —
it would make me think deeper.

It is a simple life we lived
but nobody could say that it was comfortable.
Often during life I have known God's holy help,

because I was often in the grip of a sorrow
from which I could not escape.
When the need was greatest
God would lay his merciful eye on me,
and the clouds of sorrow would be gone without a trace.
In their place would be a spiritual joy
whose sweetness I cannot describe here.

There are people who think that this island is a lonely place,
but the peace of the Lord is here.
I am living in it for more than forty years,
and I didn't see two neighbours fighting in it yet.
We helped each other
and lived in the shelter of each other.

But now my life is spent, as a candle,
and my hope is rising every day,
that I'll be called into the eternal kingdom.
May God guide me on this long road
I have not travelled before.
I think everything is folly except for loving God.

From *An Old Woman's Reflections* by Peig Sayers, translated by Seamus Ennis,
Oxford University Press, 1962.

THIRTY-FOURTH SUNDAY OF THE YEAR
Messengers of the King

INTRODUCTION AND CONFITEOR

Today we honour Christ as our King. We honour him best,
however, by helping to spread his Kingdom. We should do this col-
lectively, as members of the Church, and also individually.

Christ wants us to be messengers of his love to others, but
especially to the poor and the needy. What kind of a messenger am
I? (Pause). Christ, who forgave the good thief, will forgive us
also.

Lord Jesus, you help us to spread your Kingdom by living in
peace with others. Lord, have mercy.

Lord Jesus, you help us to spread your Kingdom by sharing with
others. Christ, have mercy.

Lord Jesus, you help us to spread your Kingdom by letting the
world see our love for each other. Lord, have mercy.

HEADINGS FOR READINGS

First Reading (2 Samuel 5:1-3). David had already been anointed king of Judah. Here we read how the northern tribes also acknowledge him as king. Thus David became the king of a united country.

Second Reading (Colossians 1:11-20). Paul gives thanks to God for having delivered us from the dominion of darkness and transferred us to the Kingdom of his Son, who is not only head of the Church but head of all creation.

Gospel (Luke 23:35-43). This tells of the mockery Christ suffered as he hung on the cross, and how in the midst of it he brought hope and salvation to one of the thieves crucified with him.

HOMILY

Once upon a time there was a prince who lived a very sheltered life. No sorrow ever touched him. When he died the people erected a lovely statue of him in the main square of the capital city. The statue was gilded all over with leaves of pure gold. It had two sapphires for eyes, and a large red ruby on the handle of the sword. Everyone who saw the statue could not fail but to admire it, and of course it was the pride and joy of the townspeople. The prince had such a happy look on his young face that they called him 'the Happy Prince'.

Now this little swallow from Northern Europe got left behind when, at the end of summer, the main flock went south to warmer lands. But then, sensing the coming of winter, he too headed south. One evening, having flown all day long, he came to rest at the base of the statue of the Happy Prince. The night was cold but dry. As he was drifting off to sleep he was surprised when a few drops fell on him. He looked up and saw to his surprise that the Happy Price was weeping.

'Why are you weeping?' asked the little swallow.

'When I was alive I saw no suffering or misery. It was all hidden from me,' said the Prince. 'But from my perch up here I see that there is a lot of unhappiness in the world. I'd like to help but I can't do anything as my feet are fastened here. I need a messenger. Would you be my messenger?'

'But I have to go to Egypt.'

'Please stay this night with me.'

'Very well, then. What can I do for you?'

'In a room there is a mother tending a sick child. She has no money with which to pay the doctor. Take the ruby from my sword and give it to her.'

The swallow removed the ruby with his beak and bore it away to the woman and she rejoiced. The doctor came and her child recovered. And the swallow came back and slept soundly. Next day he went down to the river to bathe and prepare for take-off again. He came back to say goodbye to the Happy Prince. But the prince asked him to stay another night and he agreed. Then the prince asked him to take out one of the sapphires and give it to a young man who was trying to write a play but was finding it very difficult because his hands were blue with the cold. On receiving the sapphire the young writer was able to buy firewood, and succeeded in finishing his work.

Next day it was the same story. The prince begged the swallow to stay another night, and reluctantly he agreed. This time he asked him to take out the other sapphire and give it to a little matchgirl down in the square. The little girl had sold no matches all that day and was afraid she would be beaten when she got home. Once again the swallow did as he was asked. And a strange thing happened to him. As he was running these errands of mercy, the swallow's own eyes were opened, and he saw how much poverty and suffering there was in the city. Then he was glad to stay with the prince and be his messenger. One by one, at the Prince's urging, he stripped off the leaves of gold and gave them away to the poor and the needy. Finally he arrived back one evening. As usual he came to rest at the base of the statue. But by now the statue was bare, having been stripped of all its ornaments. The night was very cold. Next morning the little swallow was found dead at the base of the statue.

The Happy prince had given away all his riches, but he could not have done so without the wings of his faithful messenger, the little swallow. Christ, our King, gave himself away totally while he lived on earth. Here surely was the strangest king of all. He was not out to conquer but to convert. He was not out to rule but to serve. He was not out to hoard possessions but to give them away. He devoted all his love, all his time, all his energy to seeking out the sick, the poor, the lost and the lonely. At the end he even gave his life away for those he loved, and he loved everybody.

Even as he died he was still giving to those who were receptive. He could not do much for the crowd. They didn't really understand what was happening. Most of them were there merely out of curiosity. And of course he could give absolutely nothing to the scoffers — the religious leaders and the soldiers. Nor could he give anything to one of the thieves, for the poor man's heart had long since turned into stone. But surprisingly he was able to enrich the other thief, the one we refer to ever since as 'the good thief'. This man's heart was still open and he realised he was desperately poor. So he reached out to Christ who gave him nothing less than paradise itself.

We firmly believe that Christ, our risen King and Saviour, lives

on in the Church. He is still as generous as ever. From his lofty
perch at the Father's right hand, he surveys the plight of all the
Father's children, all those who are now his brothers and sisters.
But his feet, so to speak, are fastened, his hands tied, and his
tongue silent. He needs messengers. He needs us. He has no hands
but ours, no feet but ours, no tongue but ours. And it is his riches,
not our own, that we are called to dispense — his love, his
forgiveness, his mercy, his good news . . .

Our first job is to transform ourselves — our hearts and our lives.
We have to try to live as he taught us: 'Seek first the Kingdom of
God, and all these other things will be given to you.' What does this
imply? It means that each day, in all our actions, we have to try
to do the will of God. This is no easy task but we have his grace
to help us. If we live like this then we will be more willing and more
capable of bringing his riches to others. I become his messenger,
not so much by undertaking all sorts of extra things, but by trying
to be a certain kind of person — a Christlike person.

But this is not something we do only as individuals. We must not
forget that together we form the Body of Christ. Hence we have to
give a collective witness to Christ. We do this firstly by being united
and by supporting one another. And secondly by a joint effort to
show our practical concern about the plight of the poor.

"There is no other way of spreading the Kingdom of God than
by the deeds and lives of individual Christians who strive each day
to do the will of God in their lives.' (Walter Ciszek SJ).

'The world is moved not only by the mighty shoves of the heroes,
but also by the tiny pushes of each honest person.' (Helen Keller).

PRAYER OF THE FAITHFUL

Let us pray to our heavenly Father who has delivered us from the
dominion of darkness and transferred us to the Kingdom of his
beloved Son.   *R*. May your Kingdom come.

For the Church: that we its members may realise that we are
spreading the Kingdom of God when we do our ordinary work
well, at home and outside the home. (Pause).   We pray to the
Lord.

For our political leaders: that they may help to spread the
Kingdom by showing special concern for the weaker and disadvantaged members of society: the little ones, the old, the sick, the handicapped . . . (Pause).   We pray to the Lord.

For those who do not acknowledge Christ as their Saviour and
King: that they may discover him in his followers. (Pause).   We
pray to the Lord.

That we may allow Christ to enrich our own lives, and then
gladly give ourselves to him as messengers of his love, peace and

forgiveness to others. (Pause).   We pray to the Lord.
   For local needs.
   Let us pray:
   Heavenly Father, we make all our prayers to you, through Jesus
your Son, who is our Brother, our Saviour and our King, and who
lives and reigns with you and the Holy Spirit, one God, for ever and
ever.

COMMUNION REFLECTION
Death — harvest time of the spirit.

On an autumn day
I took up a handful of grain
and let it slip slowly through my fingers.
And I said to myself:
'This is what it's all about.
There is no longer any room for pretense.
At harvest time the essence is revealed.
The straw and the chaff are set aside.
They have done their job.
The grain alone matters — sacks of pure gold.'

So it is when a person dies.
The essence of that person is revealed.
At the moment of death a person's character stands out.
Happy for the person if he has forged it well over the years.

Then it will not be the great achievements that will matter;
not how much money or possessions a person has amassed.
These, like the straw and the chaff, will be left behind.
It is what he has made of himself that will matter.

Death can take away from us what we have,
but it cannot rob us of what we are.
We are children of our heavenly Father,
and coheirs with Christ to the Kingdom of heaven.

Festivals

THE IMMACULATE CONCEPTION
Mary: a translucent person

INTRODUCTION AND CONFITEOR

Today we celebrate the holiness of Mary. Right from the first moment of her existence she lived in the light. No trace of darknes ever touched her soul.

We know that our souls are darkened, not only by original sin, but also by personal sin. By our Baptism we are enabled to walk in the light of Christ. Let us call to mind the sins which darken our lives and the lives of others. (Pause).

Mary, our Mother, will intercede for us as we confess our sins and ask forgiveness of God and one another.

I confess to almighty God . . .

HEADINGS FOR READINGS

First Reading (Genesis 3:9-15, 20). When man and woman disobeyed God and fell into sin, God promised salvation from sin through another man and woman, namely, Christ and his Mother.

Second Reading (Ephesians 1:3-6, 11-12). In his love for us God has adopted us as his sons and daughters. Hence we too are called to a holy and blameless life.

Gospel (Luke 1:26-38). Mary's greatness and holiness are due to God's grace and her cooperation with that grace.

HOMILY

It has been said that a saint is a window through which we get a glimpse of another world, a person through whom the light of God shines. I think it is a beautiful description of what holiness is. If it applies to a saint then surely it applies even more so to Mary whom we honour today.

One evening I was sitting on a bench watching the sun go down. As it went down it filled the world with golden light. Everything was bathed in it, especially the clouds. It was hard to imagine that anything could be more beautiful.

But then it dipped lower and lower in the western sky. The shadows lengthened. The dusk and gloom of the summer twilight enveloped all things. As the sun retreated, one by one all the colours and all the lights were extinguished. Darkness devoured them without a trace. It was hard to imagine that it was the same world I was looking at.

I continued to sit there for some time. Opposite me was a church.

It too was plunged into darkness. But then, all of a sudden, a light went on inside the church, and I found my eyes drawn to a stained-glass window. Even when the sun was shining I hadn't even noticed it. But now against the background of darkness it glowed with a beauty that was simply stunning. And the outlines of the figures on the window, which previously had been invisible, now stood out clearly. The light inside was shining, not so much on the window, as through it. No doubt that window had a certain beauty before, yet I had to wait until the sun went down and darkness set in to appreciate its true beauty. But this beauty was revealed only because there was a light within.

And I reflected that in some ways people are like stained-glass windows. Many glow and shine but only in the sunlight of the approval and recognition of others. When this approval is withdrawn, and nobody pays any attention to them, they are plunged into darkness because they do not have the light within. As these thoughts were running through my mind someone switched off the light inside the church. Now all was in darkness both within and without. How dark it is when a light goes out — darker by far than if it had never shone.

When we say that Mary was conceived without original sin what are we saying? We are saying that she was as holy as it is possible for a redeemed creature to be. Mary too had to be redeemed, but she was redeemed in advance. Unlike us, Mary was never subject to the prince of darkness — not even for a moment. From the very first moment of her existence she belonged to the Kingdom of light, that is, the Kingdom of God. The light of God's grace illuminated her from within, so that no matter how deep was the darkness that surrounded her, she was still in the light. Far from extinguishing her light, the darkness merely served to show it up.

And it was through the humble Mary that Christ's powerful light shone into our world of darkness and shadows. Christ is 'the light of the world.' He it is who 'enlightens all men'. It was his light that also illuminated the heart and soul of Mary.

Each of us was conceived and born, not only into a world darkened by many forms of evil, but personally subject to the kingdom of darkness. But at our Baptism the light of God's grace was kindled within us, and Christ our Saviour began to free us from the grip of darkness. As Peter put it: 'God has called us out of darkness into his own marvellous light.' (1 Peter 2:9). And Paul says: 'You were darkness once, but now you are light in the Lord; be like children of the light.' (Eph 5:8).

But, alas, the darkness still has power over us. The process of freeing ourselves from it through the grace of Christ is a life-long process. It cannot happen at the turn of a switch. Even though most of us are afraid of the dark and it causes us to stumble and lose our way, yet it somehow has a fascination for us. But Mary, even though her inner light always burned brightly, knows what it is to live in a world darkened by greed, hatred, pride, cruelty, and selfishness. She will help, guide and encourage us to walk in the way of Christ, which is the way of light.

In essence, what does living in the light entail? Listen to St John: 'Anyone who loves his brother is living in the light and need not be afraid of stumbling; unlike the man who hates his brother and is in darkness, not knowing where he is going because it is too dark to see.' (1 John 2:10-11).

Every time we meet Mary in the Gospels she is seen as someone who was concerned about other people. Not only did the light of God's love illuminate her own life. But it shone out through her and illuminated the lives of all those around her. She will help us to keep the light of Christ burning brightly within us, and she will encourage us to shed light into the path of others.

'Humility like darkness reveals the heavenly lights.' (Thoreau).

'The person who fears to be alone will never be anything but lonely.' (Thomas Merton).

PRAYER OF THE FAITHFUL

From her first moment Mary, the Immaculate Virgin, became a temple of God, and was filled with the light of the Holy Spirit. Let us pray that, after her example, we may walk humbly but steadfastly in the path traced out by her Son. *R.* Lord, hear us in your love.

That all Christians may experience the love of Mary in their lives and draw inspiration from her life to follow her Son more closely. (Pause). Let us pray in faith.

For all those who hold public office: that in a world darkened by greed and selfishness they may fulfil their responsibilities worthily. (Pause). Let us pray in faith.

God made Mary blessed among women. Let us pray that society and the Church may recognise the rights of women and give them their rightful place and role. (Pause). Let us pray in faith.

That like Mary we may be concerned about the needs of those around us, and thus the light of God will shine out through us. (Pause). Let us pray in faith.

For local needs.

Let us pray:

Father, in your gentle mercy, guide our wayward hearts, for we know that, left to ourselves, we cannot do your will. We ask this through Christ our Lord.

We gain a better understanding of Mary
if we look at her through the eyes of the poor,
especially the poor of the third world.

She experienced uncertainty and insecurity
when she said 'yes' to the angel.
She knew what oppression was
when she couldn't find a room in which to give birth to Jesus.
She lived as a refugee in a strange land,
with a strange language and strange customs.
She knew the pain of having a child
who does not follow the accepted path,
but who causes controversy wherever he goes.
She knew the loneliness of the widow,
and the agony of seeing her only son executed.

Mary is the friend of all the poor,
oppressed and lonely women of our times.
Every word about her in the Scriptures
points to her close connection
with all those who are rejected, despised and pushed around.

She gives hope to those who struggle for a more just world,
and challenges us all to live a simpler life,
a life of unconditional trust in God's loving care.

THE BODY AND BLOOD OF CHRIST
The Banquet of the People of God

INTRODUCTION AND CONFITEOR
We don't always appreciate the greatness of what we do when we celebrate the Eucharist. We don't appreciate our closeness to Christ, our Saviour and Friend, and our closeness to one another, as brothers and sisters in his name. (Pause).

Lord Jesus, here you speak to us the words of eternal life. Lord, have mercy.

Lord Jesus, here you heal in us the wounds of sin and division. Christ, have mercy.

Lord Jesus, here you nourish us with the bread of life as we travel towards the promised land of heaven.   Lord, have mercy.

HEADINGS FOR READINGS

First Reading (Genesis 14:18-20). A pagan priest-king by the name of Melchizedek gives bread and wine to Abraham and makes a profession of faith in the one true God. In Christian tradition this bread and wine were taken to prefigure the Eucharist.

Second Reading (1 Cor 11:23-26). When we celebrate the Eucharist we do not merely make present Christ's Body and Blood, but we re-enact the death by which he saved us.

Gospel (Luke 9:11-17). Jesus provides an extraordinary meal for the people who followed him to a lonely place. In the Eucharist the Church continues the mission of Christ to teach, heal and nourish the People of God.

HOMILY

There were at least two good reasons why Jesus should have sent those people back to their homes. Firstly, King Herod (who had already murdered his cousin, John) was expressing an interest in him. So it was surely a time for keeping a low profile. And secondly, the apostles had just returned from a mission. He wanted to give them a chance to talk about their experiences. That is why he went off to a quiet spot with them. But the people found out where he had gone and followed him.

And what was his reaction when all those people turned up? He didn't tell them to go home. He didn't even get annoyed with them. He looked at them with compassion, for he saw that they were like sheep without a shepherd. He saw that they were neglected, but at the same time he saw that they were searching for something. He looked around at them and saw that some of them were also deeply wounded.

So he gathered them around him. Picture Jesus surrounded by over five thousand people. They were drawn by the magnetism of his words and the warmth of his personality. The first thing he did was to teach them. He spoke to them about the Father's love for them. Their own teachers had abandoned them as hopeless, but he assured them that they were members of God's People. He threw open to them the door of the Kingdom of God and invited them to enter.

Then he went around and touched all those who were sick or wounded and healed them. By the tme he had finished this it was late afternoon and everybody was hungry because in their excitement they had forgotten to bring food with them. The apostles, seeing the situation, urged him to send them away. But he would not hear of sending them away. He worked a great miracle to feed them. Now they knew they were like the Israelites of old, for here was a new Moss giving them bread in the wilderness. Only when he had taught, healed and fed them did he dismiss them. How happy they must have been as they made their way back to their homes. They knew that God cared about them. They were no longer sheep without a shepherd. They had found a loving and caring shepherd who had given himself completely to them.

We are like those people in the desert. The first thing we have to realise is that we are not a bunch of individuals without any common bond. We are members of the new People of God. We are gathered in this special building we call a 'church'. The Church is of course the house of God, but it is more especially the house of God's People — their meeting place. We must be conscious of our unity every time we meet.

And of course it is Christ himself who draws us here. He is in our midst. We are gathered around him. Without him we too are no better than sheep without a shepherd. The first thing he does is teach us. When the Scriptures are read to us we hear his voice. 'Man does not live by bread alone, but by every word that comes from the mouth of God.' Christ's words are not dead words. They are living words. They console, inspire and challenge us. If we are genuinely searching for God we will listen and we will hear him speaking to us.

Then here Christ heals us, for we are all deeply wounded by sin. Christ forgives our sins and heals the wounds they leave. By bringing us together he heals us of our isolationism. He draws us out of our solitude and joins us with others. Many people today suffer from the anguish of acute loneliness. Here they are healed, for they see that they are not alone on the road of life. They have brothers and sisters who share their hopes, and who will support and encourage them. Those who are in despair are healed of their despair. Jesus assures them that their lives have a meaning and a goal. And we are all healed of our selfishness and indifference to the needs of others. We are challenged to reach out to one another in love and compassion. And of course any broken bonds are repaired, because we get the grace to seek reconciliation with anyone from whom we may be estranged. Thus the Eucharist forms us into a community of love. Today people want a Church made of friendship, of genuine contacts, and of mutual support. In it we must find what we all seek and thirst for — truth, love, friendship, and warm relationships.

Finally here we are nourished by Christ. The food he gave to the people in the desert was only a preparation for the food he gives us in the Eucharist. That food is himself. 'Unless you eat my flesh and drink my blood you shall not have life in you.' Fed on this food we can cross whatever desert life may confront us with as we make our way to the promised land of eternal life.

It looks as if at the end of the day in the desert the people went home and, as they say, that was that! But we can't do this after we have taken part in this special meal. Otherwise we are left with a community of do-nothing Christians, with a Church that only comes alive on a Sunday for a little worship. Here we do not merely re-enact the miracle of the loaves and fishes, but we re-enact the saving death of Christ. We are drawn into his death by trying when we go away from here to live a life of self-giving as he did. Thus our lives too will become an offering to the Father. The more we can die to ourselves, the more we will free ourselves from the power of death and share even now in the risen life of Christ. We leave here to become bearers of life to others. At the end of Mass the priest dismisses us. We are sent out into the world. We should always leave here with our hearts lifted up.

'In a world become a desert we thirst for comradeship.' (Antoine de Saint Exupery).

'The problem with normal people is fear. We are afraid of one another — afraid of meeting.' (Jean Vanier).

PRAYER OF THE FAITHFUL

Jesus nourished those people who followed him into the desert. In the Eucharist he nourishes all those who follow him in their lives. *R.* Lord, graciously hear us.

For the Church: that the Eucharist may form us into a community of love. (Pause). Lord, hear us.

That the well-off countries may share with the poor countries, so that none of God's children will go hungry. (Pause). Lord, hear us.

That all who are lonely may find comfort; that all who are lost may find guidance. (Pause). Lord, hear us.

That we who share in the one bread of life may be filled with Christlike love and put aside all selfish ways. (Pause). Lord, hear us.

For local needs.

Let us pray:

Lord Jesus, stay with us as our companion on the road of life. In your mercy inflame our hearts and raise up our hopes, so that in union with our brothers and sisters we may recognise you in the Scriptures and in the Breaking of Bread. Who live and reign with the Father and the Holy Spirit, one God, for ever and ever.

SIGN OF PEACE

Lord Jesus Christ, the night before you died, in order to let the apostles know the bonds of love that existed between you and them, you said to them: 'I am the vine, you are the branches;

separated from me you can do nothing; united with me you will bear much fruit.' Strengthen the bonds that unite us with you and with one another, so that we may enjoy the peace and unity of your kingdom where you live for ever and ever.

COMMUNION REFLECTION
On the night before he died,
as he shared himself under the form of bread and wine
with his disciples, Jesus said to them:
'Do this in memory of me.'

Everybody loves to be remembered.
To be forgotten is to be treated as if we never existed.
If we want to be remembered
we have a duty also to remember.
But there is an art in remembering.
Memory is a powerful thing.
Wrongly used, it can bring death rather than life.

The art of remembering consists in remembering what will help
and forgetting what will hinder.
Past failures remembered will warn us against repeating them.
Past victories remembered will spur us on to even greater ones.

Memory keeps the past alive.
It is a form of immortality.
Those we remember never die.
They continue to walk and talk with us.

Memory is the only paradise
from which we cannot be driven.

THE ASSUMPTION OF THE BLESSED VIRGIN MARY

INTRODUCTION AND CONFITEOR
Today the whole Church honours the humble maid of Nazareth through whom the world received its Saviour. We rejoice that she shares in the glory of her Son in heaven.

She is our Mother. From heaven she watches over us. She wants us to be obedient and loving children of the Father. But, alas, we often forget our dignity, and do our own will rather than the will of God. (Pause).

Let us confess our sins, sure that Mary prays with us and for us. I confess to almighty God . . .

HEADINGS FOR READINGS

First Reading (Rev. 11:19; 12:1-6, 10). As the Mother of the Redeemer, Mary was at the very heart of the struggle between good and evil, between God and Satan. However, God took special care of her.

Second Reading (1 Cor 15:20-26). Christ is the new Adam who undoes all the harm done by the old Adam. (Mary is the new Eve, who by her obedience undoes the harm done by the first Eve).

Gospel (Luke 1:36-56). Mary had no doubt about the importance of the role she had been given by God. However, she takes no credit for herself but gives all the glory to God.

HOMILY

In this feast we are celebrating Mary's assumption into heaven, where she shares fully in the glory attained by Christ her Son at the right hand of the Father. All Mary's greatness comes from her relationship with Christ. We cannot understand her or appreciate her role in the Church without keeping this in the forefront of our minds.

Adrienne (an English woman) was very interested in paintings. She admits that in the beginning she didn't know much about art, but she just loved it. One day she had a stroke of good luck. Though it made her famous, it also brought a lot of trouble on her and led to her being spurned by the art establishment of the day. In the course of some research she was doing she stumbled across a small painting which she had reason to believe was a self-portrait by Gainsborough.

She found it in a small rural antique shop. She took it home and began to clean it of its cover of dust and soot. It took a lot of time, patience and hard work to restore it. As she worked on it, however, the conviction grew within her that it was indeed an original by the master himself, though naturally she did have moments of doubt. But when she tried to interest the leading figures in the art establishment they were very dismissive both of her and the painting.

This surprised her. Thinking that the nation's museums would be only too glad to have a new Gainsborough, she sent photos of the picture to the country's most distinguished authorities on eighteenth century English paintings. But they weren't interested. They had already made up their minds to dismiss her claim. Most of the experts didn't even bother to go to see the picture itself when it was displayed in a public gallery. They were quite content to base their opinions on the photos.

The director of the National Gallery said: 'Seeing the picture wouldn't really help,' and he pronounced that it was definitely no Gainsborough. The director of the Tate Gallery said it definitely was from that period but not a Gainsborough. Most of the others that she sent the photos to were quite content to echo the opinions of the top experts.

All this didn't exactly increase Adrienne's respect for those eminent gentlemen. 'The trouble with all these museum directors,' she said, 'is that they are trying to make a personal name for themselves, the younger ones especially. They are all dying to get on television so that they can pontificate. They put their own personalities above the museum and its pictures. They do no service to art.'

But she was a very determined and dedicated lady. She didn't give up. She merely tried harder. She threw herself into a flurry of research. She had the picture X-rayed in a Scotland Yard laboratory, and under infra-red examination Gainsborough's initials came to light under the top layers of paint. She immediately sent off her findings to one of the chief experts. He displayed a polite interest but stuck to his former view that it was not an original. Next she delved into the history of that period and unearthed more evidence which more or less proved beyond doubt that she was right. One expert who accepted her findings said: 'You can't prove these things with absolute certainty, but she has got as far as one can. In fact, the evidence she has unearthed is much stronger than it is for many pictures whose authenticity is accepted without demur.'

Even so, the director of the National Gallery remained unconvinced. Which led Adrienne to conclude: 'With such people you could argue forever and it would make no difference. These people are civil servants, and all they are interested in is power.' When a celebration was held at the Royal Academy to honour her and to make public her find, the top brass from the art world, the so-called guardians of the national heritage, did not even bother to attend.

What they were celebrating at that gathering was the coming to light of an original painting by a great master. The fact that it was a self-portrait made it all the more interesting. But it was only right that Adrienne should share in some of the glory. For without her efforts, perseverence and conviction the painting would probably never have come to light.

Christ is a self-portrait of God. It was through Mary that he came to birth among us. She cared for him during all the years he remained in the shadows, unknown and unrecognised. And when at last he emerged from those shadows and came out into public view, he did not meet with universal acclaim. True, many of the ordinary people believed in him, but the religious establishment refused to believe in him. Mary suffered enormously at seeing him regarded with suspicion, declared an imposter, and eventually put to death. But all the time, in spite of darkness and difficulty, she continued to believe in him and stood by him in his hour of humiliation.

Is it not right then that she, his mother, should share in the spoils of his victory? Mary was a very humble person. She did not seek her own glory. She attributed all her greatness to the love and mercy of God. But she played her part. She did the will of God even though it meant following a path that was steep and dark. It was through her that Christ's glory was seen and recognised by those who accepted him 'as the only Son of the Father, full of grace and truth.'

Mary is our Mother. We are precious to her. Though others may not always believe in us, she believes in us. Each of us is made in the image of God. With her help we will come to believe in our human and divine dignity, and we will try to be true to it. We will then be able to help others to believe in their dignity. Then one day we can hope to share in her glory, which is the glory of her Son, who wants us too to be where he and his Mother now are.

'Mary's sanctity is the most hidden of all sanctities.' (Thomas Merton).

'Tell me what you are busy about and I will tell you what you are.' (Goethe).

PRAYER OF THE FAITHFUL

Mary shares fully in her Son's victory over sin and death. We are still straining towards the state to which she has attained. Let us pray that we may persevere. *R.* Lord, graciously hear us.

That all Christians may see heaven as their final goal and come to attain it through the prayers of Mary and the grace of her Son. (Pause). Lord, hear us.

For all in positions of power and authority: that they may not seek their own glory but serve those under them humbly as Mary served. (Pause). Lord, hear us.

For all mothers, but especially for those who have witnessed the tragic death of one or more of their children: that they may experience the power of Mary's intercession. (Pause). Lord, hear us.

That we may strive after holiness of life by seeking to do at all times, not our own will, but the will of God. (Pause). Lord, hear us.

For local needs.

Let us pray:

Lord, you looked on the lowliness of Mary your most faithful handmaid, and raised her up in glory. Raise us up also to share with her in the fulness of that redemption won for us by your Son. We ask this through the same Christ, our Lord.

COMMUNION REFLECTION

(The following is adapted from an old Hebrew prayer).

For each of us life is a journey.
Birth is the beginning of this journey,
and death is not the end but the destination.

It is a journey that takes us
from youth to age,
from innocence to awareness,
from ignorance to knowledge,
from foolishness to wisdom,
from weakness to strength and often back again,
from offence to forgiveness,
from loneliness to friendship,
from pain to compassion,
from fear to faith,
from defeat to victory and from victory to defeat,
until, looking backward or ahead,
we see that victory does not lie at some high point along the way,
but in having made the journey, stage by stage.

Mary, our mother,
you now share fully in the glory of your risen Son.
Guide us who are still on the road of life,
until we too come to share that same glory,

ALL SAINTS
Becoming real

INTRODUCTION AND CONFITEOR

Today we honour in a special way the 'little' saints, that is, those who will never be officially canonised. Let us reflect for a moment to see if we have known one such person. If so, ask yourself what was it about them that impressed you? (Pause).

To be a saint is to be Christlike. We all fall far short, even though as Christians this is supposed to be the main aim of our lives.

Lord Jesus, you call us to be poor in spirit and pure of heart. Lord, have mercy.

Lord Jesus, you call us to be gentle and merciful to others. Christ, have mercy.

Lord Jesus, you call us to hunger and thirst after right living. Lord, have mercy.

HEADINGS FOR READINGS

First Reading (Rev 7:2-4, 9-14). Here we are given a vision of the victorious followers of Christ rejoicing in his presence in the heavenly kingdom. They come from every nation, and race, and tribe, and language.

Second Reading (1 John 3:1-3). St John tells us that in heaven we will see God as he is. However, if we want to attain to this vision we must try to live like Christ.

Gospel (Matthew 5:1-12). Here Jesus stresses the qualities he wishes to see in his disciples, qualities we see exemplied in the lives of the saints.

HOMILY

Many people have a false idea of what a saint is. For them saints are people who never committed a sin in all their lives. People who were always shining with virtue — strong-willed, humble, pure, who never lost their patience, and who never thought of themselves but always of God and others. But this is a fallacy. It implies that the saints were saints from the cradle onwards. In other words, that saints were born. But the saints were *not born*. They *became saints*. They underwent a conversion — a change of heart which resulted in a change of life. This change did not happen overnight, but was the result of a long and painful struggle.

There was once a rabbit made of the most beautiful velvet you could imagine. He hadn't a crease or wrinkle, not a spot or a stain on his shiny skin. The little boy was delighted when he saw him in his stocking on Christmas morning. However, by the end of the day the rabbit had been cast aside.

For a long time he lived in a cupboard full of all kinds of toys. Some of them seemed far superior to him, especially the mechanical ones, who acted as if they were real. Realising that he was stuffed with sawdust, the rabbit had a very poor image of himself. He felt very ordinary and very insignificant among all those fancy toys. The only one who was kind to him was the Skin Horse.

The horse seemed to have acquired a lot of wisdom during his long life. He wasn't very impressed by the succession of mechanical toys he met. He saw how they were full of noise as long as the mainsprings lasted, but as soon as the latter gave way, they became utterly useless. The little rabbit then realised that they weren't real after all. But he so longed to be real.

One day he turned to the horse and asked: 'What does it mean to be real?'

'Real isn't how you are made,' answered the horse. 'It is something that happens to you. When someone loves you for a long time, not just for the use he gets out of you, but for yourself, then you become real.'

'Does it hurt to become real?' asked the rabbit.

'Sometimes it does, but it's a small price for becoming real.'

'Does it happen all at once or bit by bit?'

'It happens bit by bit, and can take a long time. That's why it doesn't often happen to people who break easily or who have to be handled very gently. Generally, by the time you are real, most of your hair will have fallen out, you eyes will have grown dim, your joints creaky, and your skin will be full of wrinkles. But these things don't matter, because when you become real you acquire another kind of beauty.'

On hearing this the rabbit longed even more ardently to become real. But the idea of growing worn and shabby made him sad. He only wished he could become real without any of these unpleasant things happening to him.

One night when the boy was going to sleep, his mother could not find his teddybear so she gave him the rabbit. That night, and for many nights afterwards, the rabbit slept in the boy's bed. At first he found it rather uncomfortable and could scarcely breath. But in time he grew to love it especially when the boy was nice to him and talked to him before falling asleep. Time went by and he was very happy, so happy that he never noticed how his lovely velvet fur was growing shabbier, his tail was coming unsewn, and his bright eyes got scratched from the boy's caresses.

One night the boy, unable to find his favourite rabbit, refused to go to sleep. His mother scolded him saying: 'But he's only a toy!' But he replied: 'He isn't just a toy. He is *real.*' On hearing this the little rabbit became very happy, for he knew that what the horse had said had come true at last. He was a toy no longer. He was real. The boy himself had said so. That night he was almost too happy to sleep. When he did eventually fall asleep his dreams were sweeter than usual.

The change of heart that we call conversion (which every saint underwent) is very clearly seen in the lives of some of the greatest names in the Church's register of saints: Francis of Assisi, Ingnatius of Loyola, Augustine of Hippo, Paul of Tarsus . . . Each of these at a certain moment in their lives heard the words of Christ: 'Repent and believe the Good News.'

This is why the lives of the saints, the 'little' ones as well as the 'great' ones, are such a challenge to us. We cannot read them without experiencing a great call to conversion — a call to rethink our basic attitudes to life, to redefine our goals, to confront our sinfulness, and to throw ourselves open to God's love and mercy. After reading the lives of the saints we see what we could be if we are willing to take the risk of total surrender to the love of God.

To become a saint is to become real. It means that the real me, which is often hidden under layers of foolishness and absurd pretense, finally emerges. All the hidden goodness and beauty that God has placed within me comes out. And it all starts with the realisation that God loves me as I am. The saints were people who believed the Good News of God's unconditional love, and who began to return his love, and found their lives changed, not overnight, but through a gradual process of growth which didn't rule out further falls. In some cases (for example that of St Peter) it took a long time. A lot of corners had to be knocked off before they became real. We all want something for nothing, quickly, and without having to work for it. But it cannot be.

As this was happening to them, the saints discovered a tremendous joy and freedom. There can be no joy for us as long as the things we do are different from the things we believe in. And there is no freedom for us outside the will of God. When we do the will of God things hum sweetly. We become like an instrument that is being played properly.

'There is nothing better in the world than to become a witness to the love of God.' (Philip Toynbee).

'Holiness means living without division between word and action.' (Henri Nouwen).

PRAYER OF THE FAITHFUL

Let us pray that, inspired by the example of the saints, and helped on by their prayers, we may seek after holiness of life with noble and generous hearts. *R.* Lord, hear us in your love.

For all the People of God: that they may learn what is pleasing to God and undertake to do it with all their strength. (Pause). We pray in faith.

For all holders of authority: that they may be gentle and fair in the exercise of that authority. (Pause). We pray in faith.

For Christians who suffer for their faith, and for all who suffer in the cause of right and truth: that the Lord may sustain them in their efforts to live the beatitudes. (Pause). We pray in faith.

That we may see holiness of life as a call to live up to our dignity as children of God and followers of Christ. (Pause). We pray in faith.

For local needs.

Let us pray:

Father, give us a love for what you command, and a longing for what you promise, so that amid this world's changes our hearts may be set on the world of lasting joy. We ask this through Christ, our Lord.

COMMUNION REFLECTION

How many times I have felt myself glow
when others recognised or praised me.
And how many times I have been plunged into gloom
when others ignored or criticised me.
Acclaim affects me like a wedding feast.
Criticism affects me like a bereavement.

But there are some who have a steady flame,
shining from deep inside them.
This is not extinguished when others ignore them,
for it is not dependent on what others think of them;
it is what they think of themselves with a quiet certainty.

We all have two potentialities within us —
to behave like a swine or a saint.
But we help people more by giving them a favourable image of
    themselves
than by constantly harping on their faults.
Each individual normally strives to be true to his best image.

The saints hold up a mirror before us.
In this mirror we get a most favourable image of ourselves.
We see what we are capable of.
All we need is the will to imitate them.